4 Ingredient Recipes for 30 Minute Meals
100 Menus with Recipes
Short-cuts • Grocery Lists
Barbara C. Jones

4-Ingredient Recipes For 30-Minute Meals

1st Printing January 2005
2nd Printing Setptember 2005

ISBN 1-931294-70-4 (Hard Bound)

ISBN 1-931294-76-3 (Paper Back)

Library of Congress Number: 2004116140

Cover and Illustrations by Nancy Bohanan
Manufactured in China
Edited, Designed and Published in the
United States of America by
Cookbook Resources, LLC
541 Doubletree Drive
Highland Village, Texas 75077
Toll free 866-229-2665
www.cookbookresources.com

cookbook resources® LLC

How often do you have dinner together as a family?

Well, having dinner together as a family is what this cookbook is all about. With 4-Ingredient Recipes For 30-Minute Meals you can get dinner on the table and serve your family in 30 minutes or less. This cookbook helps you plan simple, satisfying meals using basic ingredients and convenience foods that are readily available.

If you have looked through this cookbook, it is not hard to figure out that it is an "idea" book as much as a cookbook. It is filled with ideas about how to use today's convenience foods and what to serve with them when you are really in a hurry. What can you cook in 30 minutes when you do not even have time to think?

With ideas and recipes for family meals, 4-Ingredient Recipes For 30-Minute Meals is your secret weapon for a busy lifestyle. There are 4 ingredients or less in every recipe. Short, simple instructions make dishes easy to prepare. Great ideas for quick side dishes and desserts make it easy to grab something from the pantry. Everyday ingredients and today's convenience foods keep things very simple.

Circle family nights on the kitchen calendar in red and make them special. Making family night a special night, a time to share a meal, enriches every person at the table.

Designate one night a week as "Soup Night" or "Sandwich Night". What about "Mexican Night" or "Italian Night"?

Let the kids bring a friend home for dinner.

Have a "VIP" chair or special red plate for the person who has a birthday or does something really good that week. Talk about good grades, scoring the winning soccer goal or something funny that happened to someone.

When you don't have time to think, remember 4-Ingredient Recipes For 30-Minute Meals will help you get food on the table and the family in their chairs. It's easy and it's important to bring families to the table.

Enjoy preparing some easy meals in 30 minutes or less.

~Barbara C. Jones

About The Author

Barbara C. Jones has written 16 cookbooks for simple, delicious homecooking and she continues to find ways to make recipes easier and meals important. She recognizes the time demands we all face and strives to make our lives easier by finding shortcuts in the kitchen.

One of her most popular cookbook, The Ultimate Cooking With 4 Ingredients, has sold more than 225,000 copies and is still going strong. Many of her other cookbooks, including one of her best Easy Cooking With 5 Ingredients, focus on how to prepare recipes more quickly and with the least effort.

She is not one to minimize the importance of family meals. She raised two children and cooked breakfast, lunch and dinner for her family almost everyday during the school year. There were no McDonald's, no pizza delivery, no fast food places and no restaurants in the small town where she lived for more than 50 years. Homecooked meals were a necessity and she made them delicious, nutritious and special.

While she has had no formal or professional culinary training, she's been trained in the real world to get meals on the table before everyone goes in different directions. She has trained herself to be an excellent wife, chief cook and bottle washer and loving mother. Her qualifications are more than ample to write cookbooks for real people living in the real world.

Cookbook Resources is grateful to her for the contributions she has made to our publishing program.

Sheryn R. Jones,
Publisher

Contents

Ranch-Style Sausage and Grits

1 cup quick-cooking grits
1 (16 ounce) package bulk pork sausage
1 cup salsa
1 (8 ounce) package shredded cheddar cheese, divided

- Preheat oven to 350°. Cook grits according to package directions and set aside. In skillet, brown and cook sausage. Drain and crumble.
- In skillet, combine grits, sausage, salsa and half cheese and spoon into greased 2-quart baking dish.
- Bake 15 minutes and remove from oven. Top with remaining cheese and bake another 5 minutes. Serve hot.

Cheesy Scrambled Eggs

Butter
Eggs
Milk
Shredded cheddar cheese

- Scramble as many eggs as needed and mix with a little milk. In skillet with a little butter, pour eggs and cook slowly.
- When eggs are not runny, sprinkle cheese over half and fold remaining eggs on top. Cook 1 to 2 minutes more to melt cheese. Remove from heat and serve.

Hot Buttermilk Biscuits

1 cup butter, softened, divided
2 cups flour
¾ cup buttermilk

- Preheat oven to 425°. Cut ½ cup butter into flour with pastry blender or by hand until mixture resembles coarse meal. Stir in buttermilk and mix until dry ingredients are moist.
- Turn dough on floured surface and knead 3 or 4 times. Roll dough to ¾-inch thickness and cut with biscuit cutter or glass.
- Place on lightly greased cookie sheet and bake for 12 to 15 minutes. Use remaining butter for table.

Tip: To make buttermilk, mix 1 cup milk with 1 tablespoon lemon juice or vinegar and let milk sit for about 10 minutes.

Sliced Honeydew Melon

1 ripe honeydew melon, chilled

- Peel and slice honeydew melon in 8 slices.

Tip: If honeydew melons are not in season, get 1 or 2 (16 ounce) jars refrigerated mango slices. They are delicious.

When I think of grits for breakfast, I think of the delicious grits you get in the South. Grits go with anything and everything you order for breakfast. My husband thinks a southern breakfast tops any breakfast anywhere—anytime!

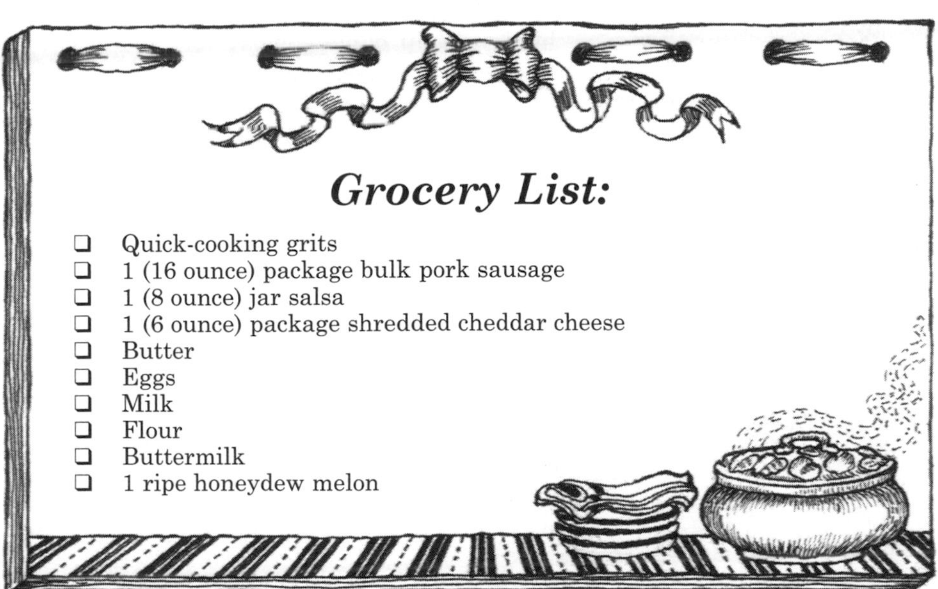

Grocery List:

- ❑ Quick-cooking grits
- ❑ 1 (16 ounce) package bulk pork sausage
- ❑ 1 (8 ounce) jar salsa
- ❑ 1 (6 ounce) package shredded cheddar cheese
- ❑ Butter
- ❑ Eggs
- ❑ Milk
- ❑ Flour
- ❑ Buttermilk
- ❑ 1 ripe honeydew melon

Sunrise Olé

Breakfast Tacos
Crispy Bacon Slices
Chilled Cantaloupe Slices
Hot Flour Tortillas with Honey Butter

Breakfast Tacos

4 eggs, scrambled
1 (8 ounce) package shredded cheddar cheese
1 (16 ounce) jar chunky salsa
1 (12 count) package flour tortillas

- Scramble eggs and mix with a little milk. In skillet with a little butter, pour eggs and cook slowly.
- When eggs are not runny, sprinkle cheese over half and fold remaining eggs on top. Cook 1 to 2 minutes more to melt cheese and remove from heat.
- Wrap 5 to 6 tortillas in a slightly damp paper towel and warm them in microwave on HIGH for 45 seconds. Scoop eggs into tortilla, cover with salsa and roll up. Serve with extra tortillas and lots of butter.

Tip: To serve more than 4, just double everything and let each person fill their own tortilla.

Crispy Bacon Slices

½ to 1 (16 ounce) package sliced bacon

◆ Fry ½ pound bacon for 4 people or 1 pound for 8 people.
My bunch always wants leftover bacon sitting on the stove so they can "graze" as long as it lasts.

Chilled Cantaloupe Slices

1 cantaloupe, chilled

◆ Peel chilled cantaloupe, slice in about 8 slices and place in dish with lid. Refrigerate.
You just can't beat a good chilled cantaloupe for breakfast, lunch or a late-night snack.

Hot Flour Tortillas with Honey Butter

◆ Warm several flour tortillas as directed in Breakfast Tacos and spread with lots of butter mixed with honey.

If you would like a touch of something sweet, make honey-butter recipe in "South of the Border Breakfast" (p. 17) and spread on warm tortillas.

Grocery List:

- ❑ Eggs
- ❑ 1 (8 ounce) package shredded cheddar cheese
- ❑ 1 (16 ounce) jar chunky salsa
- ❑ 1 (12 count) package 8-inch flour tortillas
- ❑ Package sliced bacon
- ❑ 1 or 2 cantaloupes
- ❑ Butter
- ❑ Honey

Belgian Waffles and Maple Syrup

1 (6 or 8 count) package frozen Belgian waffles
1 (8 ounce) bottle maple or raspberry syrup
Sliced strawberries, raspberries or blueberries
Butter

- Preheat oven to 350°. Heat waffles according to package directions and serve with maple or raspberry syrup and butter.

Crispy Bacon

1 (16 ounce) package sliced bacon

- In skillet over medium heat, fry bacon and drain on paper towels. (Buy pre-cooked bacon if you don't want to fry bacon.)

Fried or Scrambled Eggs, *optional*

Eggs
Butter
Milk

- Fry or scramble number of eggs you need. Add a little butter or spray skillet before frying eggs. Scramble eggs with a little milk before cooking.

Spiced Pears

1 (15 ounce) can pear halves with syrup
⅓ cup packed brown sugar
½ teaspoon ground nutmeg
½ teaspoon ground cinnamon

- Drain pears, reserve syrup and set pears aside.
- In saucepan, combine syrup, brown sugar and spices and heat to boiling. Reduce heat and simmer uncovered about 10 minutes. Stir frequently.
- Add pears and simmer another 5 minutes or until pears heat through. To serve, remove pears with slotted spoon and serve with waffles.

To make your own waffles, use a buttermilk waffle and pancake mix. Instead of adding whole eggs, I add only egg yolks to the batter, beat egg whites and fold them into batter last. This makes a lighter and fluffier waffle. The only problem is that you can eat twice as many waffles as you thought you could—or should!

Grocery List:

- ❑ 1 (6 or 8 count) package frozen Belgian waffles
- ❑ 1 (8 ounce) bottle maple syrup
- ❑ 1 (8 ounce) bottle raspberry syrup
- ❑ Butter
- ❑ 1 (16 ounce) package sliced bacon
- ❑ Eggs, optional
- ❑ Milk, optional
- ❑ 1 (15 ounce) can pear halves
- ❑ Brown sugar
- ❑ Nutmeg
- ❑ Cinnamon

Biscuits and Gravy Special

Quick, Creamy Biscuits
Creamy Baked Eggs, optional
Sausage and Classic Cream Gravy
Strong Coffee, Espresso or Latte

Quick, Creamy Biscuits

2½ cups biscuit mix
1 (8 ounce) carton whipping cream

- ◆ Preheat oven to 375°. Mix biscuit mix and cream. Place on floured board. Knead several times.
- ◆ Pat out to ½-inch thickness. Cut with biscuit cutter or 2-inch glass and place biscuits on non-stick baking sheet.
- ◆ Bake for 12 to 15 minutes or until light brown.

Creamy Baked Eggs, *optional*

4 eggs
4 tablespoons whipping cream or half-and-half
4 tablespoons cracker crumbs, divided
4 tablespoons shredded cheddar cheese, divided

- ◆ Preheat oven to 350°. Grease 4 muffing cups and place 1 egg in each. Add 1 tablespoon each of cream, crumbs and cheese for each egg. Sprinkle with a little salt and pepper.
- ◆ Bake for 12 to 20 minutes until eggs are set and baked to consistency desired.

Sausage and Classic Cream Gravy

Pork sausage or thick-sliced bacon
Sausage or bacon drippings
3 tablespoons flour
½ teaspoon salt
½ teaspoon pepper
1½ cups milk

- Fry sausage or bacon until crispy. Drain pieces well on paper towels. Pour all but 2 tablespoons pan drippings away.
- Make the gravy in same skillet used to fry sausage or bacon. Leave about 1 to 2 tablespoons pan drippings in skillet for that special seasoning. Sprinkle flour, salt and pepper in drippings over medium heat and stir to mix well.
- Turn heat to high and slowly pour milk into skillet while stirring constantly until gravy thickens.
- When gravy reaches right consistency, pour into bowl and serve with biscuits.

Strong Coffee, Espresso or Latte

1 pot fresh espresso or extra-strong coffee, brewed
Milk

- While coffee is brewing, pour milk in small saucepan and place on low heat until steaming. For those who want latte, pour two-thirds steaming milk into cup and one-third coffee. Sweeten according to taste.

Grocery List:

- ❑ Biscuit mix
- ❑ 1 (8 ounce) carton whipping cream
- ❑ Eggs
- ❑ Cracker crumbs
- ❑ 1 (8 ounce) package shredded cheddar cheese
- ❑ Pork sausage or thick-sliced bacon
- ❑ Flour
- ❑ Milk
- ❑ Coffee

Celebration Brunch

Maple-Syrup Peppered Bacon
Creamy, Rich, Hot Biscuits
Strawberry Butter
Eggs Florentine

Maple-Syrup Peppered Bacon

Thick-sliced bacon
Maple syrup
Cracked black pepper

- Preheat oven to 375°. Place bacon slices in baking pan and pour a little maple syrup over each slice. Turn bacon over to coat both sides. Grind black pepper over bacon. Put bacon in oven to cook for 20 to 30 minutes until crispy. Check bacon as it cooks.

Creamy, Rich, Hot Biscuits

2 cups flour
3 teaspoons baking powder
½ teaspoon salt
1 (8 ounce) carton whipping cream

- Preheat oven to 350°. Combine flour, baking powder and salt. In mixing bowl, beat whipping cream only until it holds shape. Combine flour mixture and cream and mix with fork.
- Put dough on lightly floured board and knead it for about 1 minute. Pat dough to ¾-inch thickness. Cut out biscuits with small biscuit cutter or glass and place on baking sheet. Bake for about 12 minutes or until light brown.

Strawberry Butter

1 (10 ounce) package frozen strawberries with juice
1 cup unsalted butter, softened
1 cup powdered sugar

- Place all ingredients in food processor or mixer and process until mixture blends. Spread on hot biscuits.

Eggs Florentine

Base:
1 teaspoon beef bouillon granules
2 (10 ounce) packages frozen, chopped spinach

Filling:
4 eggs
Salt and pepper
4 tablespoons whipping cream
1 cup shredded cheddar cheese

- Sprinkle bouillon over spinach in 1-quart, microwave-safe bowl and microwave on HIGH according to package directions. Cool slightly and drain thoroughly on several paper towels. Squeeze to remove all juice.
- Place spinach in bottom of 4 ramekins in baking pan. Gently crack egg, pour over spinach and salt and pepper. Pour 1 tablespoon whipping cream into each ramekin and top with cheese.
- Stick toothpick gently into yolk before putting into microwave. Place wax paper over ramekins and cook on HIGH for 2 minutes, turn ramekins and cook additional 2 minutes or until eggs set and cook as desired.

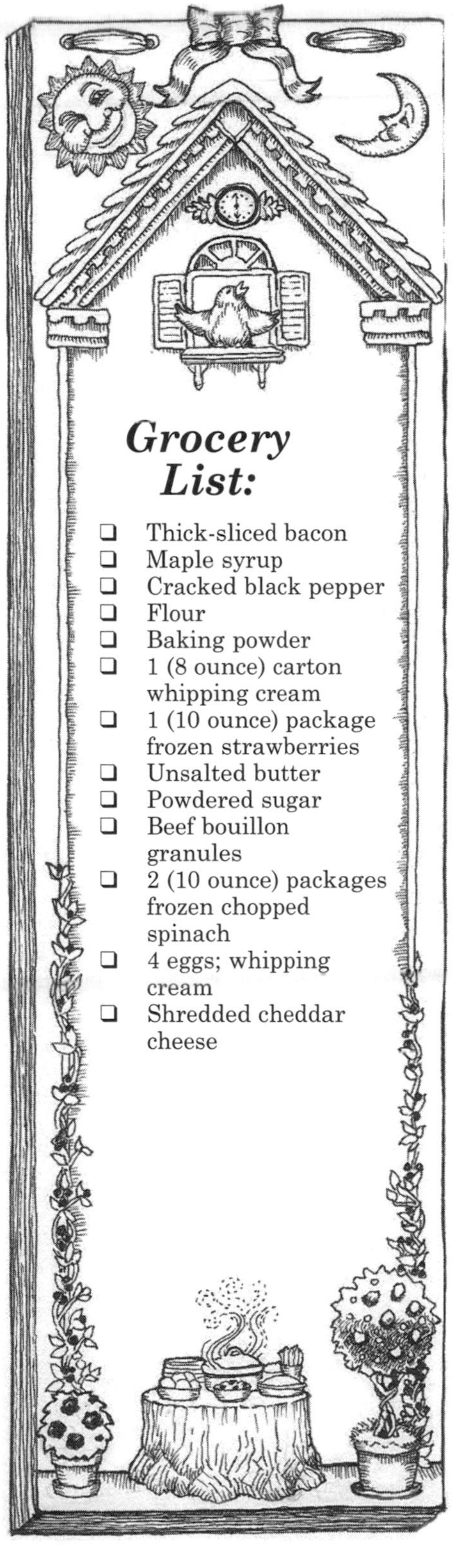

Tex-Mex Warmer

6 flour tortillas
1 (14 ounce) jar Pace® Mexican Creations™ roasted ranchero cooking sauce
6 large eggs
1 (8 ounce) package shredded cheddar-jack cheese

- Preheat oven to 250°. On large baking sheet, heat tortillas in oven 10 to 15 minutes.
- In large 12-inch skillet, pour cooking sauce and heat to boiling. Remove from heat.
- Break each egg separately in custard cup. With large spoon, make well in sauce in skillet and add an egg. Repeat for each egg.
- Cover and simmer about 5 minutes or until egg whites set. Remove from heat and sprinkle cheese over each egg. Cover just until cheese melts.
- Remove tortillas from oven. Serve 1 egg on each tortilla, spoon sauce over all and serve immediately.

Sausages, Flour Tortillas and Honey Butter

2 (8 ounce) packages fully cooked heat-and-serve sausage links, heated
Flour tortillas, warmed

Honey Butter:
½ cup (1 stick) whipped butter, softened
¼ cup honey
1 tablespoon lemon juice
¼ cup packed brown sugar

◆ Heat sausages according to package directions. Combine honey-butter ingredients and spread on tortillas. Add 1 sausage link to each tortilla, roll and serve.

Mexican Fruit Salad

1 (15 ounce) can pineapple chunks, drained, chilled
1 pint fresh strawberries, stemmed, halved, chilled
1 ripe papaya, peeled, seeded, cubed, chilled

◆ In chilled salad bowl, combine all ingredients and serve with Jalapeno-Citrus Dressing.

Jalapeno-Citrus Dressing

⅓ cup honey
2 mild jalapeno peppers, seeded, minced
½ cup orange juice
2 tablespoons lemon juice

◆ Combine all ingredients and mix well. Serve over Mexican Fruit Salad.

  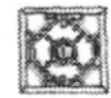

This Southwest-style breakfast only tastes like it took hours to prepare! If you're not a fan of jalapenos, skip the Jalapeno-Citrus Dressing. I'm not much into jalapenos at breakfast, but I have served this to some who eat jalapenos at every meal.

See page 18 for Grocery List

South-of-the-Border Breakfast Grocery List:

- ❑ 1 (10 count) package flour tortillas
- ❑ 1 (14 ounce) jar Pace® Mexican Creations™ roasted ranchero cooking sauce
- ❑ 6 large eggs
- ❑ 1 (8 ounce) package shredded cheddar-jack cheese
- ❑ 2 (8 ounce) packages Jimmy Dean® fully cooked heat-and-serve sausage links
- ❑ 1 (12 count) package flour tortillas
- ❑ 1 (7 ounce) carton whipped butter
- ❑ Honey
- ❑ Lemon juice
- ❑ Brown sugar
- ❑ 1 (15 ounce) can pineapple chunks
- ❑ 1 pint fresh strawberries
- ❑ 1 ripe papaya
- ❑ 2 jalapeno peppers
- ❑ Orange juice

See page 16

Breakfast Bake Grocery List:

- ❑ 2 (15 ounce) cans corned beef hash
- ❑ Butter
- ❑ 1 dozen eggs
- ❑ Half-and-half cream
- ❑ Brown sugar
- ❑ Chopped pecans
- ❑ Bread slices
- ❑ Juice
- ❑ Coffee

See page 19

Corned Beef Hash Bake

2 (15 ounce) cans corned beef hash, slightly warmed
Butter
6 to 8 eggs
⅓ cup half-and-half cream

- Preheat oven to 350°. Spread corned beef hash in greased 9 x 13-inch baking pan. Pat down with back of spoon and make 6 to 8 deep hollows in hash large enough to accommodate 1 egg.
- Fill hollows with dab of butter. Pour eggs into each hollow and cover eggs with 1 to 2 tablespoons of cream. Bake uncovered for 15 to 20 minutes or until eggs are set as desired. Divide into squares to serve.

Praline Toast

½ cup (1 stick) butter, softened
1 cup packed brown sugar
⅓ cup finely chopped pecans
Bread slices

- Combine butter, sugar and pecans. Spread on bread slices. Toast in broiler until brown and bubbly.

See page 18 for Grocery List

Crazy Toaster Morning

Quick French Toast Sticks and Maple Syrup
Pineapple-Island Spread
Peanut Butter Spread
Fresh Fruit

Quick French Toast Sticks and Maple Syrup

4 eggs
1 cup half-and-half cream
2 thick slices bread, cut into 3 strips each
Maple syrup

- Preheat oven to 350°. Beat eggs, cream and pinch of salt. Heat a little oil in skillet. Dip bread into batter and allow batter to soak in.
- Fry bread in skillet until brown on both sides. Transfer to baking pan and bake for about 4 minutes or until puffed. Powdered sugar is really good sprinkled on top. Serve with syrup.

Fresh Fruit

Serve fresh or canned fruit of your choice.

Pineapple-Island Spread

2 (8 ounce) packages cream cheese, softened
1 (8 ounce) carton sour cream
1 (8 ounce) can crushed pineapple with juice
½ cup finely chopped pecans

◆ Combine cream cheese and sour cream and beat until creamy. Fold in pineapple with juice and pecans. Chill and serve with French toast or plain toast and fresh fruit.

Peanut Butter Spread

1 (8 ounce) package cream cheese, softened
1⅔ cups creamy peanut butter
½ cup powdered sugar
1 tablespoon milk

◆ Beat all ingredients together in mixing bowl. Spread over apple slices or toast.

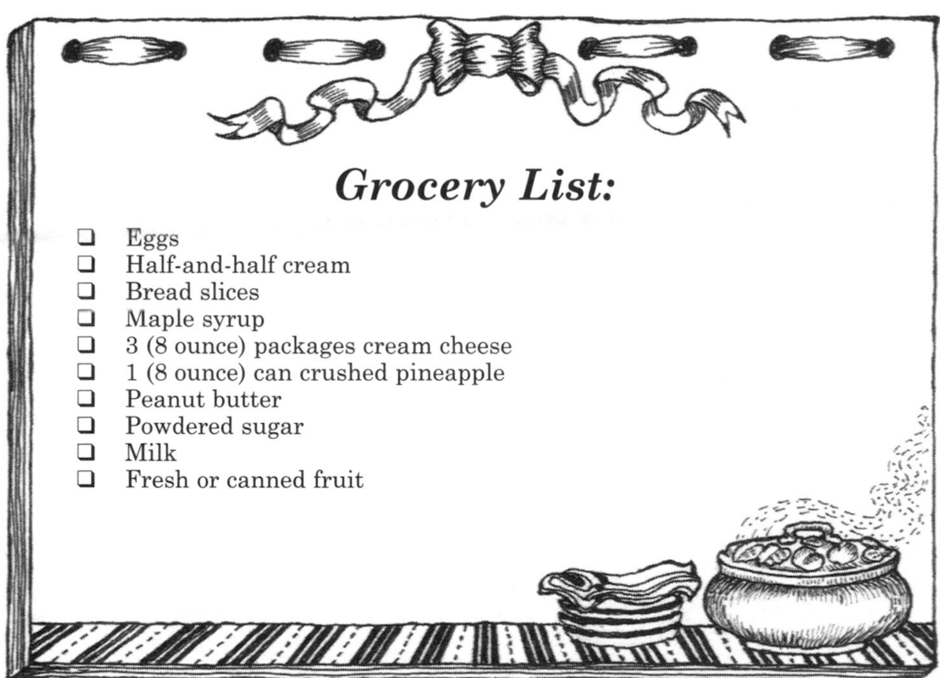

Grocery List:

- ❑ Eggs
- ❑ Half-and-half cream
- ❑ Bread slices
- ❑ Maple syrup
- ❑ 3 (8 ounce) packages cream cheese
- ❑ 1 (8 ounce) can crushed pineapple
- ❑ Peanut butter
- ❑ Powdered sugar
- ❑ Milk
- ❑ Fresh or canned fruit

A Fruity Quick-Start Breakfast

Maple Custard over Fruity Waffles
Strawberry-Yogurt Smoothie

Maple Custard

¾ cup cold milk
¼ cup maple-flavored syrup
1 (4 ounce) package vanilla-flavored instant pudding and pie filling

- In medium bowl, combine milk and syrup and stir.
- Add pudding mix and beat with wire whisk until well blended.
- Refrigerate mixture until ready to use.
- Makes 4 servings.

Fruity Waffles

1 (10 count) box frozen, prepared waffles, thawed
1 cup bananas, sliced
1 cup blueberries
Maple custard-pudding mixture

- Cut 1 waffle into 6 wedges and arrange in star shape on serving plate. Repeat with rest of waffles.
- Toss bananas and blueberries. Spoon ½ cup fruit mixture over waffle pieces on each plate.
- Top each with ¼ cup maple custard-pudding mixture and serve immediately

Tip: Substitute your favorite cut-up fresh fruit for the bananas and blueberries.

Strawberry-Yogurt Smoothie

1½ cups cold milk
1½ teaspoons Crystal Light tangerine-strawberry soft drink mix
1 (8 ounce) container vanilla yogurt
1 cup frozen whole strawberries

◆ Combine all ingredients in blender, cover and blend on HIGH speed until smooth. Makes about 4 (8 ounce) servings.

Grocery List:

- ❑ Milk
- ❑ Maple-flavored syrup
- ❑ 1 (4 ounce) package vanilla-flavored instant pudding and pie filling
- ❑ 1 (10 count) box frozen, prepared waffles
- ❑ Bananas
- ❑ Fresh or frozen blueberries
- ❑ Frozen whole strawberries
- ❑ Crystal Light tangerine-strawberry soft drink mix
- ❑ 1 (8 ounce) container vanilla yogurt

Grab-and-Go Breakfast

English Muffin Breakfast Sandwich
Fresh Fruit Medley
Mocha Coffee or Juice

English Muffin Breakfast Sandwich

4 to 6 eggs
1 package English muffins, halved, toasted
1 package pre-cooked bacon slices, halved
1 (16 ounce) package cheese slices

- Prepare eggs in skillet over medium heat and stir often. Season according to taste.
- Heat bacon in microwave according to package directions.
- Spoon egg mixture onto muffin half, add cheese slice and bacon and top with top half of muffin.

A great sandwich for people "on-the-go"! Place it on a napkin or paper plate and take it with you. Add a banana or other small fruit to complete your meal. What a great way to start the day!

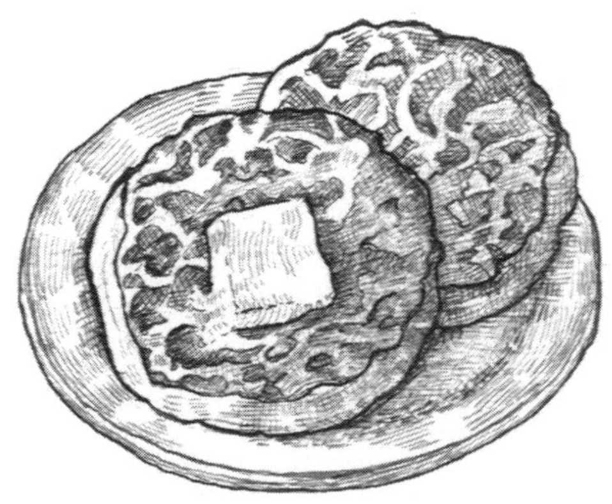

Fresh Fruit Medley

Fresh strawberries
Bananas, sliced
Green or red grapes, seedless
Fresh kiwi, peeled, sliced

- Combine all fruit in bowl and serve or have them ready to grab on the way out the door.

Mocha Yummy

1 cup milk
1 banana
1 teaspoon instant coffee granules
½ cup frozen vanilla yogurt

- Place milk, peeled banana, coffee granules and frozen yogurt into blender or food processor.
- Blend until mixture is smooth and serve immediately.

Tip: Season to taste with sugar substitute and garnish with sliced banana.

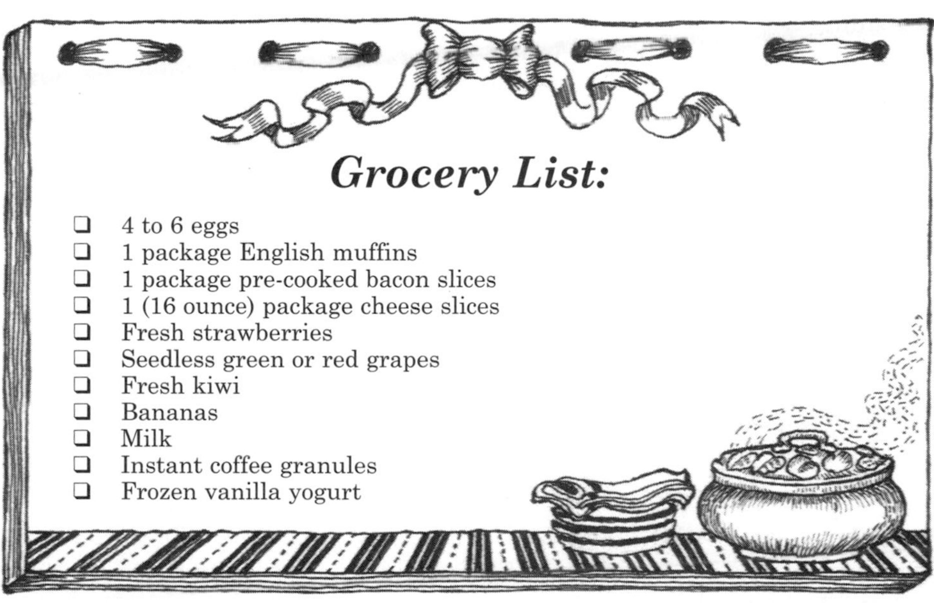

Grocery List:

- ❑ 4 to 6 eggs
- ❑ 1 package English muffins
- ❑ 1 package pre-cooked bacon slices
- ❑ 1 (16 ounce) package cheese slices
- ❑ Fresh strawberries
- ❑ Seedless green or red grapes
- ❑ Fresh kiwi
- ❑ Bananas
- ❑ Milk
- ❑ Instant coffee granules
- ❑ Frozen vanilla yogurt

It's-A-Wrap Breakfast

Scrambled Breakfast Wrap
Lemony-Orange Blend
Fresh Fruit

Scrambled Breakfast Wrap

1 medium green pepper, finely chopped
4 eggs
½ cup thick n' chunky salsa
4 to 6 flour tortillas

- ◆ Cook and stir green peppers in hot oil in large skillet on medium heat for 3 to 4 minutes or until peppers are crisp-tender.
- ◆ Add eggs and mix well. Cook for 3 to 5 minutes and stir often.
- ◆ Add salsa, reduce heat to low and simmer for 2 minutes. Stir occasionally.
- ◆ Spoon one-fourth egg mixture on each tortilla and roll up.

Fresh Fruit

Cantaloupe
Honeydew melon
Clementine oranges
Red delicious apples

- ◆ Slice melons and put 1 serving each in plastic bags. Have oranges and apples ready with paper towels for each so everyone can grab a good snack on the way out the door.

Lemony-Orange Blend

1 tub lemonade-flavored powdered drink mix
2 cups (16 ounces) cold water
2 cups (16 ounces) orange juice

- Place drink mix in plastic or glass pitcher, add water and stir until mix dissolves.
- Stir in orange juice and cover. Refrigerate until ready to serve.

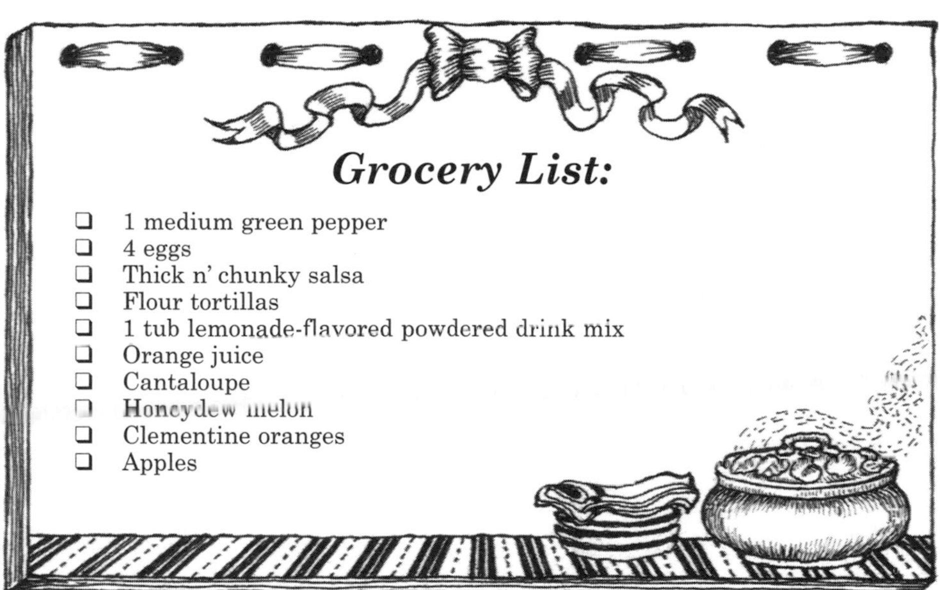

Grocery List:

- ❑ 1 medium green pepper
- ❑ 4 eggs
- ❑ Thick n' chunky salsa
- ❑ Flour tortillas
- ❑ 1 tub lemonade-flavored powdered drink mix
- ❑ Orange juice
- ❑ Cantaloupe
- ❑ Honeydew melon
- ❑ Clementine oranges
- ❑ Apples

Peachy, Light and Easy Breakfast

Peach Melba Breakfast Shortcake
Bacon Slices or Sausage
Café Au Lait or Lemon-Banana Shake

Peach Melba Breakfast Shortcake

1 (10 count) box frozen, prepared waffles, thawed, lightly toasted
½ cup cottage cheese
½ cup fruit and bran cereal with peaches, raisins, almonds
1 (16 ounce) can peach slices

- Top each waffle with cottage cheese, cereal and fruit.
- Serve immediately.

Tip: Substitute peaches with your favorite fruit.

Bacon Slices or Sausage

1 package precooked bacon slices or sausage links

- Prepare bacon slices or sausage links in microwave-safe dish according to package directions.

Lemon-Banana Shake

1 (16 ounce) can frozen lemonade concentrate, thawed
1 banana, sliced
Vanilla ice cream
2 cups milk

- In blender, combine lemonade concentrate and banana.
- Add at least 2 scoops of vanilla ice cream. Add more if thicker consistency is desired.
- Blend thoroughly.

Café Au Lait

1 cup ground coffee
1 quart (4 cups) cold water
1 quart (4 cups) milk, warmed

- Brew coffee in coffee maker.
- When brewing is complete, pour equal amounts of coffee and hot milk into 8 ounce mugs.
- Sweeten coffee according to taste.

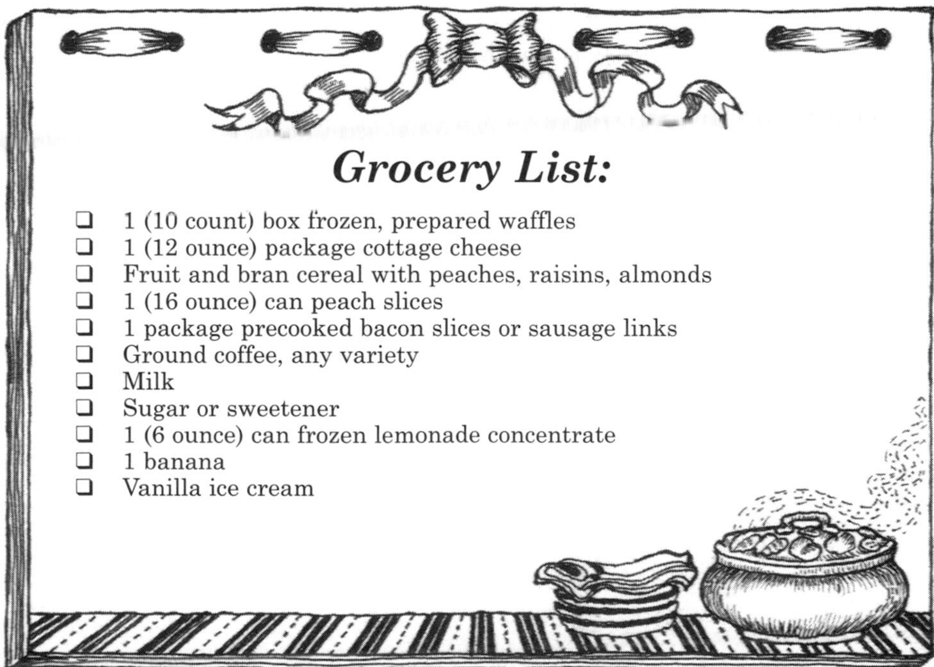

Grocery List:

- ❑ 1 (10 count) box frozen, prepared waffles
- ❑ 1 (12 ounce) package cottage cheese
- ❑ Fruit and bran cereal with peaches, raisins, almonds
- ❑ 1 (16 ounce) can peach slices
- ❑ 1 package precooked bacon slices or sausage links
- ❑ Ground coffee, any variety
- ❑ Milk
- ❑ Sugar or sweetener
- ❑ 1 (6 ounce) can frozen lemonade concentrate
- ❑ 1 banana
- ❑ Vanilla ice cream

Great Day in the Morning

Breakfast Taquitos
Breakfast Frittata
Tropical Fruit
Blueberry Muffins and Butter

Breakfast Taquitos

1 (25 ounce) package frozen breakfast taquitos, thawed

- ◆ Place the number of taquitos you want to serve on baking sheet and heat according to package directions.

Breakfast Frittata

2 medium zucchini, diced, dried with paper towels
1 cup finely diced fresh mushrooms
2 ripe avocados, peeled, cubed
5 eggs, 1½ cups shredded Swiss cheese

- ◆ In large skillet with a little oil over medium heat, cook zucchini and mushrooms 4 to 5 minutes or just until tender. Remove from heat and sprinkle with salt and pepper. Place cubed avocado over top of vegetable mixture.
- ◆ In mixing bowl, beat eggs and about 1 cup water (or milk) until frothy and pour over ingredients in skillet. Return to medium heat, cover and cook 5 minutes or until eggs set. Top with cheese, cover and cook 1 minute more or just until cheese melts. Cut in wedges to serve.

Tropical Fruit

1 (24 ounce) jar refrigerated tropical mixed fruit
Flaked coconut, optional

- Transfer fruit to serving bowl, sprinkle flaked coconut and serve chilled.

There are many canned fruits in jars on the market. The best choices are the refrigerated chunky mixed fruits and the frozen fruits.

Blueberry Muffins and Butter

2 (4 count) packages bakery blueberry muffins
Butter

- Warm muffins in oven at 350° for 5 to 10 minutes.

Frittatas, compared to omelets, are fun to make for breakfast. You don't have to flip them over or make just 1 per person. You can cut the frittata into wedges in the skillet and put it right on the table. This recipe makes enough for 4 to 6 servings—all in about 12 minutes.

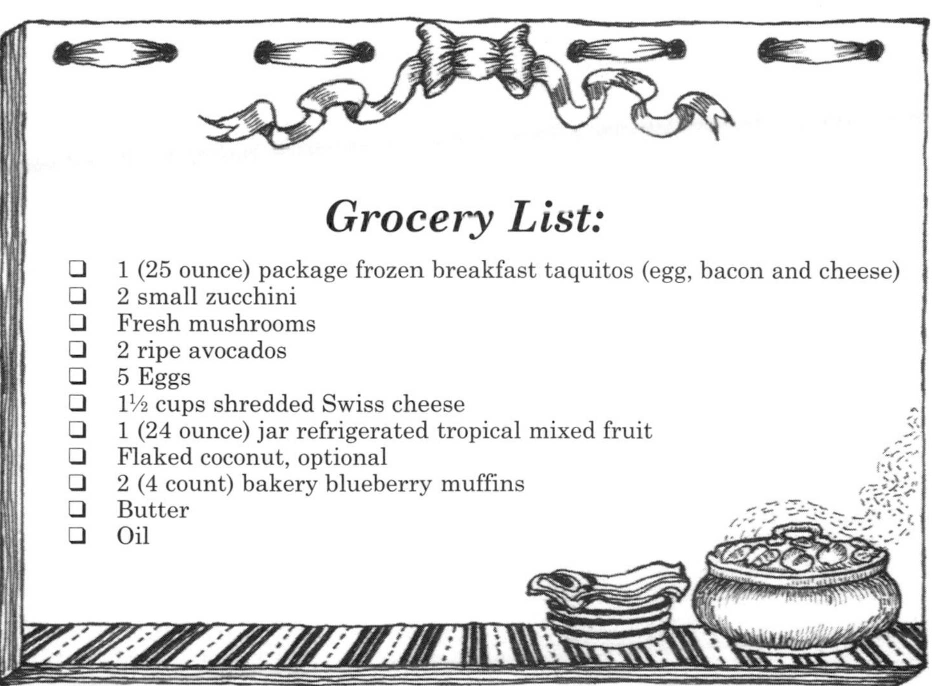

Grocery List:

- ❑ 1 (25 ounce) package frozen breakfast taquitos (egg, bacon and cheese)
- ❑ 2 small zucchini
- ❑ Fresh mushrooms
- ❑ 2 ripe avocados
- ❑ 5 Eggs
- ❑ 1½ cups shredded Swiss cheese
- ❑ 1 (24 ounce) jar refrigerated tropical mixed fruit
- ❑ Flaked coconut, optional
- ❑ 2 (4 count) bakery blueberry muffins
- ❑ Butter
- ❑ Oil

Pineapple-Cheese Casserole

2 (20 ounce) cans pineapple chunks, drained
1 cup sugar, 5 tablespoons flour
1½ cups shredded cheddar cheese
1 stack round buttery crackers, crushed
½ cup (1 stick) butter, melted

- Preheat oven to 350°. In sprayed 9 x 13-inch baking dish, layer ingredients in following order: pineapple, sugar-flour mixture, shredded cheese and cracker crumbs. Drizzle melted butter over casserole.
- Bake 25 minutes or until casserole bubbles around edges.

Yes, I know this recipe has 6 ingredients, but it is such a great dish I knew you would want it. It is not the usual breakfast fare, but it is a great change of pace, is really easy to make and a great way to serve fruit for breakfast. It is also a great dish to serve for lunch with a bowl of soup.

Creamy Baked Eggs, optional

4 eggs
4 tablespoons half-and-half
4 tablespoons buttery cracker crumbs
4 tablespoons shredded cheddar cheese

- Preheat oven to 325°. In each of 4 sprayed muffin cups, place 1 egg and sprinkle with salt and pepper. Add 1 tablespoon each of cream, crumbs and cheese.
- Bake 15 to 18 minutes or until eggs set. To remove from muffin cups, slip knife around edge and remove carefully with large spoon.

Crispy Toast and Cinnamon Butter

1 loaf oatnut bread
1 (.75 ounce) carton buttery spread
½ cup packed brown sugar
¾ teaspoon cinnamon

◆ Toast bread on both sides. Mix buttery spread, brown sugar and cinnamon and spread on toast.

Bananas

1 bunch bananas

◆ Slice or serve whole in fruit bowl.

The Pineapple-Cheese Casserole is practically a meal in itself. Top it off with a banana and you have a hearty, filling breakfast for family or guests.

Grocery List:

- ❑ 2 (20 ounce) cans pineapple chunks
- ❑ Sugar
- ❑ Flour
- ❑ 1 (8 ounce) package shredded cheddar cheese
- ❑ 1 box round buttery crackers
- ❑ Butter
- ❑ 4 Eggs
- ❑ Half-and-half
- ❑ Oatnut bread
- ❑ Buttery spread
- ❑ Brown Sugar
- ❑ Cinnamon
- ❑ Bananas

Easy Meaty Minestrone

2 (20 ounce) cans minestrone soup
1 (15 ounce) can pinto beans with liquid
1 (18 ounce) package frozen Italian meatballs, thawed
1 (5 ounce) package grated parmesan cheese

- ◆ In large saucepan, combine soups, beans, meatballs and ½ cup water. Bring to boil, reduce heat to low-medium and simmer about 15 minutes.
- ◆ To serve, sprinkle each serving with parmesan cheese.

Cornbread Muffins

2 (8 ounce) packages corn muffin mix
⅔ cup milk
2 eggs

- ◆ Preheat oven to 400°. In mixing bowl, combine all ingredients and pour into sprayed 12 to 14-count muffin pan.

Tip: You just can't have too many muffins. To make cornbread instead of muffins, pour batter into greased 9 x 13-inch baking pan and bake according to package directions.

Lemon Cookies

½ cup (1 stick) butter, softened
1 cup sugar
2 tablespoons lemon juice
2 cups flour

- Preheat oven to 350°. Cream butter, sugar and lemon juice while slowly stirring in flour. Drop by teaspoons onto ungreased cookie sheet. Bake at 350° for 14 to 15 minutes.

This is a quick meal for a drizzly, cold winter day. Let everybody pitch in to help. It is mostly opening cans and jars, so who can complain about that? The meaty, minestrone soup and cornbread make a stick-to-your-ribs meal, so let everybody know to save room for a delicious dessert.

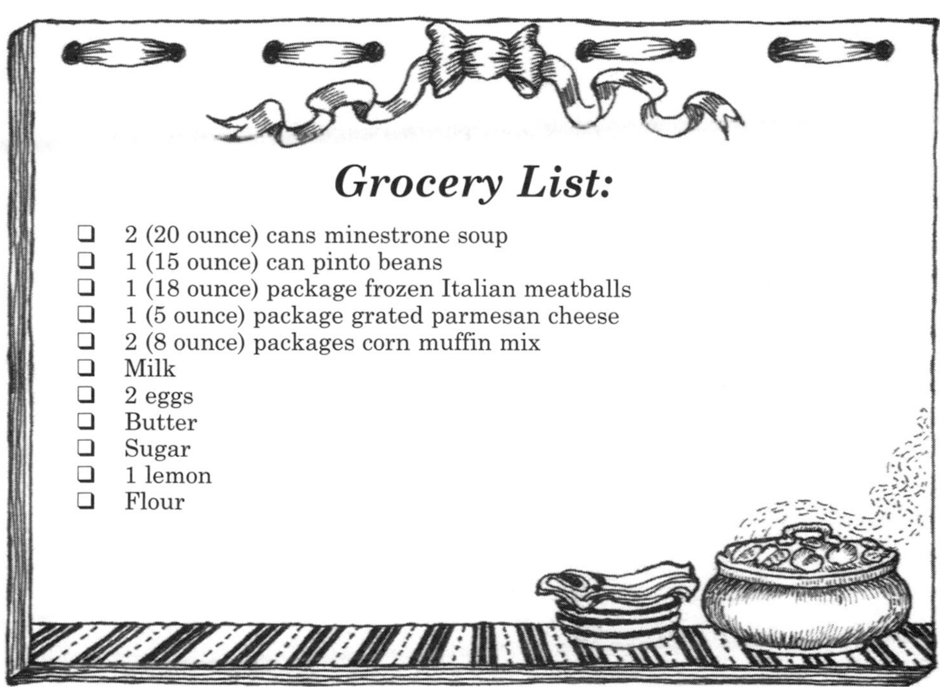

Grocery List:

- ❑ 2 (20 ounce) cans minestrone soup
- ❑ 1 (15 ounce) can pinto beans
- ❑ 1 (18 ounce) package frozen Italian meatballs
- ❑ 1 (5 ounce) package grated parmesan cheese
- ❑ 2 (8 ounce) packages corn muffin mix
- ❑ Milk
- ❑ 2 eggs
- ❑ Butter
- ❑ Sugar
- ❑ 1 lemon
- ❑ Flour

Favorites Make the Soup

Spaghetti Soup
Hush Puppies and Oyster Crackers
Deviled Eggs
Peach Cobbler and Vanilla Ice Cream

Spaghetti Soup

1 (7 ounce) package pre-cut spaghetti
1 (18 ounce) package frozen, cooked meatballs, thawed
1 (28 ounce) jar spaghetti sauce
1 (15 ounce) can Mexican stewed tomatoes

- In soup pot or kettle with 3 quarts boiling water and a little salt, cook spaghetti about 6 minutes (no need to drain).
- When spaghetti is done, add meatballs, spaghetti sauce and stewed tomatoes and cook until mixture heats through.

Tip: To garnish each soup bowl, sprinkle with 2 tablespoons mozzarella cheese, cheddar or Monterey Jack cheese or whatever you have in refrigerator.

Hush Puppies and Oyster Crackers

Frozen hush puppies
1 (10 ounce) bag oyster crackers

- Warm frozen hush puppies in oven or whip up a batch of corn muffins with just 1 egg, ⅓ cup milk and corn muffin mix. With such a big pot of soup, you may want both! Oyster crackers work well also.

Deviled Eggs

6 hard-boiled eggs
3 tablespoons sweet pickle relish
3 tablespoons mayonnaise
½ teaspoon mustard

◆ Peel eggs and cut in half lengthwise. Take yolks out and mash with fork. Add relish, mayonnaise and mustard to yolks and mix well. Place mixture back into egg white halves. Sprinkle with paprika if you like.

Peach Cobbler

1 (32 ounce) frozen peach cobbler, thawed
Vanilla ice cream

◆ Heat cobbler according to package directions. Add a scoop of ice cream while cobbler is warm.

Did you ever try breaking up dried spaghetti? When I do, sticks fly all over the kitchen. Thank goodness for pre-cut pasta. And what a time-saver ready-cooked meatballs are! I could have saved half my lifetime spent making meatballs if I had ready-cooked meatballs. Enjoy these little time-savers whenever you can.

Grocery List:

- ❑ 1 (7 ounce) package pre-cut spaghetti
- ❑ 1 (18 ounce) package frozen meatballs
- ❑ 1 (28 ounce) jar spaghetti sauce
- ❑ 1 (15 ounce) can Mexican stewed tomatoes
- ❑ 1 (8 ounce) package shredded mozzarella cheese, optional
- ❑ 1 (16 ounce) package frozen hush puppies
- ❑ 1 (10 ounce) package oyster crackers
- ❑ 6 eggs
- ❑ Pickle relish
- ❑ Mayonnaise and mustard
- ❑ 1 (32 ounce) frozen peach cobbler
- ❑ Vanilla ice cream

Steakhouse Stew

1 pound boneless beef sirloin steak, cubed
1 (15 ounce) can stewed tomatoes
2 (10 ounce) cans soup: 1 can French onion and 1 can tomato
1 (16 ounce) package frozen stew vegetables, thawed

- In skillet with a little oil, cook steak cubes until juices evaporate. Transfer to soup pot or roaster.
- Add 1 cup water, tomatoes, soups and vegetables and heat to boiling. Reduce heat to low and cook on medium for about 15 minutes or until vegetables are tender.

Spicy Cornbread Twists

½ cup (1 stick) butter, melted
¾ cup yellow cornmeal
½ teaspoon cayenne pepper
1 (11 ounce) can refrigerated soft breadsticks

- Preheat oven to 375°. Melt butter in pie plate in oven. Remove plate from oven.
- In small mixing bowl, combine cornmeal and cayenne pepper and spread on piece of wax paper. Roll breadsticks in melted butter, then in cornmeal mixture.
- Twist breadsticks according to package directions, place on baking sheet and bake 16 to 18 minutes or until breadsticks are light brown.

Pear and Cheese Salad

Shredded lettuce
1 or 2 (15 ounce) cans pear halves
1 (8 ounce) package shredded cheddar cheese

- On individual salad plates, place shredded lettuce and top with 2 pear halves. Sprinkle with cheese.

Chocolate Drops

1 (12 ounce) package milk chocolate chips
⅔ cup chunky peanut butter
4¼ cups Cocoa Krispie cereal

- In double boiler, melt chocolate chips and stir in peanut butter. Gently fold in cereal. Press into 9 x 9-inch pan and cut into bars.

When the autumn leaves or snowflakes drop, this stew supper will warm you down to your toes. Warm your oven while you put the stew together and it just takes a couple of minutes to roll the breadsticks in cornmeal. Canned pears are a great fruit for wintertime and who can turn down chocolate?

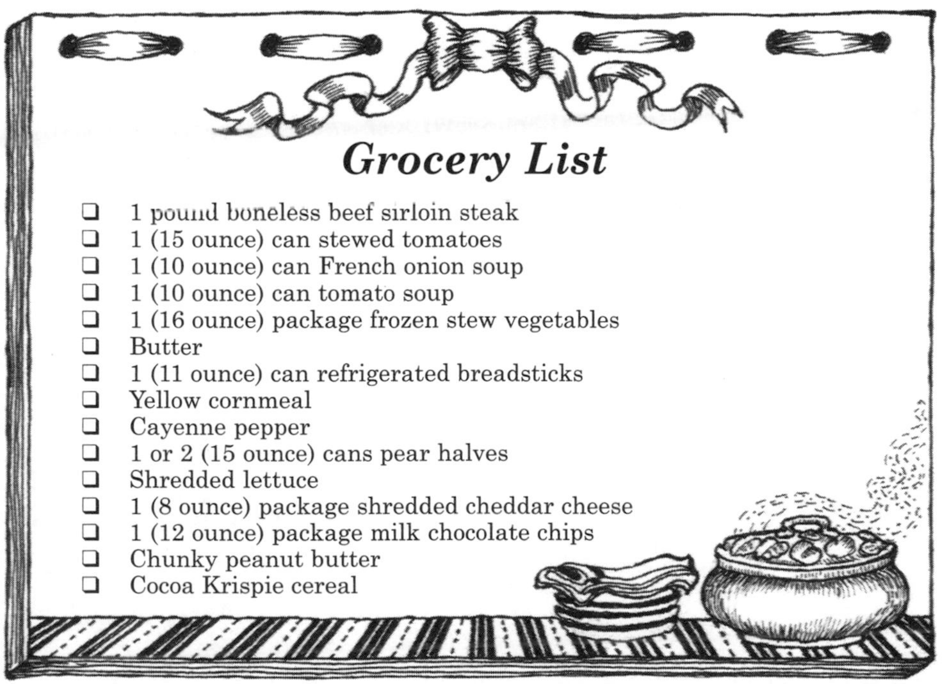

Grocery List

- ❑ 1 pound boneless beef sirloin steak
- ❑ 1 (15 ounce) can stewed tomatoes
- ❑ 1 (10 ounce) can French onion soup
- ❑ 1 (10 ounce) can tomato soup
- ❑ 1 (16 ounce) package frozen stew vegetables
- ❑ Butter
- ❑ 1 (11 ounce) can refrigerated breadsticks
- ❑ Yellow cornmeal
- ❑ Cayenne pepper
- ❑ 1 or 2 (15 ounce) cans pear halves
- ❑ Shredded lettuce
- ❑ 1 (8 ounce) package shredded cheddar cheese
- ❑ 1 (12 ounce) package milk chocolate chips
- ❑ Chunky peanut butter
- ❑ Cocoa Krispie cereal

Warm-Your-Soul Soup

3 (14 ounce) cans chicken broth
2 (15 ounce) cans Italian stewed tomatoes
1 onion and 1 rib celery, chopped
1 (8 ounce) package fettuccine

- In large soup kettle, combine chicken broth, tomatoes, onion, celery and 2 cups water. Bring to boil, reduce heat and simmer until onion and celery are tender-crisp.
- Add fettuccine and cook according to package directions. Season with salt and pepper to taste.

Tip: You may also add 1 (12 ounce) can chicken or turkey. "Warm your soul" a little more and add about ¼ teaspoon cayenne pepper.

Broccoli-Chicken Salad

3 to 4 boneless, skinless chicken breasts, cooked, cubed, chilled
2 cups fresh broccoli florets, chilled
1 sweet red bell pepper, seeded, chopped, chilled
1 cup chopped celery, chilled

- Combine chicken, broccoli, bell pepper and celery. Toss with honey mustard dressing or mayonnaise and refrigerate.

Sesame Breadsticks, Crackers or Cornbread

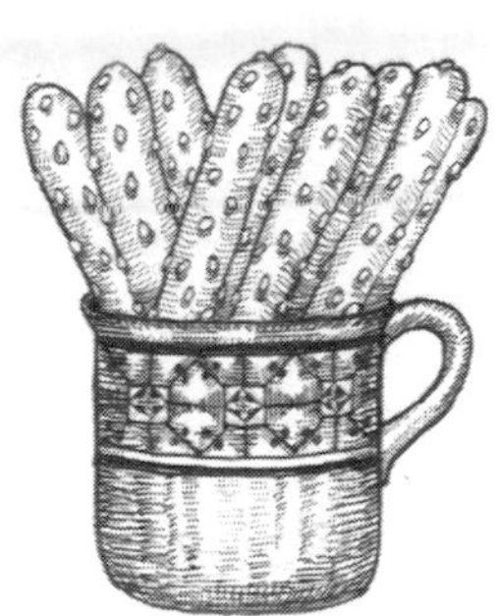

Bakery sesame breadsticks or crackers
Or 1 (8 ounce) package corn muffin mix

- Serve breadsticks or crackers on serving tray. Corn muffin mix requires 1 egg and ⅓ cup milk. Prepare batter for muffins or pour into 1 (8-inch) square pan.

Pecan Pie

1 (32 ounce) frozen pecan pie, thawed
Whipped topping

- Heat according to package directions and serve.

The addition of fettuccine in this soup makes it a hearty, robust meal-in-a-bowl.

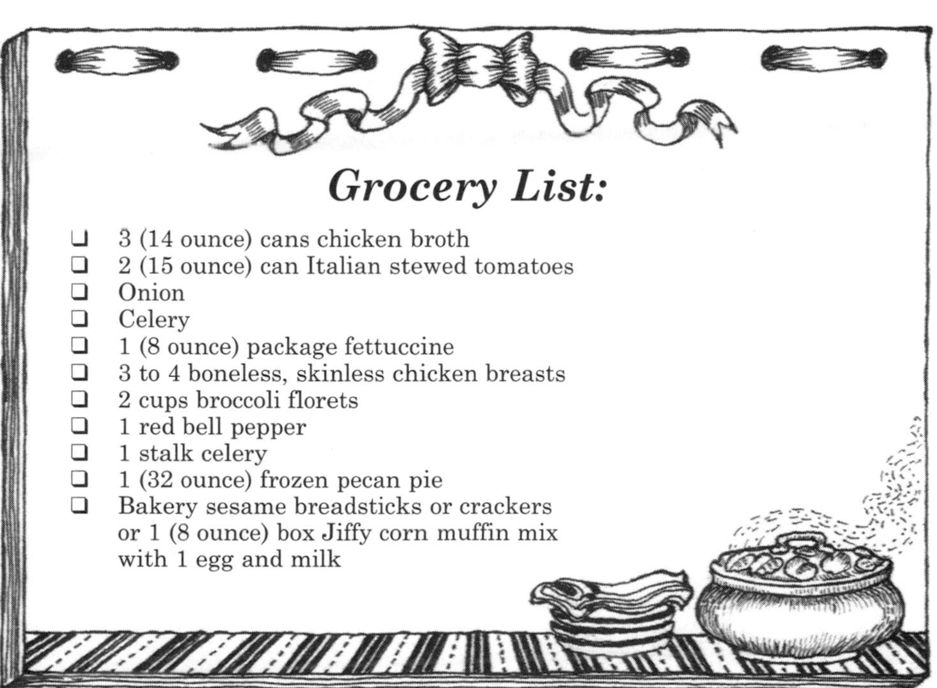

Feel-Better-Soup Night

Chicken and Noodle Supper
Mixed Green Salad with Creamy Ranch Dressing
Texas Toast
Ambrosia Dessert

Chicken and Noodle Supper

1 (3 ounce) package chicken-flavored ramen noodles, broken
1 (10 ounce) package frozen green peas, thawed
1 (4 ounce) jar sliced mushrooms, drained
3 cups cooked, cubed chicken

- In large saucepan, heat 2¼ cups water to boiling.
- Add ramen noodles, contents of seasoning packet and peas. (It's better if you add 2 teaspoons butter.) Heat to boiling, reduce heat to medium and cook about 5 minutes.
- Stir in mushrooms and chicken and continue cooking over low heat until all ingredients heat through. To serve, spoon into serving bowl.

Mixed Green Salad with Creamy Ranch Dressing

1 (10 ounce) package mixed salad greens
2 tomatoes
1 (8 ounce) bottle creamy ranch salad dressing
1 (6 ounce) box seasoned croutons

- Combine chilled salad greens and chopped tomatoes. When ready to serve, toss with just enough dressing to moisten greens. Top with seasoned croutons.

Texas Toast

1 (10 ounce) package frozen Texas toast

◆ Heat according to package directions.

Ambrosia Dessert

2 (11 ounce) cans mandarin oranges, drained, chilled
1 (20 ounce) can pineapple tidbits, drained, chilled
1 (7 ounce) can flaked coconut, chilled
1 cup miniature marshmallows

◆ In bowl with lid, combine oranges, pineapple and coconut. Fold in marshmallows (make sure marshmallows are separated so they do not stick together). Refrigerate.

We have a wealth of good recipes that can be used with ramen noodles. You could actually substitute cooked pork roast for the chicken and use the pork-flavored ramen noodles with the same vegetables. When you are in a hurry, ramen noodles can be the foundation for lots of interesting dishes.

Grocery List:

- ❑ 3 to 4 chicken breasts, cooked, cubed or deli chicken
- ❑ 1 (3 ounce) package chicken-flavored ramen noodles
- ❑ 1 (10 ounce) package frozen green peas
- ❑ 1 (4 ounce) can sliced mushrooms
- ❑ 1 (10 ounce) package mixed salad greens
- ❑ 2 tomatoes
- ❑ Creamy ranch salad dressing
- ❑ 1 (6 ounce) box seasoned croutons
- ❑ 1 (10 ounce) package frozen Texas toast
- ❑ 2 (11 ounce) cans mandarin oranges
- ❑ 1 (20 ounce) can pineapple tidbits
- ❑ 1 (7 ounce) can flaked coconut
- ❑ Miniature marshmallows

Sunday Night Supper

Cheesy Chicken Soup
Cream Cheese Sandwiches
Ranch Dip and Veggies
Dutch-Apple Pie and Butter-Pecan Ice Cream

Cheesy Chicken Soup

1 (10 ounce) can fiesta nacho cheese soup
1 (10 ounce) can cream of chicken soup
2 (14 ounce) cans chicken broth, 1 cup half-and-half
2 (12 ounce) cans chunk white chicken breast with broth

◆ In saucepan over medium heat, combine all ingredients and stir until soup is hot.

Tip: For pretty garnish, place a few sprigs fresh parsley on top of each serving.

Cream Cheese Sandwiches

2 (8 ounce) packages cream cheese, softened
1 (4 ounce) can chopped black olives
¾ cup chopped pecans
Pumpernickel rye bread with crust

◆ In mixing bowl with mixer, beat cream cheese with 2 tablespoons water or milk. Stir in olives and pecans.

◆ Spread mixture on slices of pumpernickel rye bread and cut in 3 finger strips.

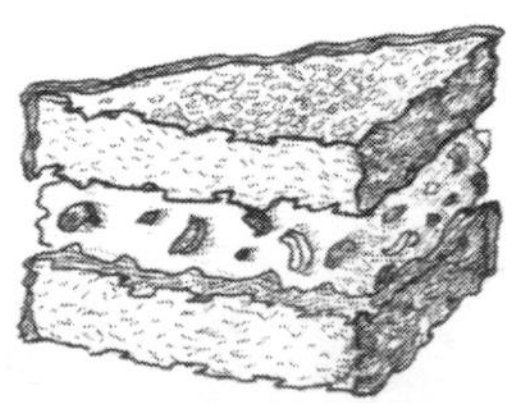

Ranch Dip and Veggies

1 stalk celery
1 bunch fresh cauliflower and broccoli florets
1 (16 ounce) package baby carrots
Ranch dip

- Wash and cut several celery ribs in about 3 to 4 pieces.
- Place on serving plate with cauliflower, broccoli and carrots.

Dutch-Apple Pie with Butter-Pecan Ice Cream

1 (45 ounce) frozen Dutch-apple pie, thawed
Butter-pecan ice cream

- Serve pie topped with ice cream.

It's "wind-down" time from the weekend and "get-ready" time for Monday. This Cheesy Chicken Soup makes the switch a little easier and puts everyone in a better mood.

Grocery List:

- ❑ 1 (10 ounce) can fiesta nacho cheese soup
- ❑ 1 (10 ounce) can cream of chicken soup
- ❑ 2 (14 ounce) cans chicken broth
- ❑ Half-and-half
- ❑ 2 (12 ounce) cans chunk white chicken breast with broth
- ❑ 2 (8 ounce) packages cream cheese
- ❑ 1 (4 ounce) can chopped black olives
- ❑ ¾ cup chopped pecans
- ❑ Loaf pumpernickel rye bread
- ❑ 1 stalk celery
- ❑ Cauliflower
- ❑ Broccoli
- ❑ 1 (16 ounce) package baby carrots
- ❑ Ranch dip
- ❑ 1 (45 ounce) frozen Dutch-apple pie
- ❑ 1 quart butter-pecan ice cream

Winter Wonders

Speedy Taco Soup
Cream-Style Corn Sticks
Greens and Artichoke Salad
Margarita Pie

Speedy Taco Soup

2 (14 ounce) cans chicken broth
1 (12 ounce) can chunk chicken breast with broth
1 (16 ounce) jar mild thick, chunky salsa
1 (15 ounce) can whole kernel corn with liquid

- In large saucepan, combine broth, chicken with broth, salsa and corn. Heat to boiling, reduce heat and simmer 15 minutes.

Cream-Style Corn Sticks

2 cups biscuit mix
3 fresh green onions, finely chopped
1 (8 ounce) can cream-style corn
½ cup (1 stick) butter, melted

- Preheat oven to 400°. In medium bowl, combine biscuit mix, green onions and cream-style corn and stir well.
- On floured surface, roll out dough and cut into 3 x 1-inch strips. Roll dough in melted butter, place on greased baking sheet and bake 15 to 17 minutes. Garnish with crushed chips, optional.

Greens and Artichoke Salad

1 (10 ounce) package spring-mix salad greens
1 (14 ounce) jar artichoke hearts, drained, chopped
2 tomatoes, chopped, drained
1 (8 ounce) bottle Catalina salad dressing

- In salad bowl, toss all ingredients with dressing just before serving.

Margarita Pie

1 (8 ounce) package cream cheese, softened
⅓ cup sugar
2 (½ ounce) envelopes dry margarita mix
1 (8 ounce) carton whipped topping
1 (9 inch) ready shortbread piecrust

- In mixing bowl, whip cream cheese until fluffy, add sugar and margarita mix and beat until smooth. Fold in whipped topping and mix well. Pour into piecrust and freeze.

Few people agree on an exact recipe for taco or tortilla soup, but this one is guaranteed fast and easy! I really don't know how we managed before salsa was available in the supermarket. When winter comes, be sure you have these ingredients on hand.

Grocery List:

- ❑ 2 (14 ounce) cans chicken broth
- ❑ 1 (12 ounce) can chunk chicken breast with broth
- ❑ 1 (16 ounce) jar mild thick, chunky salsa
- ❑ 1 (15 ounce) can whole kernel corn
- ❑ 2 cups biscuit mix
- ❑ 1 (8 ounce) can cream-style corn
- ❑ Green onions
- ❑ Butter
- ❑ 1 (10 ounce) package spring-mix salad greens
- ❑ 1 (14 ounce) jar artichoke hearts
- ❑ 2 vine-ripened tomatoes
- ❑ 1 (8 ounce) bottle Catalina salad dressing
- ❑ 1 (8 ounce) package cream cheese
- ❑ Sugar
- ❑ 2 (½ ounce) envelopes dry margarita mix
- ❑ 1 (8 ounce) carton whipped topping
- ❑ 1 (9 inch) ready shortbread piecrust

Quick-Winter Date

Beefy Vegetable Soup
Cornbread
Potato Skins and Stuffed Celery
Vanilla Layer Cake

Beefy Vegetable Soup

1 pound lean ground beef
1 (46 ounce) can cocktail vegetable juice
1 (1 ounce) packet onion soup mix
1 (3 ounce) package beef-flavored ramen noodles
1 (16 ounce) package frozen mixed vegetables

- In large soup pot or kettle over medium heat, cook beef until no longer pink. Drain. Stir in cocktail juice, soup mix, contents of noodle seasoning packet and mixed vegetables.
- Heat mixture to boiling, reduce heat and simmer uncovered 6 minutes or until vegetables are tender-crisp. Return to boiling, stir in noodles and cook 3 minutes.

Cornbread

1 or 2 (8 ounce) boxes Jiffy corn muffin mix
⅓ cup milk
1 egg
Butter

- Prepare mix according to package directions and pour into greased muffin pan. Or you can use both boxes and pour into greased 7 x 11-inch baking pan and cut cornbread in squares.

Potato Skins

4 slices bacon, fried crisp, drained, crumbled
4 baked potatoes
1 cup shredded cheddar cheese

- Fry bacon in skillet or microwave, drain and crumble. Slice potatoes lengthwise and microwave for 3 minutes. Scoop out potato, leaving ¼ inch of potato on skins.
- Fill each potato skin with cheese and bacon. Cover with paper towel and microwave for 30 seconds or until cheese melts.

Stuffed Celery

1 stalk celery
1 (16 ounce) carton pimento cheese

- Break off celery ribs and cut in 3-inch pieces. Fill generously with cheese.

Vanilla Layer Cake

1 (22 ounce) frozen vanilla layer cake, thawed

- Slice and serve on dessert plates.

There are as many recipes for vegetable soup as there are minutes in a year, but not every pot of soup needs to simmer for hours. With today's high-quality, convenient products, we can whip up a hearty pot of soup in a few minutes! With this recipe, meat, vegetables and even pasta are ready in minutes. It's homemade goodness from the pantry and freezer!

Grocery List:

- ❑ 1 pound lean ground beef
- ❑ 1 (46 ounce) can cocktail vegetable juice
- ❑ 1 (1 ounce) packet onion soup mix
- ❑ 1 (3 ounce) package beef flavored ramen noodles
- ❑ 1 (16 ounce) package frozen mixed vegetables
- ❑ 1 or 2 (8 ounce) boxes Jiffy corn muffin mix
- ❑ Milk
- ❑ 1 Egg
- ❑ Butter
- ❑ Celery
- ❑ 1 (16 ounce) carton pimento cheese
- ❑ Bacon
- ❑ 4 Potatoes
- ❑ 1 (8 ounce) package shredded cheddar cheese
- ❑ 1 (22 ounce) frozen vanilla layer cake

Chicken Supper in Minutes

Skillet Chicken and Peas
Spinach-Strawberry Salad
Buttered French Bread
Coffee Mallow

Skillet Chicken and Peas

4 or 5 boneless, skinless chicken breast halves
2 (10 ounce) cans cream of chicken soup
½ teaspoon EACH paprika and black pepper
2 cups uncooked instant rice
1 (10 ounce) package frozen green peas

- Heat a little oil in very large skillet. Add chicken and cook until well browned.
- Transfer chicken to plate and keep warm. To skillet, add soup, 1¾ cups water, paprika and pepper. Heat to boiling and stir in rice and peas; reduce heat. Top with chicken and cook on low heat for 15 minutes.

Spinach-Strawberry Salad

1 (10 ounce) package baby spinach
1 pint fresh strawberries, halved
½ cup slivered almonds, toasted
1 (8 ounce) bottle poppy seed salad dressing

- In salad bowl, combine spinach and strawberries and toss. When ready to serve, toss with dressing and sprinkle almonds on top.

Buttered French Bread

1 loaf frozen, garlic French bread

- Preheat oven to 325°. Place slices on baking sheet and heat 15 minutes.

Coffee Mallow

3 cups miniature marshmallows
½ cup brewed, strong coffee
1 (8 ounce) carton whipping cream
½ teaspoon vanilla

- In large saucepan, combine marshmallows and coffee. On very low heat and stirring constantly, cook until marshmallows melt. Cool mixture (it will cool faster if you will place it in freezer for few minutes). Fold in whipped cream and vanilla and spoon into individual dessert glasses.

How can you beat having the chicken, rice and vegetable cook right in the skillet? (If you have an electric skillet, you might want to use it because they are usually larger.) All you need now is a good salad and hot bread. But don't give up on dessert – Coffee Mallow is easy and delicious!

Grocery List:

- ❑ 4 or 5 boneless, skinless chicken breast halves
- ❑ 2 (10 ounce) cans cream of chicken soup
- ❑ Paprika and black pepper
- ❑ 1 box instant rice
- ❑ 1 (10 ounce) package frozen green peas
- ❑ 1 (10 ounce) package baby spinach
- ❑ 1 pint fresh strawberries
- ❑ ½ cup slivered almonds
- ❑ 1 (8 ounce) bottle poppy seed salad dressing
- ❑ 1 loaf garlic French bread
- ❑ 1 (10 ounce) package miniature marshmallows
- ❑ ½ cup strong coffee
- ❑ 1 (8 ounce) carton whipping cream
- ❑ Vanilla

Razzleberry Jiffy Chicken Dinner

Sweet-and-Sour Chicken-Veggies
Tossed Green Salad
Toasted French Bread
Razzleberry Pie

Sweet-and-Sour Chicken-Veggies

1 (.03 ounce) package chicken-flavored ramen noodles
1 (16 ounce) package frozen broccoli, cauliflower and carrots
⅔ cup sweet and sour sauce plus 1 tablespoon soy sauce
3 cooked boneless, skinless chicken breast halves, cut into strips

- In saucepan, cook noodles and vegetables in 2 cups water (reserve seasoning packet) for 3 minutes or until liquid absorbs.
- Add seasoning packet, sweet and sour sauce and a little salt and pepper.
- Add chicken strips and heat and stir well.

Tossed Green Salad

1 (10 ounce) package fancy salad greens mix
1 seedless cucumber, sliced
1 bunch fresh green onions
Seasoned croutons

- In salad bowl, toss all ingredients with favorite dressing.

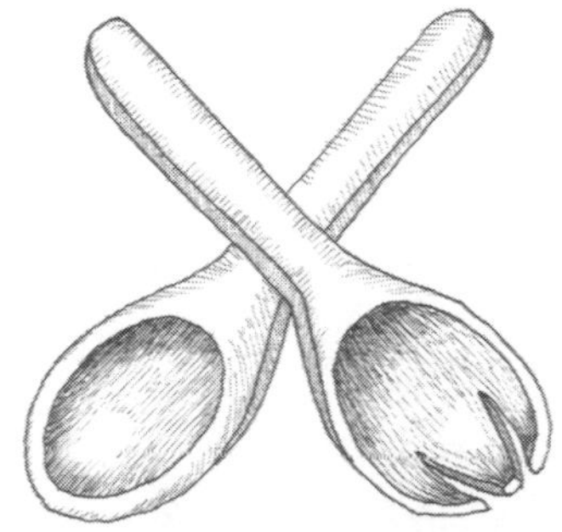

Toasted French Bread

1 loaf French bread, unsliced
½ cup (1 stick) butter, softened
¾ cup parmesan cheese
¾ teaspoon garlic powder

- Slice bread in half lengthwise, then slice each half to make 4 pieces.
- In bowl, combine butter, parmesan cheese and garlic powder and spread on bread slices. Use all the mixture.
- Place bread on baking sheet and bake at 325° about 20 minutes or until top browns.

Razzleberry Pie

1 (42 ounce) frozen razzleberry pie, thawed

- Serve on dessert plates.

This "one-dish" chicken menu is ready in a jiffy and clean-up is easy, too! Toasted French bread with parmesan cheese is a crunchy addition to the meal and works well with the salad.

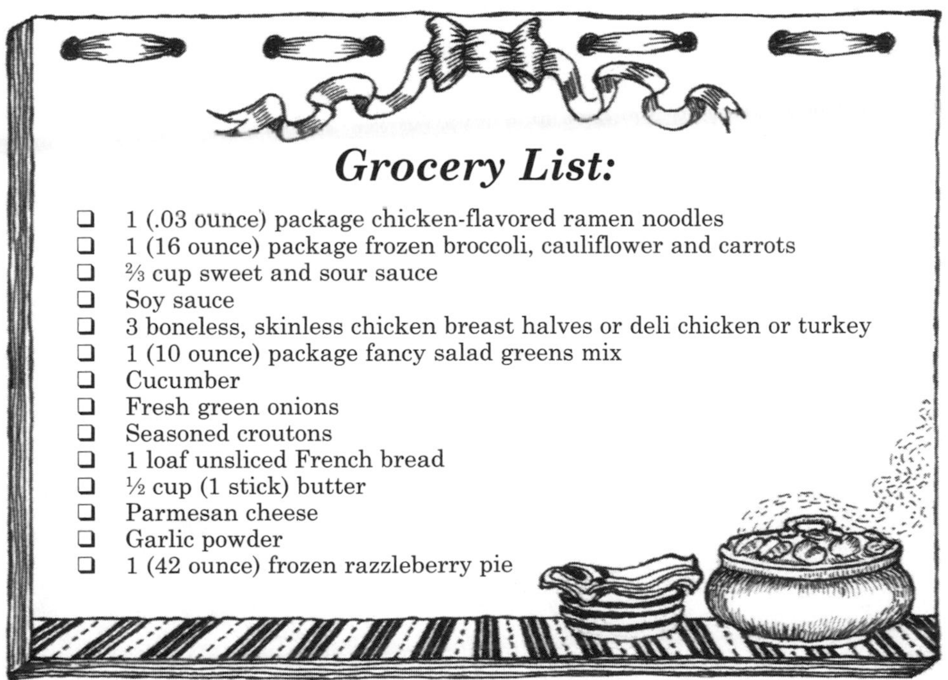

Grocery List:

- ❑ 1 (.03 ounce) package chicken-flavored ramen noodles
- ❑ 1 (16 ounce) package frozen broccoli, cauliflower and carrots
- ❑ ⅔ cup sweet and sour sauce
- ❑ Soy sauce
- ❑ 3 boneless, skinless chicken breast halves or deli chicken or turkey
- ❑ 1 (10 ounce) package fancy salad greens mix
- ❑ Cucumber
- ❑ Fresh green onions
- ❑ Seasoned croutons
- ❑ 1 loaf unsliced French bread
- ❑ ½ cup (1 stick) butter
- ❑ Parmesan cheese
- ❑ Garlic powder
- ❑ 1 (42 ounce) frozen razzleberry pie

Chicken Parmesan and Spaghetti

1 (14 ounce) package frozen, cooked, breaded chicken cutlets, thawed
1 (28 ounce) jar spaghetti sauce
1 (5 ounce) package shredded parmesan cheese, divided
1 (8 ounce) package spaghetti, cooked

- Preheat oven to 400°. In buttered 9 x 13-inch baking dish, place chicken cutlets and top each with about ¼ cup spaghetti sauce and heaping tablespoon parmesan cheese. Bake 15 minutes.
- Place cooked spaghetti on serving platter and top with cutlets. Sprinkle remaining cheese over each cutlet. Heat remaining spaghetti sauce and serve with chicken and spaghetti.

Spinach Souffle

2 (12 ounce) packages frozen spinach souffle, thawed

- While spaghetti and chicken cook, remove tray from both outer cartons, then remove film covers.
- Microwave on high 15 to 16 minutes and stir both trays after 10 minutes of cooking. (Microwave wattage may vary time.) Souffle is done when it bubbles around edges and knife inserted in center comes out clean.

This souffle is delicious and way too much trouble to make from scratch.

Tossed Green Salad

1 (10 ounce) bag Italian blend mixed salad greens
1 seedless cucumber, sliced
1 rib celery, sliced
2 small zucchini, sliced

◆ In salad bowl, combine mixed greens, cucumber, celery and zucchini and toss. Dress with creamy Italian or favorite dressing.

Rice Pudding

2 (16 ounce) cartons refrigerated rice pudding
1 cup chopped pecans, toasted

◆ Spoon pudding into dessert bowls and garnish with toasted pecans.

This meal is a nice change of pace from the traditional spaghetti and meatballs. Cooked, breaded chicken cutlets are great frozen entrees and the spinach souffle is simply fabulous! Those cartons of refrigerated rice pudding (also tapioca pudding) are deliciously creamy and good without being a "too-sweet" dessert.

Grocery List:

- ❑ 1 (14 ounce) package frozen, cooked, breaded chicken cutlets
- ❑ 1 (28 ounce) jar spaghetti sauce
- ❑ 1 (5 ounce) package shredded parmesan cheese
- ❑ 1 (8 ounce) package spaghetti
- ❑ 2 (12 ounce) packages frozen spinach souffle
- ❑ 1 (10 ounce) bag Italian blend mixed salad greens
- ❑ 1 cucumber
- ❑ 1 rib celery
- ❑ 2 small zucchini
- ❑ 1 (8 ounce) bottle creamy Italian dressing
- ❑ 2 (16 ounce) cartons refrigerated rice pudding
- ❑ 1 cup chopped pecans
- ❑ Buttered and sliced frozen French bread, optional

Dinner on the Run

Skillet Chicken and More
Cauliflower and Green Peas
Dinner Rolls
Corn Flake Cookies

Skillet Chicken and More

4 boneless, skinless chicken breast halves
2 (10 ounce) cans cream of chicken soup
2 cups uncooked, instant white rice
1 (16 ounce) package frozen broccoli florets

- In very large skillet (or electric skillet) with a little oil, brown chicken breasts on both sides and simmer 10 minutes. Remove chicken and keep warm.
- To skillet, add soup and 2 cups water. Heat to boiling.
- Stir in instant rice and broccoli florets. Top with chicken sprinkled with a little black pepper and paprika. Cover dish and cook on low 15 minutes or until liquid evaporates.

Cauliflower and Green Peas

1 (16 ounce) package frozen cauliflower, thawed
¼ cup (½ stick) butter
1 cup chopped celery
1 (15 ounce) can green peas

- Cook cauliflower according to package directions and drain. Saute celery in butter and stir in peas and cauliflower. Heat thoroughly.

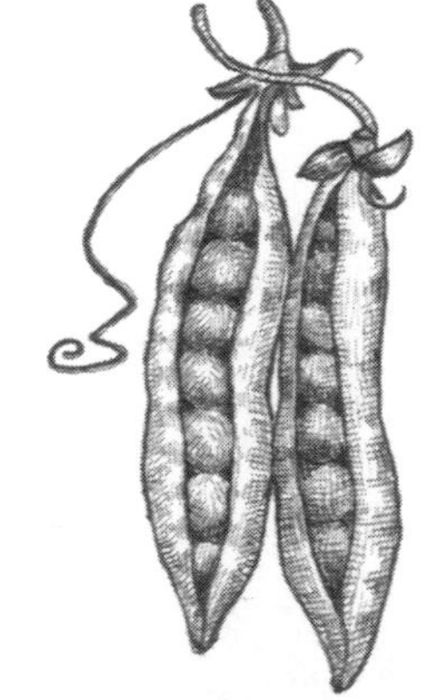

Dinner Rolls

1 (14 ounce) package frozen dinner rolls, thawed
Butter

◆ Preheat oven to 375°. Heat rolls according to package directions and serve with butter.

Corn Flake Cookies

1 (12 ounce) package chocolate chips
¾ cup peanut butter
3½ to 4 cups corn flakes, crushed

◆ Melt chocolate chips in double boiler; remove from heat and stir in peanut butter. When mixed thoroughly, gently stir in corn flakes and drop by teaspoon on wax paper.

In between soccer practice and the PTA meeting, you'll still have time to cook a hot meal with this great Skillet Chicken. With hot rolls and cookies, they'll wonder how you did it all.

Grocery List:

- ❑ 4 boneless, skinless chicken breast halves
- ❑ 2 (10 ounce) cans cream of chicken soup
- ❑ 1 (28 ounce) package instant white rice
- ❑ 1 (16 ounce) package frozen broccoli florets
- ❑ Black pepper
- ❑ Paprika
- ❑ 1 (16 ounce) package frozen cauliflower
- ❑ Butter
- ❑ Celery
- ❑ 1 (15 ounce) can green peas
- ❑ 1 (14 ounce) package frozen dinner rolls
- ❑ 1 (12 ounce) package chocolate chips
- ❑ Peanut butter
- ❑ Cornflakes

Dinner in a Skillet

Chicken and the Works
Butter Rolls
Cheese-Topped Tomatoes
Haystacks

Chicken and the Works

6 boneless, skinless chicken breast halves with paprika
2 (10 ounce) cans cream of chicken soup
2 cups uncooked, instant white rice
1 (10 ounce) package frozen green peas, thawed

- Sprinkle chicken with black pepper and paprika and brown in large, 12-inch skillet with little oil. Reduce heat, cover and simmer about 15 minutes. Transfer chicken to plate and keep warm.
- Add soups, 2 cups water and mix well. Heat to boiling and stir in rice and green peas. Top with chicken breasts, cover and simmer over low heat about 10 minutes.

Butter Rolls

2 cups biscuit mix
1 (8 ounce) carton sour cream
½ cup (1 stick) butter, melted
Honey

- Preheat oven to 375°.
- In mixing bowl, combine all ingredients and mix well.
- Spoon butter into 8 to 10 greased muffin pans and bake 12 to 14 minutes or until rolls brown lightly. Serve with butter and a little honey.

Cheese-Topped Tomatoes

Shredded lettuce
2 or 3 vine-ripened tomatoes
1 (8 ounce) package shredded mozzarella cheese

◆ Place shredded lettuce on individual salad plates. Slice tomatoes and place 2 or 3 slices on each plate. Cover tomatoes with mozzarella cheese.

Haystacks

1 (12 ounce) package butterscotch chips
1 cup salted peanuts
1½ cups chow mein noodles

◆ Melt butterscotch chips in top of double boiler. Remove from heat and stir in peanuts and noodles. Drop by teaspoons on wax paper.

What a deal... practically a whole meal in a skillet. (Make sure it's a really big skillet.) And rolls to die for and the always-great tomatoes topped with yummy cheese. The Haystacks are the fun thing to make. In fact, this is a good time to let the kids take over the dessert.

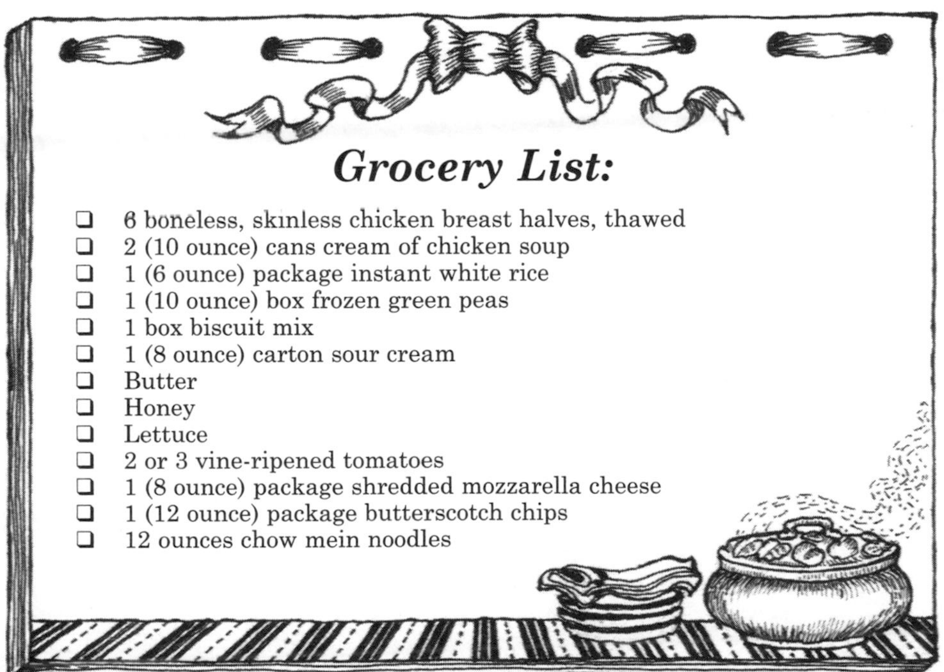

Grocery List:

- ❑ 6 boneless, skinless chicken breast halves, thawed
- ❑ 2 (10 ounce) cans cream of chicken soup
- ❑ 1 (6 ounce) package instant white rice
- ❑ 1 (10 ounce) box frozen green peas
- ❑ 1 box biscuit mix
- ❑ 1 (8 ounce) carton sour cream
- ❑ Butter
- ❑ Honey
- ❑ Lettuce
- ❑ 2 or 3 vine-ripened tomatoes
- ❑ 1 (8 ounce) package shredded mozzarella cheese
- ❑ 1 (12 ounce) package butterscotch chips
- ❑ 12 ounces chow mein noodles

Rainy Night Special

Creamy Mushroom Chicken
Chicken Couscous and Hot Buttered Rolls
Tomato-Pesto Salad
Cherry-Crunch Pie

Creamy Mushroom Chicken

4 boneless, skinless chicken breast halves
1 (10 ounce) can cream of mushroom soup
1 (4 ounce) can sliced mushrooms, drained
½ cup milk

- Sprinkle chicken liberally with seasoned salt and black pepper. In skillet over high heat with a little oil, brown chicken on both sides.
- While chicken browns, combine mushroom soup, mushrooms and milk in saucepan and heat just enough to mix well. Pour over chicken breasts, reduce heat to low and simmer covered for 15 minutes.

Chicken Couscous

1 (5.7 ounce) package chicken-flavored couscous

- Cook couscous according to package directions.
- To serve, place couscous on serving platter with chicken breasts on top. Pour sauce into gravy boat to spoon over chicken and couscous.

Hot Buttered Rolls

1 (14 ounce) package bakery potato dinner rolls
Butter

- Preheat oven to 375°. Heat rolls in oven until they brown lightly.

Tomato-Pesto Salad

4 to 5 vine-ripened tomatoes
8 ounces fresh mozzarella cheese
½ cup prepared, refrigerated pesto sauce
Extra virgin olive oil

- Slice tomatoes, arrange in circle on serving plate and overlap slightly.
- Place slice cheese on each tomato slice and top with scant 1 tablespoon pesto sauce. Lightly drizzle olive oil over all and add salt and pepper to taste.

Cherry-Crunch Pie

1 (37 ounce) frozen cherry crunch pie, thawed
Whipped topping or ice cream

- Warm pie according to package directions. Top with whipped topping or ice cream.

In today's "fast-food" world, any home-cooked meal is comfort food! Warm up an evening with this Creamy Mushroom Chicken and spectacular sides.

Grocery List:

- ❑ 4 boneless, skinless chicken breast halves
- ❑ 1 (10 ounce) can cream of mushroom soup
- ❑ 1 (4 ounce) can sliced mushrooms
- ❑ Milk
- ❑ Butter
- ❑ 1 (5.7 ounce) package chicken-flavored couscous
- ❑ 4 to 5 vine-ripened tomatoes
- ❑ 8 ounces fresh mozzarella cheese
- ❑ 1 (8 ounce) carton refrigerated pesto sauce
- ❑ Extra virgin olive oil
- ❑ 1 (14 ounce) package bakery potato dinner rolls
- ❑ 1 (37 ounce) Mrs. Smith's frozen cherry-crunch pie
- ❑ Whipped topping or ice cream

Alfredo Chicken

5 or 6 boneless, skinless chicken breast halves
1 (16 ounce) package frozen broccoli florets, thawed
1 sweet red bell pepper, seeded, chopped
1 (16 ounce) jar alfredo sauce

- ◆ Preheat oven to 375°. In large skillet with a little oil, brown and cook chicken breasts until juices run clear. Transfer to greased 9 x 13-inch baking dish.
- ◆ Microwave broccoli according to package directions and drain. (If broccoli stems are extra long, trim and discard.) Spoon broccoli and bell pepper over chicken.
- ◆ In small saucepan, heat alfredo sauce with ¼ cup water. Pour over chicken and vegetables. Cover and bake for 15 to 20 minutes.

This chicken-broccoli dish can be "dressed up" a bit by sprinkling a little shredded parmesan cheese over top after casserole is removed from oven.

Italian Corn

1 (16 ounce) package frozen whole kernel corn
2 slices bacon, cooked, diced
1 small onion, chopped
1 (15 ounce) can Italian stewed tomatoes

- ◆ Place all ingredients in 2-quart pan and cook until most of liquid in tomatoes cooks out. Add salt and pepper to taste.

Cheese Drops

2 cups biscuit mix
⅔ cup milk
⅔ cup shredded sharp cheddar cheese
¼ cup (½ stick) butter, melted

- Preheat oven to 375°. Mix biscuit mix, milk and cheese. Drop 1 heaping tablespoon dough onto greased baking pan and bake for 10 minutes or until slightly brown.
- While warm, brush tops of biscuits with melted butter.

Porcupine Clusters

¼ cup light corn syrup
1 (12 ounce) package white chocolate morsels
2 cups chow mein noodles
¾ cup salted peanuts

- On low heat, melt corn syrup and white chocolate chips. (You can use dark chocolate chips if you like.)
- Pour over noodles and peanuts, mix well and drop by teaspoon on wax paper. Refrigerate to set.

Boneless, skinless chicken breasts are terrific time-savers. Always keep a big bag in the freezer to prepare one of our easy chicken recipes. Plan ahead by removing frozen chicken from freezer in the morning and thawing in refrigerator. Couscous is also a big favorite of mine—it replaces rice with lots of pizzazz!

Grocery List:

- ❑ 5 to 6 boneless, skinless chicken breast halves
- ❑ 1 (16 ounce) package frozen broccoli florets
- ❑ 1 sweet red bell pepper
- ❑ 1 (16 ounce) jar alfredo sauce
- ❑ 1 (16 ounce) package frozen whole kernel corn
- ❑ 2 bacon slices
- ❑ 1 onion
- ❑ 1 (16 ounce) can Italian stewed tomatoes
- ❑ Bisquick
- ❑ Milk
- ❑ 1 (8 ounce) package shredded, sharp cheddar cheese
- ❑ Butter
- ❑ Light corn syrup
- ❑ 1 (12 ounce) package white chocolate morsels
- ❑ 2 cups chow mein noodles
- ❑ ¾ cup salted peanuts

Merry Berry Chicken Tonight

Spiced Chicken
Roasted-Garlic Rice and Mushrooms
Merry Berry Salad
Banana Cream Pie

Spiced Chicken

Spice Mix:
1 tablespoon paprika
1 teaspoon ground cumin
½ teaspoon cayenne pepper
½ teaspoon each coriander and oregano

Chicken:
4 or 5 boneless, skinless chicken breasts, split in half lengthwise
Extra-virgin olive oil
Spice mix

- ◆ In small bowl, combine paprika, cumin, cayenne pepper, coriander, oregano and 1 teaspoon salt.
- ◆ In large shallow baking dish, place chicken pieces and drizzle with olive oil to coat. Rub each piece liberally with spice mix and let stand about 10 minutes.
- ◆ Heat large skillet over medium to high heat and brown chicken pieces. Reduce heat, cover and simmer about 10 minutes on each side. Transfer to serving platter.

Roasted-Garlic Rice and Mushrooms

2 (6 ounce) packages roasted garlic rice
Butter
2 (4 ounce) cans sliced mushrooms, drained

- ◆ Cook rice according to package directions. Stir in mushrooms.

Merry Berry Salad

1 (10 ounce) package salad mixed greens
1 red apple and 1 green apple, unpeeled, diced
1 (8 ounce) package shredded parmesan cheese
¾ cup Craisins®

◆ In salad bowl, toss all ingredients with poppy seed dressing.

Tip: To keep apples from turning dark, sprinkle peeled fruit with a little lemon juice. Once they are in the salad with the dressing, they will be fine, so try to put this salad together as quickly as you can.

Banana Cream Pie

1 (42 ounce) frozen banana cream pie, thawed

◆ Slice and serve.

After you catch those chickens, rub'em down good with this spicy and very tasty seasoning combination. This is a fun menu with the Merry Berry Salad and the Banana Cream Pie—nobody can turn this dinner down.

Grocery List:

- ❑ Paprika
- ❑ Ground cumin
- ❑ Cayenne pepper
- ❑ Ground coriander
- ❑ Ground oregano
- ❑ 4 or 5 boneless, skinless chicken breasts
- ❑ Extra-virgin olive oil
- ❑ 2 (6 ounce) packages Uncle Ben's Roasted Garlic Rice
- ❑ Butter
- ❑ 2 (4 ounce) cans sliced mushrooms
- ❑ 1 (10 ounce) package salad mixed greens
- ❑ 1 red apple, 1 green apple
- ❑ 1 (8 ounce) package shredded parmesan cheese
- ❑ Craisins® (sweetened, dried cranberries)
- ❑ 1 (8 ounce) bottle poppy seed dressing
- ❑ 1 (42 ounce) frozen banana cream pie

It's a Wrap

Sweet 'N Spicy Chicken
Hot Cooked Rice
Cauliflower and Broccoli in 3-Cheese Sauce
Green Goddess Salad
Butterscotch Pudding Cups

Sweet 'N Spicy Chicken

1 pound boneless, skinless chicken breasts, cubed
1 (1.25 ounce) packet taco seasoning
1 (16 ounce) jar chunky salsa
1 (8 ounce) jar peach preserves

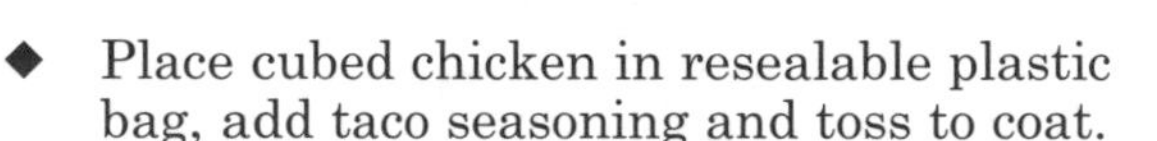

- Place cubed chicken in resealable plastic bag, add taco seasoning and toss to coat.

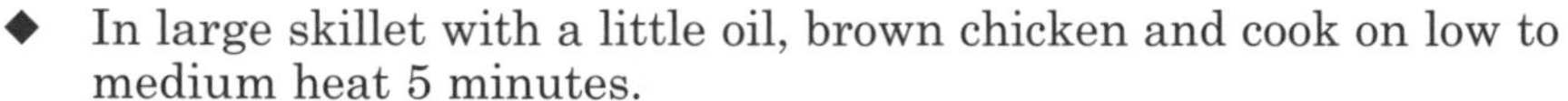

- In large skillet with a little oil, brown chicken and cook on low to medium heat 5 minutes.
- In saucepan, combine salsa, preserves and ¼ cup water. Heat and stir until salsa and preserves mix well. Stir into skillet with chicken.
- Bring mixture to boil. Reduce heat, cover and simmer 15 minutes.

Hot Cooked Rice

2 cups uncooked, instant white rice
Butter
1½ cups chopped walnuts
1 bunch green onions, chopped

- Cook rice according to package directions. Stir in walnuts and onions and serve chicken over rice.

Cauliflower and Broccoli in 3-Cheese Sauce

1 (19 ounce) package frozen cauliflower and broccoli in 3-cheese sauce

- Heat according to package directions.

Green Goddess Salad

1 (10 ounce) package fancy greens
2 cups fresh broccoli florets
2 tomatoes, chopped, drained
1 (16 ounce) bottle green goddess salad dressing

- In large salad bowl, combine greens, broccoli and tomatoes and toss with dressing to taste.

Butterscotch Pudding Cups

6 (4 ounce) butterscotch pudding cups, chilled
Sugar cookies

- Serve as is or in dessert cups with sugar cookies.

This chicken has the flavor to get your attention and is quick and easy to make! Delightful veggies in cheese sauce and a green salad are perfect sides. If you can't eat a meal without bread and butter, try a 12-ounce tray of frozen yeast rolls. They are very good.

Grocery List:

- ❑ 1 pound boneless, skinless chicken breasts
- ❑ 1 (1.25 ounce) packet taco seasoning
- ❑ 1 (16 ounce) jar chunky salsa
- ❑ 1 (8 ounce) jar peach preserves
- ❑ 1 (28 ounce) package instant white rice
- ❑ Butter
- ❑ 1½ cups chopped walnuts
- ❑ 1 bunch green onions
- ❑ 1 (19 ounce) package frozen cauliflower and broccoli in 3-cheese sauce
- ❑ 1 (10 ounce) package fancy greens
- ❑ 2 cups fresh broccoli florets
- ❑ 2 tomatoes
- ❑ 1 (16 ounce) bottle green goddess salad dressing
- ❑ 6 (4 ounce) butterscotch pudding cups, chilled
- ❑ Sugar cookies

Chili-Pepper Chicken

¼ cup (½ stick) butter
6 boneless, skinless chicken breast halves
1 (6 ounce) box Shake'n Bake chicken coating mix
1 (16 ounce) jar mild salsa

- Preheat oven to 400°. In 9 x 13-inch glass baking dish, melt butter in oven and remove.
- In shallow bowl, place coating mix and coat each chicken breast on both sides.
- Place chicken in buttered baking dish and arrange so pieces are not touching.
- Bake 20 minutes or until chicken browns lightly. Serve with heaping spoon of salsa.

Tip: Chicken coating mixes are available in a variety of flavors, including mild.

Deli-Pasta Salad

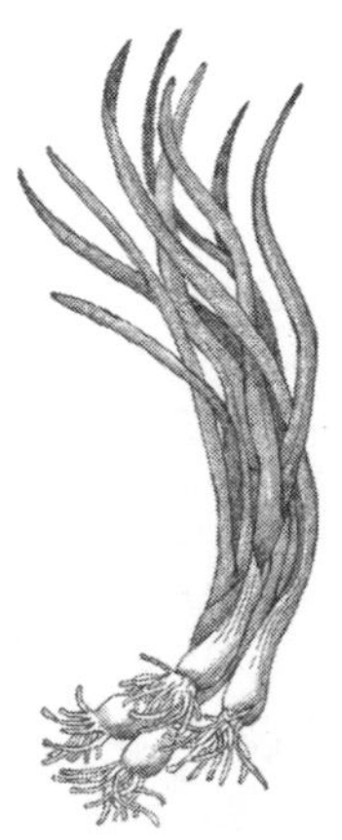

1 (24 ounce) carton deli-pasta salad
1 bunch fresh green onions, sliced
1 (4 ounce) jar chopped pimento, well drained
3 vine-ripened tomatoes

- In salad bowl, combine pasta salad, green onions and pimento. Quarter each tomato and place around edge of salad.

Corn-on-the-Cob

1 (8 count) package frozen corn-on-the-cob halves, thawed
Butter
Salt and pepper

- Boil corn according to package directions. Serve with melted butter, salt and pepper.

Pound Cake Deluxe

1 (10-inch) round bakery pound cake
1 (20 ounce) can crushed pineapple with juice
1 (5.1 ounce) package coconut instant pudding mix
1 (8 ounce) carton whipped topping

- Slice cake horizontally to make 3 layers.
- Mix pineapple, pudding and whipped topping and blend well.
- Spread mixture on each layer and top of cake. Sprinkle coconut on top layer if desired. Refrigerate.

Chicken seasoning and coating mix is an easy way to prepare tender, juicy chicken without frying. I prefer the spicy varieties for extra flavor and "kick." Frozen corn on the cob is nutritious and ready after only 5 minutes of boiling time. The only time my son didn't beg for corn on the cob was when he was 5 and had his 2 front teeth missing!

Grocery List:

- ❑ Butter
- ❑ 6 boneless, skinless chicken breast halves
- ❑ 1 (6 ounce) box Shake'n Bake chicken coating mix
- ❑ 1 (16 ounce) jar mild salsa
- ❑ 1 (24 ounce) carton deli-pasta salad
- ❑ 1 bunch fresh green onions
- ❑ 1 (4 ounce) jar chopped pimento
- ❑ 3 vine-ripened tomatoes
- ❑ 1 (8 count) package frozen corn-on-the-cob halves
- ❑ 1 (10-inch) round bakery pound cake
- ❑ 1 (20 ounce) can crushed pineapple
- ❑ 1 (5.1 ounce) package coconut instant pudding mix
- ❑ 1 (8 ounce) carton whipped topping

Tony's Supper

Jambalaya
Spinach-Strawberry Salad
Buttered French Bread
Banana Cream Pudding

Jambalaya

1 (8 ounce) package Tony Chachere's® jambalaya mix
1 (6 ounce) package frozen, cooked chicken breast strips, thawed
1 (11 ounce) can mexicorn
1 (2.25 ounce) can chopped black olives

- In soup pot or large saucepan, combine jambalaya mix and 2¼ cups water. Heat to boiling, reduce heat and cook slowly 5 minutes.
- Add chopped chicken, corn and black olives. Heat to boiling, reduce heat and simmer about 20 minutes. (You could also add leftover ham or sausage.)

Tip: I think any Creole would suggest adding 1 tablespoon lemon juice. It gives a lively tang to the jambalaya. If you are serving more than 4, double this recipe.

Spinach-Strawberry Salad

1 (10 ounce) package fresh, baby spinach
1 pint fresh strawberries, washed, halved
½ cup slivered almonds, toasted
1 (8 ounce) bottle poppy seed salad dressing

- In salad bowl, combine spinach and strawberries and refrigerate.
- When ready to serve, toss spinach and strawberries with about ⅓ of dressing (more if you like). Sprinkle slivered almonds over top.

Tip: To toast almonds, heat in oven 5 minutes along with bread.

Buttered French Bread

1 loaf frozen, buttered garlic French bread

- Preheat oven to 325°. Place slices on baking sheet and heat 15 to 20 minutes.

Banana Cream Pudding

6 (4 ounce) banana cream pudding cups, chilled

- Serve as is or in dessert bowl.

Louisiana jambalaya is delicious and full of flavor. After you try Tony Chachere's® jambalaya mix, you'll be on a first-name basis with this well-seasoned Creole. With Buttered French Bread and a fancy salad, you are all set for a wonderful meal.

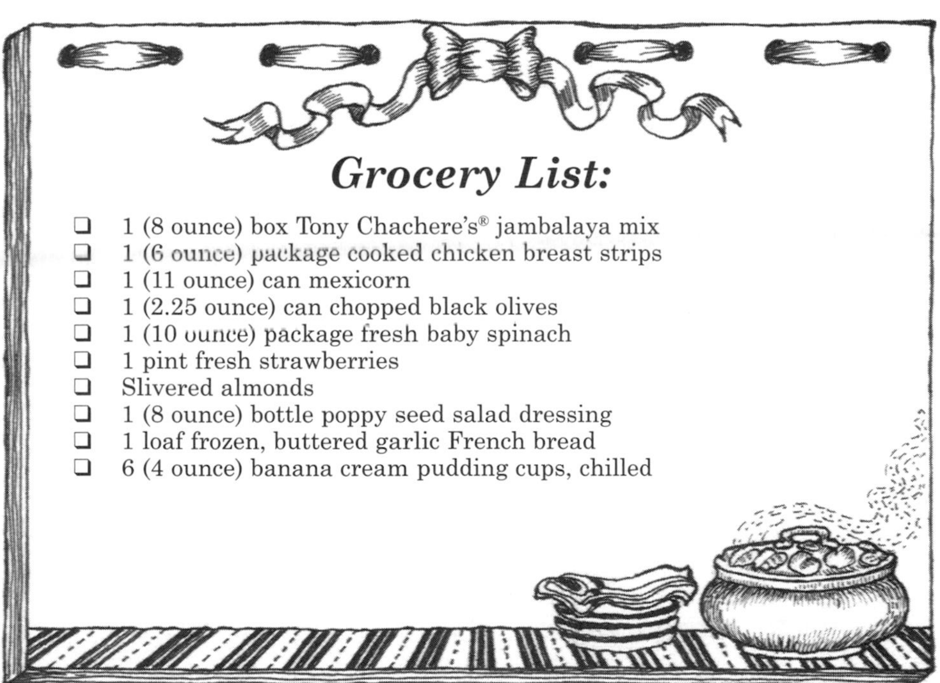

Grocery List:

- ❑ 1 (8 ounce) box Tony Chachere's® jambalaya mix
- ❑ 1 (6 ounce) package cooked chicken breast strips
- ❑ 1 (11 ounce) can mexicorn
- ❑ 1 (2.25 ounce) can chopped black olives
- ❑ 1 (10 ounce) package fresh baby spinach
- ❑ 1 pint fresh strawberries
- ❑ Slivered almonds
- ❑ 1 (8 ounce) bottle poppy seed salad dressing
- ❑ 1 loaf frozen, buttered garlic French bread
- ❑ 6 (4 ounce) banana cream pudding cups, chilled

Home-Style Family Favorite

Fried Chicken Breasts
Ranch-Style Mashed Potatoes
Creamy Biscuits and
Country-Style Cream Gravy
3-Bean Salad

Fried Chicken Breasts

4 to 6 boneless, skinless chicken breast halves
2 eggs, beaten
Salt and pepper
30 saltine crackers, finely crushed

- Pound chicken breasts to ¼-inch thickness and cut in half if chicken breasts are very large.
- In shallow bowl, combine beaten eggs, salt, pepper and 3 tablespoons water. Dip chicken in egg mixture and in crushed crackers to coat well.
- Deep fry until golden brown. Drain on paper towels.

If you do not want to deep-fry chicken, place about 3 tablespoons oil in large, heavy skillet and fry chicken with less oil.

Ranch-Style Mashed Potatoes

1 packet ranch-style dressing mix
¼ cup (½ stick) butter, melted
¾ cup sour cream
5 to 6 cups prepared, instant mashed potatoes with no salt or butter

- In large, heavy saucepan over low heat, combine all ingredients. Stir until potatoes heat through.

Creamy Biscuits

2½ cups biscuit mix
1 (8 ounce) carton whipping cream

- Preheat oven to 375°. Mix biscuit mix and cream. Place on floured board. Knead several times. Pat out to ½-inch thickness.
- Cut with biscuit cutter or 2-inch glass and place biscuits on non-stick baking sheet. Bake for 12 to 15 minutes or until light brown.

Country-Style Cream Gravy

3 tablespoons flour
½ teaspoon salt
½ teaspoon pepper
1½ cups milk

- Make gravy in same skillet used to fry chicken. Leave about 2 tablespoons pan drippings in skillet for that special seasoning. Sprinkle flour, salt and pepper in drippings over medium heat and stir to mix well.
- Turn heat to high and slowly pour milk into skillet while stirring constantly until gravy thickens. When gravy reaches right consistency, pour into bowl and serve with biscuits.

3-Bean Salad

2 (15 ounce) cans 3-bean salad, chilled

- Refrigerate cans the day before serving. Pour into a pretty crystal bowl.

Who doesn't like real, homemade fried chicken? This may not be your grandmother's recipe, but you will love the great crunch you get with the breading of saltine crackers. My son would tell me very quickly that we have to have biscuits and gravy over everything with this menu!

Grocery List:

- ❑ 4 to 6 boneless, skinless chicken breast halves
- ❑ 2 eggs
- ❑ 1 box saltine crackers
- ❑ 1 box instant mashed potatoes
- ❑ 1 packet ranch-style dressing mix
- ❑ Butter
- ❑ ¾ cup sour cream
- ❑ Bisquick
- ❑ 1 (8 ounce) carton whipping cream
- ❑ Flour
- ❑ Milk
- ❑ 2 (15 ounce) cans 3-bean salad

Hot Corn Bake

3 (15 ounce) cans whole kernel corn, drained
1 (10 ounce) can cream of corn soup
1 cup hot, chunky salsa
1 (8 ounce) package shredded Mexican 4-cheese blend

◆ Preheat oven to 375°. Combine corn, corn soup, salsa and half cheese and mix well. Pour into buttered 3-quart baking dish and bake for 25 minutes. Remove from oven and sprinkle remaining cheese over casserole.

Chicken-Fried Chicken and Cream Gravy

1 (24 ounce) package frozen chicken fried chicken breasts, thawed
2 (12 ounce) jars chicken cream gravy

◆ Thaw and heat chicken according to package directions. Pour gravy into small saucepan and heat.

Creamy Mashed Potatoes

1 (32 ounce) package refrigerated home-style mashed potatoes

◆ Heat and eat!

Tip: I believe that the best way to heat mashed potatoes like these is in the microwave. If your microwave doesn't have a turntable, be sure to turn and stir potatoes once or twice during cooking.

Dinner Rolls

1 (14 ounce, 15 count) package frozen dinner rolls, thawed
Butter

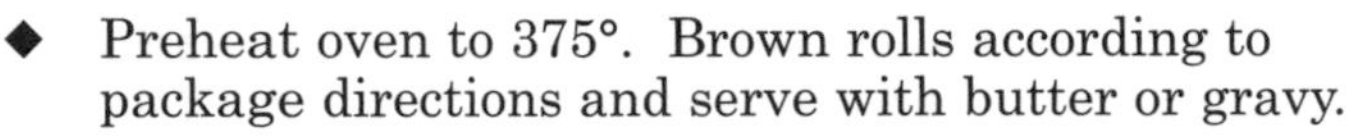

◆ Preheat oven to 375°. Brown rolls according to package directions and serve with butter or gravy.

Broccoli-Pepper Salad

5 cups cut broccoli florets, stemmed
1 sweet red bell pepper, julienned
1 cup diagonally sliced celery
1 (8 ounce) package Monterey jack cheese, cubed

◆ In bowl with lid, combine all ingredients and mix well. Toss with honey-mustard salad dressing.

Tip: If you want a little crunch, add handful of dry roasted sunflower kernels.

Lemon Meringue Pie

1 (36 ounce) frozen lemon meringue pie, thawed

◆ Serve on dessert plates.

This is one of my all-time favorite family menus. Who doesn't like fried chicken and gravy over hot rolls? What a treat! This will be a special request by everyone and is a fast and easy way to serve fried chicken.

Grocery List:

- ❑ 3 (15 ounce) cans whole kernel corn
- ❑ 1 (10 ounce) can cream of corn soup
- ❑ Salsa
- ❑ 1 (8 ounce) package shredded Mexican 4-cheese blend
- ❑ 1 (24 ounce) package frozen chicken fried chicken breasts
- ❑ 2 (12 ounce) jars chicken cream gravy
- ❑ 1 (32 ounce) package refrigerated home-style mashed potatoes
- ❑ 1 (14 ounce) package frozen dinner rolls, thawed
- ❑ Butter
- ❑ 1 or 2 bunches fresh broccoli
- ❑ 1 sweet red bell pepper
- ❑ Celery
- ❑ 1 (8 ounce) package shredded Monterey Jack cheese
- ❑ 1 (16 ounce) jar honey-mustard salad dressing
- ❑ Dry roasted sunflower kernels, optional
- ❑ 1 (36 ounce) frozen lemon meringue pie

Chicken and Wild Rice Special

1 (6 ounce) package long grain and wild rice mix
4 to 5 boneless, skinless chicken breast halves
2 (10 ounce) cans French onion soup
1 red and 1 green bell pepper, julienned

- In saucepan, cook rice according to package directions and keep warm.
- In large skillet with a little oil over medium to high heat, brown chicken breasts on both sides.
- Add soups, ¾ cup water and bell peppers. Reduce heat to low or medium, cover and cook 15 minutes.
- To serve, place rice on serving platter with chicken breasts on top. Serve sauce in gravy boat to spoon over chicken and rice.

Tip: For a thicker sauce, spoon 2 or 3 tablespoons sauce in small bowl and stir in 2 tablespoons flour. Mix well and stir in onion soup. Heat and stir constantly until sauce thickens.

Creamed-Spinach Bake

1 (16 ounce) package frozen chopped spinach
2 (3 ounce) packages cream cheese, softened
3 tablespoons butter
1½ cups Italian-style seasoned breadcrumbs

- Preheat oven to 375°. In saucepan, cook spinach with ½ cup water 6 minutes and drain.
- Add cream cheese and butter. Heat and stir until they melt.
- Into greased 2-quart baking dish, spoon mixture and sprinkle with breadcrumbs and a little salt. Bake about 15 minutes or until crumbs brown lightly.

Sliced Tomatoes Plus

2 to 3 vine-ripened tomatoes
1 (16 ounce) carton small-curd cottage cheese
Shredded cheddar cheese
Dash seasoned salt

- Wash tomatoes and cut in thick slices. Place on serving plate or individual salad plates.
- Top with 1 tablespoon cottage cheese, 1 tablespoon cheddar and dash seasoned salt.

Tip: Add fresh green onion to each serving.

Chocolate Pudding

6 (4 ounce) chocolate pudding cups, chilled

- Serve in containers or dessert bowls.

Chicken and rice are always good together and this recipe is no exception. Paired with the Creamed-Spinach Bake and tomatoes, this menu is pleasing to the eye and the palate! Even kids who don't like spinach like this Spinach Bake, so you have a really good chance for a round of applause.

Grocery List:

- ❑ 1 (6 ounce) package long grain and wild rice mix
- ❑ 4 to 5 boneless, skinless chicken breast halves
- ❑ 2 (10 ounce) cans French onion soup
- ❑ 1 red and 1 green bell pepper
- ❑ 1 (16 ounce) package frozen chopped spinach
- ❑ 2 (3 ounce) packages cream cheese, softened
- ❑ Butter
- ❑ 1½ cups Italian-style seasoned breadcrumbs
- ❑ 2 to 3 vine-ripened tomatoes
- ❑ 1 (16 ounce) carton small-curd cottage cheese
- ❑ 1 (8 ounce) package shredded cheddar cheese
- ❑ Seasoned salt
- ❑ 6 (4 ounce) chocolate pudding cups

Speedy Gonzales Enchilada Night

Spanish Rice
Hurry-Up Chicken Enchiladas
Black Bean Salad
Coconut-Cream Dessert

Spanish Rice

6 tablespoons (¾ stick) butter, melted
1 onion, chopped
2 cups cooked white rice
1 (10 ounce) can chopped diced tomatoes and green chilies, drained

◆ Preheat oven to 375°. In bowl, combine butter, onion, rice, tomatoes and green chilies. Add a little salt and pepper or 1 teaspoon seasoned salt. Spoon mixture into buttered 3-quart baking dish. Cover and cook for 25 minutes.

Hurry-Up Chicken Enchiladas

2 cups cooked chicken breasts, cubed
2 (10 ounce) cans soup: 1 cream of chicken soup and 1 fiesta nacho cheese soup
1 (16 ounce) jar chunky salsa, divided
8 (6 inch) flour tortillas

◆ In saucepan, heat and stir chicken, chicken soup and ¾ cup salsa. Spoon about ½ cup chicken mixture down center of each tortilla. Use all of chicken mixture. Roll up tortilla around filling and place seam side down in sprayed 9 x 13-inch glass baking dish.

◆ In saucepan, combine fiesta nacho soup, remaining salsa and ½ cup water and pour over enchiladas. Cover with wax paper and microwave on HIGH 5 minutes or until filling bubbles. (Turn baking dish several times during cooking.)

Black Bean Salad

2 (15 ounce) cans black beans, rinsed, drained, chilled
2 (11 ounce) cans mexicorn, drained, chilled
1 green bell pepper, chopped
1 small red onion, chopped, chilled

Dressing:
1 (8 ounce) bottle garlic vinaigrette salad dressing

- In bowl with lid, combine all salad ingredients and cover with dressing.

Tip: If possible, make this salad the morning you wish to serve it. If not, make the salad first and place in freezer about 20 minutes. It will be ready for your 30-minute meal.

Coconut-Cream Dessert

1 (20 ounce) can coconut pie filling, chilled
1 (8 ounce) carton chocolate whipped topping
2 or 3 (.06 ounce) bite-size, milk chocolate candy bars, crumbled
Sugar cookies

- Fill sherbet dishes (the number you will be serving) with chilled coconut pie filling and top with chocolate whipped topping.
- Sprinkle candy bars over whipped topping. Serve with cookies.

Tip: Crumble a cookie in bottom of sherbet dish, then layer other ingredients.

This is a quick and easy way to get enchiladas on the table in a flash. The 5-minute coconut cream dessert is the perfect complement.

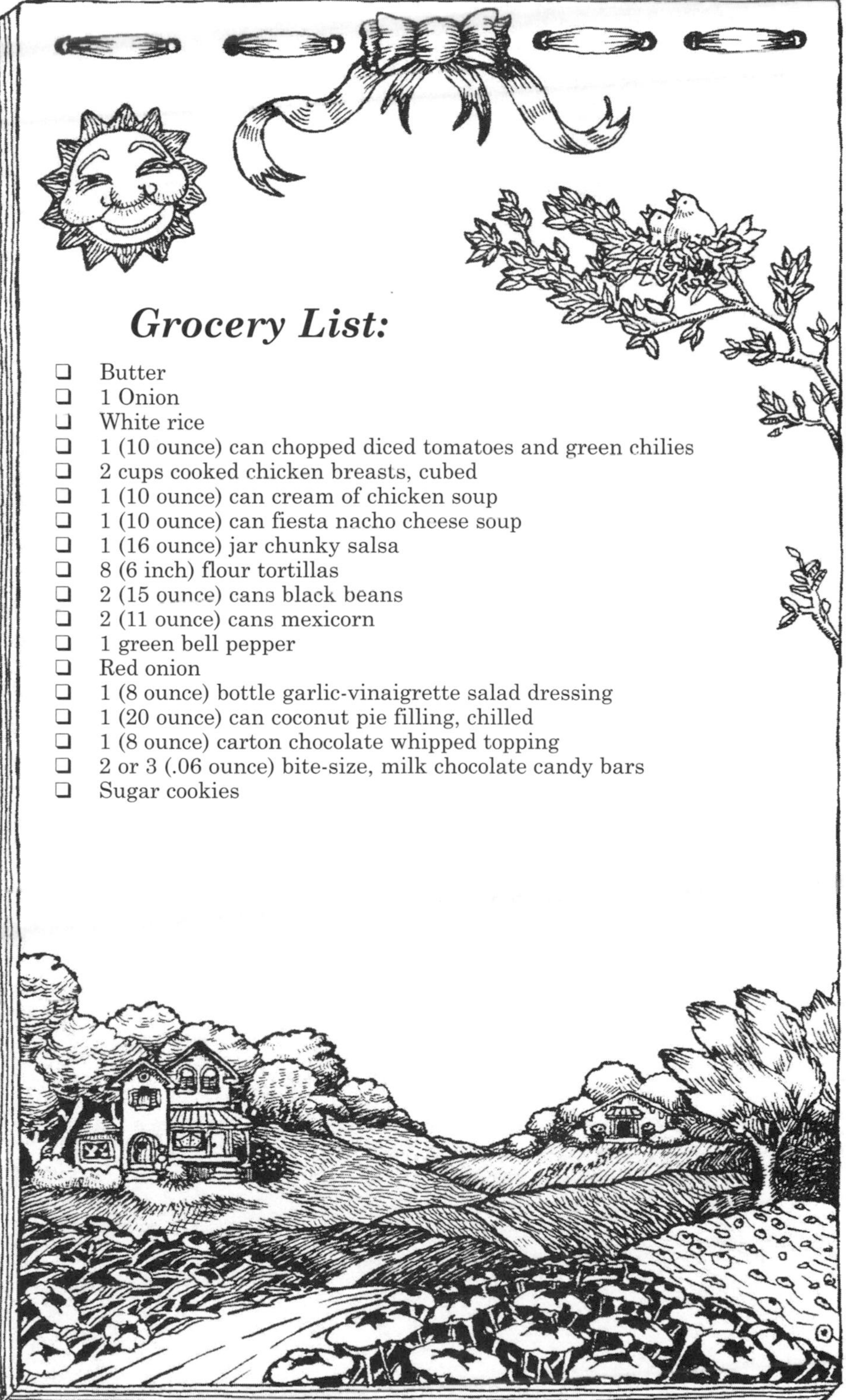

Grocery List:

- ❑ Butter
- ❑ 1 Onion
- ❑ White rice
- ❑ 1 (10 ounce) can chopped diced tomatoes and green chilies
- ❑ 2 cups cooked chicken breasts, cubed
- ❑ 1 (10 ounce) can cream of chicken soup
- ❑ 1 (10 ounce) can fiesta nacho cheese soup
- ❑ 1 (16 ounce) jar chunky salsa
- ❑ 8 (6 inch) flour tortillas
- ❑ 2 (15 ounce) cans black beans
- ❑ 2 (11 ounce) cans mexicorn
- ❑ 1 green bell pepper
- ❑ Red onion
- ❑ 1 (8 ounce) bottle garlic-vinaigrette salad dressing
- ❑ 1 (20 ounce) can coconut pie filling, chilled
- ❑ 1 (8 ounce) carton chocolate whipped topping
- ❑ 2 or 3 (.06 ounce) bite-size, milk chocolate candy bars
- ❑ Sugar cookies

Quick Tex-Mex Supper

Cheese Enchiladas
Chili-Baked Beans
Tossed Salad Surprise
Pecan Tarts

Cheese Enchiladas

10 corn tortillas
1 (12 ounce) package shredded Mexican 4-cheese blend, divided
1 onion, chopped
2 (10 ounce) cans enchilada sauce

- Wrap 5 tortillas in slightly damp paper towel, place between 2 salad plates and microwave on HIGH 30 to 40 seconds. Repeat with remaining tortillas.
- On each tortilla, place about ⅓ cup cheese and 1 tablespoon onion. Roll up.
- On sprayed 9 x 13-inch baking dish, place tortillas seam side down and pour enchilada sauce on top.
- Sprinkle with remaining cheese and onions, cover and microwave on MEDIUM 5 to 6 minutes. If microwave does not have turntable, turn tortillas once during cooking.

Chili-Baked Beans

2 (15 ounce) cans pinto beans with jalapeno peppers, drained
1 (15 ounce) can chili without beans
¼ cup packed brown sugar
1 teaspoon chili powder

- In heavy saucepan over low heat, combine all ingredients, heat and stir until mixture bubbles.

Tossed Salad Surprise

1 (10 ounce) package spring-mix salad greens
½ small jicama, peeled, julienned
1 red onion, sliced
2 small zucchini, sliced

- In salad bowl, toss greens, jicama, red onion slices and tomatoes. Spoon about 2 tablespoons honey mustard dressing on each serving.

Pecan Tarts

1 or 2 (6 count) packages bakery pecan tarts
1 (8 ounce) carton frozen whipped topping, optional

- Place tarts on individual dessert plates and serve and add whipped topping.

Chicken enchiladas in the microwave—what could be faster? The kids can help assemble this Tex-Mex meal. Jicama adds sweetness and a healthy crunch to the salad.

Grocery List:

- ❑ 10 corn tortillas
- ❑ 1 (12 ounce) package shredded Mexican 4-cheese blend
- ❑ 1 onion
- ❑ 2 (10 ounce) cans enchilada sauce
- ❑ 2 (15 ounce) cans pinto beans with jalapeno peppers
- ❑ 1 (15 ounce) can chili without beans
- ❑ ¼ cup brown sugar
- ❑ 1 teaspoon chili powder
- ❑ 1 (10 ounce) package spring-mix salad greens
- ❑ 1 jicama
- ❑ 1 red onion
- ❑ 2 zucchini
- ❑ 1 (16 ounce) jar refrigerated honey mustard dressing
- ❑ 1 (6 count) package bakery pecan tarts
- ❑ 1 (8 ounce) carton frozen whipped topping, optional

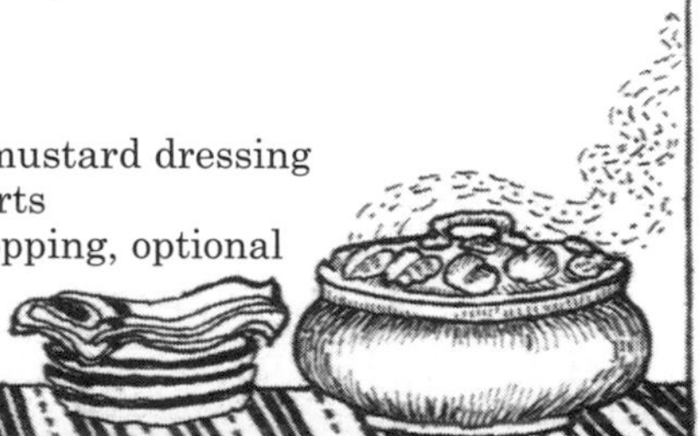

Chicken Quesadillas

1 (7 ounce) package frozen, cooked chicken breast strips, thawed
1 (10 ounce) can cheddar cheese soup
1 (16 ounce) jar hot, chunky salsa, slightly drained, divided
8 to 10 (8 inch) flour tortillas

- Preheat oven to 400°. Cut chicken strips into much smaller pieces (almost shredded). In bowl, combine soup and salsa and mix well. Lay tortillas out on flat surface and spoon ¼ to ⅓ cup mixture on half of each tortilla to within ½ inch of edge.
- Sprinkle slivers of chicken over cheese mixture. Fold tortillas over, moisten edges with a little water and press edges of tortillas to seal. Place on 2 baking sheets and bake 5 to 6 minutes or until tortillas brown.

Mexican-Fiesta Rice

1 (6 ounce) package Mexican fiesta rice
2 tablespoons butter
1 cup chopped celery
1 (8 ounce) package cubed Mexican processed cheese

- In saucepan, heat 2 cups water to boiling and add rice and butter. Return to boiling, reduce heat and simmer 5 minutes. Stir occasionally.
- Add celery, stir to mix and place in serving dish. Sprinkle with Monterey Jack cheese.

Guacamole Salad

Shredded lettuce
1 (16 ounce) carton frozen guacamole, thawed
1 bunch fresh green onions, chopped
Tortilla chips

◆ For each serving, place shredded lettuce on salad plate with about ⅓ cup guacamole on top. Place green onions with each salad.

Strawberry Shortcake

1 (20 ounce) frozen strawberry shortcake, thawed

◆ Serve on dessert plates.

To serve a large crowd, make full-size quesadillas with 10-inch tortillas. Cover bottom tortilla generously with filling (leave ½ inch around edge) and place another tortilla on top. Press down on top tortilla with wide spatula so cheese will hold the tortillas together. Flip quesadilla and brown the other side. It's about as easy as it gets.

Grocery List:

- ❑ 1 (7 ounce) package frozen, cooked chicken breast strips
- ❑ 1 (10 ounce) can cheddar cheese soup
- ❑ 1 (16 ounce) jar hot, chunky salsa
- ❑ 12 (8 inch) flour tortillas
- ❑ 1 (6 ounce) package Mexican fiesta rice
- ❑ Butter
- ❑ Celery
- ❑ 1 (8 ounce) package cubed Mexican processed cheese
- ❑ 1 (16 ounce) carton frozen guacamole
- ❑ Lettuce
- ❑ 1 bunch fresh green onions
- ❑ Tortilla chips
- ❑ 1 (20 ounce) frozen strawberry shortcake

Believe-It-Or-Not Nachos

Deluxe Dinner Nachos
Corn-On-The-Cob
Quesadilla Rolls
Key Lime Pie

Deluxe Dinner Nachos

Nachos:
1 (14 ounce) package tortilla chips, divided
1 (12 ounce) package cubed, processed cheese, divided
1 (8 ounce) can chopped jalapenos, divided

Deluxe Dinner Topping:
1 (11 ounce) can mexicorn with liquid
1 (15 ounce) can jalapeno pinto beans, drained
2 cups skinned, chopped rotisserie chicken
1 bunch fresh green onions, chopped

- In sprayed baking dish, place about three-quarters of tortilla chips in bottom of dish. Sprinkle half cheese and about 3 jalapenos on top. Heat at 400° just until cheese melts.
- Combine mexicorn, beans and rotisserie chicken in saucepan. Heat over medium heat, stirring constantly, until mixture is hot. Spoon mixture over nachos, place dish in oven and heat for about 10 minutes.
- Sprinkle remaining cheese and green onions over top and serve immediately. Garnish with remaining jalapenos, remaining tortillas and salsa.

Corn-on-the-Cob

4 to 8 ears fresh or frozen corn-on-the-cob
Butter

- Boil corn until tender. Serve with butter.

Quesadilla Rolls

2 (9 ounce) packages frozen qucsadilla rolls

◆ Heat according to package directions.

Key Lime Pie

1 (42 ounce) frozen key lime pie

◆ Serve according to package directions.

The kids will call you "Super Mom" for this dinner!

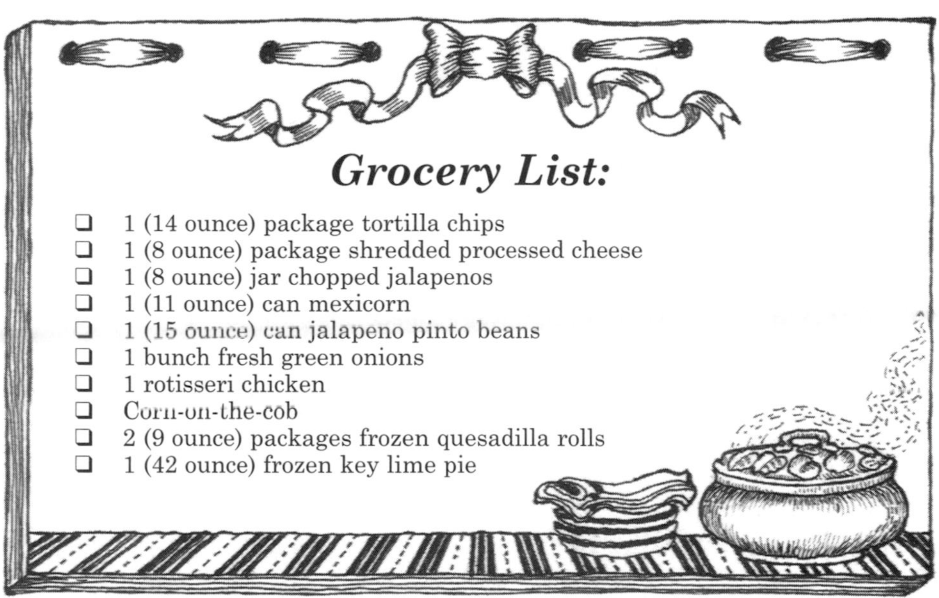

Chicken and Rice Special

Savory Chicken and Mushrooms
Cottage Dip with Veggies
Hot Buttered Rice
Lemon Tarts

Savory Chicken and Mushrooms

1 (16 ounce) package frozen chopped onions and peppers
1 (8 ounce) package fresh mushrooms, sliced
1 (10 ounce) can cream of mushrooms soup with 1 cup milk
1 rotisserie chicken

- In large skillet with a little oil, cook onions, peppers and mushrooms about 5 minutes or until onions are translucent and stir frequently.
- Stir in mushroom soup and milk, mix well and add chicken pieces and seasonings. (Minced garlic, seasoned salt and black pepper are always good.)
- Boil, reduce heat and cook for about 10 minutes. Serve over hot, cooked rice.

Cottage Dip with Veggies

1 (16 ounce) carton small-curd cottage cheese, drained
1 (1 ounce) envelope dry onion soup mix
Mayonnaise
Garlic powder

Veggies:
Broccoli florets
Carrot sticks
Celery sticks
Cauliflower

- Blend all ingredients well and serve with veggies.

Hot Buttered Rice

3 cups instant white rice
2 tablespoons butter
¾ teaspoon salt
3 cups water

◆ Cook according to package directions.

Lemon Tarts

1 (¾ ounce) box instant lemon pudding mix
1 (8 ounce) package graham cracker tart shells
1 (8 ounce) carton whipped topping

◆ Whip pudding mix and water until thick according to package directions and spoon into tart shells. Top with whipped topping.

When you buy that rotisserie chicken, your only problem is deciding how you are going to embellish "that bird" and magically transform it into a dinner with added vegetables or starches so the whole family says "It's a winner!".

Grocery List:

- ❑ 1 (16 ounce) package frozen chopped onions and peppers
- ❑ 1 (8 ounce) package fresh mushrooms
- ❑ 1 (10 ounce) can cream of mushroom soup
- ❑ Milk
- ❑ 1 rotisserie chicken
- ❑ 1 (14 ounce) box instant rice
- ❑ Butter
- ❑ 1 (16 ounce) carton small curd cottage cheese
- ❑ 1 (1 ounce) package dry onion soup mix
- ❑ Mayonnaise
- ❑ Garlic powder
- ❑ Radishes
- ❑ 1 (8 ounce) package graham cracker tart shells
- ❑ 1 (¾ ounce) box instant lemon pudding mix
- ❑ 1 (8 ounce) carton whipped topping
- ❑ Vegetable assortment for dipping

Chicken Sizzle

Cheesy Chicken And Potatoes
Out-Of-Sight Asparagus
Peachy Cottage Cheese
Strawberry Cake

Cheesy Chicken and Potatoes

1 (20 ounce) package frozen hash browns with peppers and onions, thawed
2 to 2½ cups bite-size chunks rotisserie chicken
1 bunch green onions, sliced
1 cup shredded cheddar cheese

- Add a little oil to large skillet over medium-high heat and cook potatoes for 7 minutes, turning frequently. Add seasonings (1 tablespoon minced garlic and 2 teaspoons paprika), if you like.
- Add chicken, green onions and 1/3 cup water and cook 5 to 6 minutes. Remove from heat and stir in cheese. Serve immediately right from skillet.

Tip: If you have any leftover ham, cube it and add to this dish. Use it to make a heartier meal or as a substitute for chicken.

Out-Of-Sight Asparagus

1 bunch fresh asparagus
2 tablespoons extra virgin olive oil
1 to 1½ teaspoons dried basil
1 teaspoon salt

- Wash asparagus and spread in foil-lined 7 x 11-inch baking dish. Spread olive oil over asparagus with fingers to coat.
- Sprinkle basil and salt over asparagus. Bake uncovered at 400° for 12 minutes. Serve immediately.

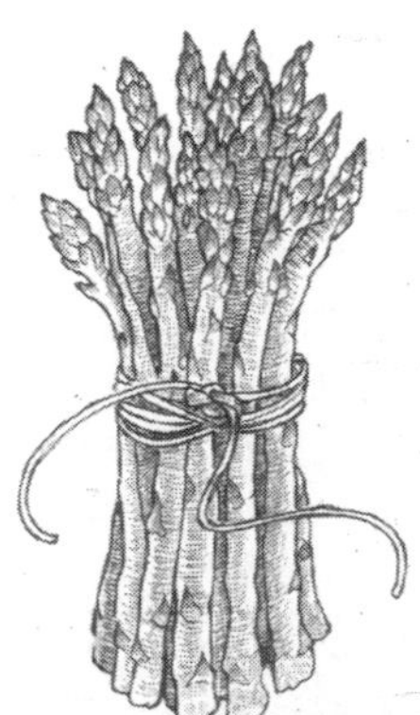

Peachy Cottage Cheese

Shredded lettuce
1 or 2 (15 ounce) cans peach halves
1 (16 ounce) carton small-curd cottage cheese
¼ cup dried craisins

◆ Place about ½ shredded lettuce on individual salad plates with 1 or 2 peach halves. Spoon 1 heaping tablespoon cottage cheese over peaches and sprinkle craisins over top.

Tip: If serving more than 4 people, 2 cans peaches are needed.

Strawberry Cake

1 (38 ounce) bakery strawberry cake
1 (16 ounce) can strawberry icing
1 pint fresh strawberries, sliced

◆ Place strawberry cake on cake plate and spread with icing. Garnish with fresh strawberries.

Tip: If you don't want to take the time to ice the cake, buy frozen, sweetened strawberries and spoon strawberries and juice over top of each slice of cake. A lemon or pound cake will also work great.

This is rotisserie chicken to the rescue! The cheese, chicken and potatoes are a great combination for a very pleasing dish that can be made in less than 20 minutes. The asparagus is superb and this is a recipe you will use repeatedly because it is so easy and so quick.

Grocery List:

- ❑ 1 (20 ounce) package frozen hash brown potatoes with onions and peppers
- ❑ 1 rotisserie chicken
- ❑ 1 bunch fresh green onions
- ❑ 1 (8 ounce) package shredded cheddar cheese
- ❑ 1 bunch fresh asparagus
- ❑ Extra virgin oil
- ❑ Dried basil
- ❑ 1 or 2 (15 ounce) cans peach halves
- ❑ 1 (16 ounce) carton small-curd cottage cheese
- ❑ 1 package dried craisins
- ❑ 1 (38 ounce) bakery strawberry cake
- ❑ 1 (16 ounce) can strawberry icing

Mac Cheese and Chicken

1½ cups small elbow macaroni
1 (12 ounce) can evaporated milk
½ to ⅔ cup hot chipotle salsa
2 cups skinned, cut-up rotisserie chicken

- ◆ Cook macaroni in 2 cups water according to package directions and drain well. Add evaporated milk and chipotle salsa and cook over medium heat about 10 minutes, stirring frequently. (There will still be liquid in mixture.)
- ◆ Stir in rotisserie chicken and heat until chicken heats thoroughly. Fold in cheddar cheese, stir constantly and cook 1 minute. Serve immediately.

Sugar Snap Peas

1 (16 ounce) package frozen sugar snap peas, thawed
1 tablespoon butter

- ◆ Cook according to package directions.

Niblet Corn in Butter Sauce

1 (19 ounce) package frozen niblet corn in butter sauce, thawed

- ◆ Cook according to package directions.

Hot Rolls

1 (20 ounce) package frozen hot rolls, thawed

◆ Heat according to package directions.

Vanilla Pudding and Chocolate Cookies

1 or 2 (3.4 ounce) boxes instant French vanilla pudding
2 cups cold milk

◆ Mix and beat according to package directions. Spoon into sherbet dishes and refrigerate. Serve with Oreo cookies.

Who had the brilliant idea of preparing rotisserie chicken in our supermarkets? I'd like to give them a hearty handshake! What a concept for creating quick, new ways to "dress up" a chicken! The first time I bought a rotisserie chicken I thought I was splurging. After tasting it and realizing how easy it is, I decided it's a bargain!

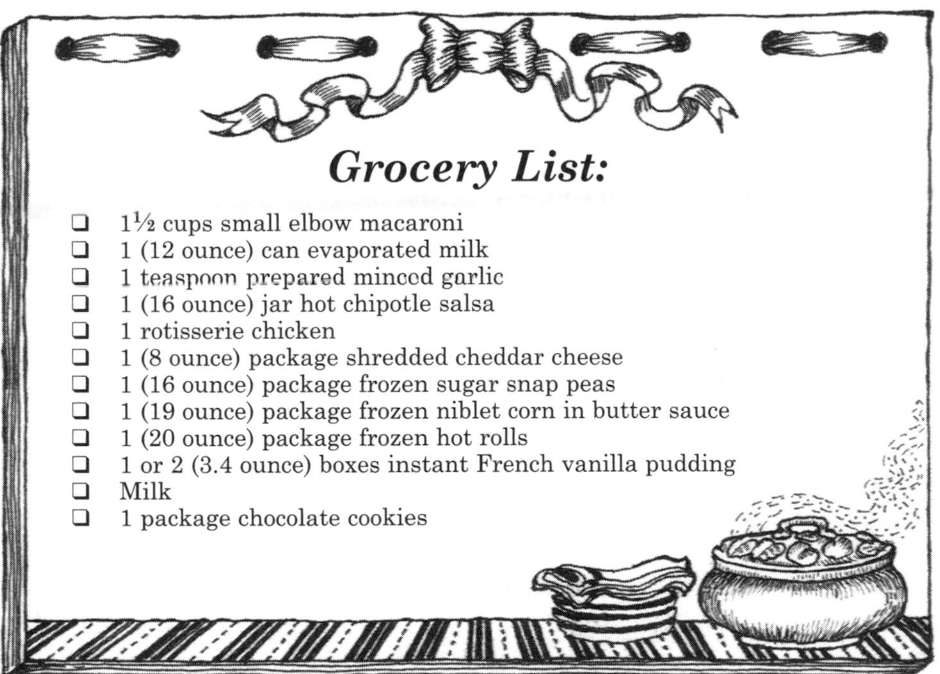

Grocery List:

- ❑ 1½ cups small elbow macaroni
- ❑ 1 (12 ounce) can evaporated milk
- ❑ 1 teaspoon prepared minced garlic
- ❑ 1 (16 ounce) jar hot chipotle salsa
- ❑ 1 rotisserie chicken
- ❑ 1 (8 ounce) package shredded cheddar cheese
- ❑ 1 (16 ounce) package frozen sugar snap peas
- ❑ 1 (19 ounce) package frozen niblet corn in butter sauce
- ❑ 1 (20 ounce) package frozen hot rolls
- ❑ 1 or 2 (3.4 ounce) boxes instant French vanilla pudding
- ❑ Milk
- ❑ 1 package chocolate cookies

Calico Corn

2 ribs celery, sliced
3 (11 ounce) cans mexicorn, drained
1 (10 ounce) can fiesta nacho cheese soup
1 cup coarsely crushed buttery crackers

- Preheat oven to 375°. Saute celery in 2 tablespoons (¼ stick) butter. In bowl, combine mexicorn, sauteed celery and cheese soup. Mix well and pour into buttered 7 x 11-inch baking dish.
- Sprinkle crushed crackers over casserole and bake uncovered 20 to 25 minutes or until crumbs brown lightly.

Cracked-Pepper Turkey Breast

1 (2½ to 3 pound) refrigerated, cracked-pepper turkey breast
1 (16 ounce) jar hot chipotle salsa
1 (8 ounce) package shredded 4-cheese blend

- Slice enough turkey for each person. Spoon 1 heaping tablespoon chipotle salsa over each slice and sprinkle a little cheese over top.

This is a delicious turkey breast that can be served many ways. Leftovers are great in turkey sandwiches and turkey casserole.

French Fries

1 (32 ounce) package frozen french fries

- Place as many fries as you need on a baking sheet and bake according to package directions.

Peanut Clusters

1 (24 ounce) package almond bark (white chocolate)
1 (12 ounce) package milk chocolate chips
3 cups salted peanuts

- In double boiler, melt almond bark and chocolate chips and stir in peanuts quickly. Drop by teaspoons on wax paper. Refrigerate 20 minutes (while you are eating).

Refrigerated turkey breasts are boneless and skinless and no trouble at all. If you prefer to serve the turkey hot, just place the slices in oven-safe dish, pour a jar or two of turkey gravy over turkey slices, cover with foil and heat in oven 15 to 20 minutes along with corn. Substitute 1 quart refrigerated macaroni and cheese or deli pasta salad for fries, if desired.

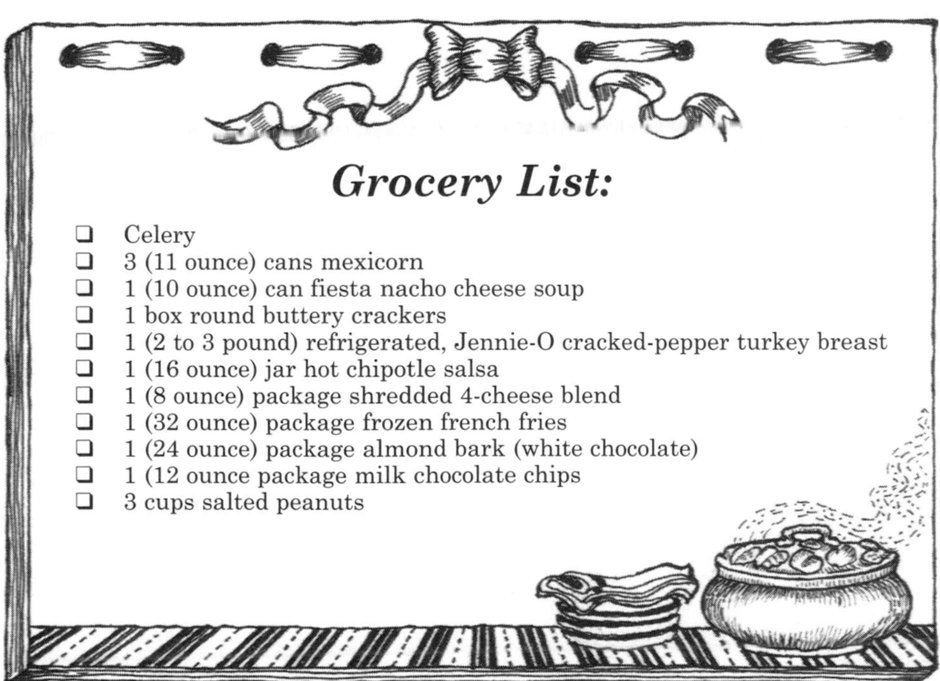

Grocery List:

- ❑ Celery
- ❑ 3 (11 ounce) cans mexicorn
- ❑ 1 (10 ounce) can fiesta nacho cheese soup
- ❑ 1 box round buttery crackers
- ❑ 1 (2 to 3 pound) refrigerated, Jennie-O cracked-pepper turkey breast
- ❑ 1 (16 ounce) jar hot chipotle salsa
- ❑ 1 (8 ounce) package shredded 4-cheese blend
- ❑ 1 (32 ounce) package frozen french fries
- ❑ 1 (24 ounce) package almond bark (white chocolate)
- ❑ 1 (12 ounce package milk chocolate chips
- ❑ 3 cups salted peanuts

It's-Not-Thanksgiving Turkey

Oven-Fried Turkey
Broccoli and Wild Rice
Elvis' Favorite Salad
German Chocolate Cake

Oven-Fried Turkey

1 to 1½ pounds turkey tenderloins, thawed
1 (5.5 ounce) package baked chicken coating mix

- Preheat oven to 400°. Place all tenderloins strips on several pieces paper towels to partially dry them. Pour chicken coating mix into shallow bowl and press both sides of each piece of turkey into seasoned coating.
- Place in large greased baking pan without pieces touching. Bake 20 minutes or until turkey is light brown.

Broccoli and Wild Rice

2 (10 ounce) packages frozen chipped broccoli, thawed
1 (6 ounce) box long grain and wild rice
1 (8 ounce) package cubed processed cheese
1 (10 ounce) can cream of chicken soup

- Preheat oven to 350°. Cook broccoli and rice according to package directions. Combine broccoli, rice, cheese and chicken soup and pour into buttered 2-quart casserole dish. Cover and bake 25 minutes or until bubbly.

Elvis' Favorite Salad

Several lettuce leaves
1 (15 ounce) can peach halves, drained
1 (16 ounce) carton small-curd cottage cheese

- Place a lettuce leaf on individual salad plates with 1 or 2 peach halves.
- Spoon heaping tablespoon cottage cheese in center of each peach half.

German Chocolate Cake

1 (52 ounce) refrigerated or frozen German chocolate cake, thawed

- Serve on dessert plates.

The cakes that we can buy in the major food chains are very good. Some may be frozen, some not, but if you are buying one that is not frozen, be sure to check the date.

Grocery List:

- ❑ 1 to 1½ pounds turkey tenderloins
- ❑ 1 (5.5 ounce) package baked chicken coating mix
- ❑ 2 (10 ounce) packages frozen chopped broccoli
- ❑ 1 (6 ounce) box long grain and wild rice
- ❑ 1 (8 ounce) package cubed processed cheese
- ❑ 1 (10 ounce) can cream of chicken soup
- ❑ Lettuce
- ❑ 1 (15 ounce) can peach halves
- ❑ 1 (16 ounce) carton small-curd cottage cheese
- ❑ 1 (52 ounce) refrigerated or frozen German chocolate cake

First Fall Supper

Turkey Casserole
Almond Green Beans & Garlic Breadsticks
Cheese-Topped Pear Slices
Carrot Cake

Turkey Casserole

1 (6 ounce) package herb-seasoned stuffing mix
1 cup canned whole cranberry sauce
6 (¼-inch thick) slices deli turkey
1 (15 ounce) jar turkey gravy

- Preheat oven to 375°. Prepare stuffing according to package directions.
- In medium bowl, combine prepared stuffing and cranberry sauce and set aside.
- In buttered 9 x 13-inch baking dish, place slices of turkey and pour gravy over turkey. Spoon stuffing mixture over casserole. Bake about 15 minutes or until hot and bubbly.

Almond Green Beans

⅓ cup almonds, slivered
¼ cup (½ stick) butter
1 teaspoon garlic salt
2 tablespoons lemon juice
1 (16 ounce) package frozen green beans

- In saucepan, saute almonds in butter. Add garlic salt and lemon juice and cook until almonds turn golden brown.
- Add green beans to almond-butter mixture and pour in ⅓ cup water. Cook for about 10 minutes. Beans should be tender-crisp.

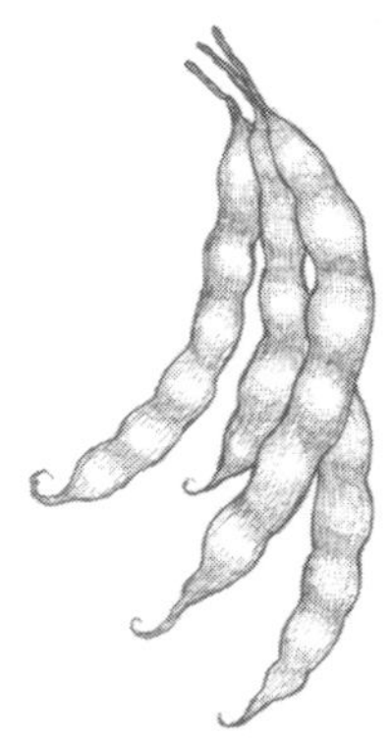

Garlic Breadsticks

1 (12 ounce) package frozen garlic breadsticks

- Heat according to package directions.

Cheese-Topped Pear Slices

Shredded lettuce
1 or 2 (15 ounce) cans pear halves, drained
Small-curd cottage cheese
Honey-mustard dressing

- On individual salad plates, place shredded lettuce and 2 pear halves.
- Top each pear half with heaping tablespoon cottage cheese and pour small amount dressing over cottage cheese.

Carrot Cake

1 (52 ounce) frozen bakery carrot cake, thawed

- Serve on dessert plates.

Turkey is not just a fall dish. This lean, economical meat is available year-round and it's delicious any time!

Grocery List:

- ❑ 1 (6 ounce) package herb-seasoned stuffing mix
- ❑ 1 (16 ounce) can whole cranberry sauce
- ❑ 6 (¼-inch thick) slices deli turkey
- ❑ 1 (15 ounce) jar turkey gravy
- ❑ ⅓ cup slivered almonds
- ❑ Butter
- ❑ Garlic salt
- ❑ Lemon juice
- ❑ 1 (16 ounce) package frozen green beans
- ❑ 1 (12 ounce) package frozen garlic breadsticks
- ❑ Head lettuce
- ❑ 1 or 2 (15 ounce) cans pear halves
- ❑ 1 (16 ounce) carton small curd cottage cheese
- ❑ 1 (16 ounce) jar honey-mustard dressing
- ❑ 1 (52 ounce) frozen bakery carrot cake

Turkey for Lunch

4 (thick sliced) cooked, smoked deli turkey breast slices
1 (8 ounce) package cream cheese, softened
¼ cup mayonnaise
1½ cups hot, chunky salsa

- Place chicken slices on serving platter. In mixing bowl with mixer, combine cream cheese and mayonnaise. Fold in salsa.
- Place about one-fourth cream cheese mixture on each slice chicken. Serve cold.

Tip: Garnish each serving with pimento-stuffed green olives, if desired.

Pasta Salad

1 (7.5 ounce) box Suddenly Pasta Salad
½ cup mayonnaise
2 ribs celery, chopped
½ sweet red bell pepper, chopped

- Boil pasta in 3 quarts water for about 15 minutes, drain and rinse in cold water. Stir in seasoning mix, mayonnaise, green onions and bell pepper and refrigerate.

Swiss Spinach Salad

1 (10 ounce) bag baby spinach
½ red onion, chopped
1 (8 ounce) package shredded Swiss cheese
½ cup sunflower seeds, toasted

◆ In salad bowl, combine spinach, onion and Swiss cheese. Toss with Wild Berry Vinaigrette. Sprinkle sunflower seeds over top of salad.

Croissants

1 (7 ounce, 8 count) package mini-croissants

◆ Warm, if desired, and arrange on serving tray.

Croissants are the perfect touch for a luncheon.

Chocolate Meringue Pie

1 (36 ounce) frozen chocolate meringue pie, thawed

◆ Serve on dessert plates.

The cooked turkey breast we can buy today is worth serving all summer! You can also buy Louis Rich® or Jennie-O® brand whole turkey breasts and keep on hand to slice for sandwiches. Besides this Relish Tray Deluxe, try the relish used in "Party Dinner" on page 152. It's great too!

Grocery List:

- ❑ 4 (thick sliced) cooked, smoked deli turkey breast slices
- ❑ 1 (8 ounce) package cream cheese
- ❑ Mayonnaise
- ❑ 1 (16 ounce) jar hot, chunky salsa
- ❑ 1 (7.5 ounce) box Suddenly Pasta Salad
- ❑ Celery
- ❑ Red bell pepper
- ❑ 1 (10 ounce) bag baby spinach
- ❑ Red onion
- ❑ 1 (8 ounce) package shredded Swiss cheese
- ❑ Sunflower seeds
- ❑ 1 package small croissants
- ❑ 1 (36 ounce) frozen chocolate meringue pie

Feast for the Day

Cheese Ravioli and Zucchini
Caesar Salad
Texas Garlic Toast
Cherry Crisp with Ice Cream

Cheese Ravioli and Zucchini

1 (25 ounce) package fresh cheese-filled ravioli
4 small zucchini, sliced
2 ribs celery, sliced diagonally
1 (26 ounce) jar marinara sauce

- Cook ravioli according to package directions and drain. Return to saucepan and keep warm. (If you prefer, you can use frozen chicken ravioli.)
- Place zucchini and celery in another saucepan and pour marinara sauce over vegetables. Cook and stir over medium-high heat about 8 minutes or until vegetables are crisp-tender.
- Spoon marinara-vegetable mixture over ravioli and toss gently. Pour into serving bowl and garnish with shredded parmesan if desired.

Caesar Salad

2 (8 ounce) packages romaine lettuce
1 (8 ounce) package shredded mozzarella cheese
1 (8 ounce) bottle Caesar dressing
1 (6 ounce) box seasoned croutons

- Combine lettuce and cheese and toss with dressing. Sprinkle croutons over salad.

Texas Garlic Toast

1 (11 ounce) package frozen garlic toast, thawed

- Heat according to package directions.

Frozen garlic toast is usually heavily buttered. If you prefer less butter, buy a loaf of Italian bread. Slice it yourself, spread with a little butter and sprinkle with garlic.

Cherry Crisp with Ice Cream

1 (20 ounce) can cherry pie filling
¾ cup granola
Vanilla ice cream

- Spoon cherry pie filling into individual custard cups and sprinkle granola over pie filling. Place scoop ice cream on top of each serving.

Substitute any flavor pie filling in this recipe. If you don't have granola on hand, crumble several shortbread pecan cookies or use a handful of any granola-type cereal.

This cheese ravioli is a meal in itself, but the Caesar salad and garlic toast are "icing on the cake!" This is an easy last-minute meal with plenty of flavor and variety.

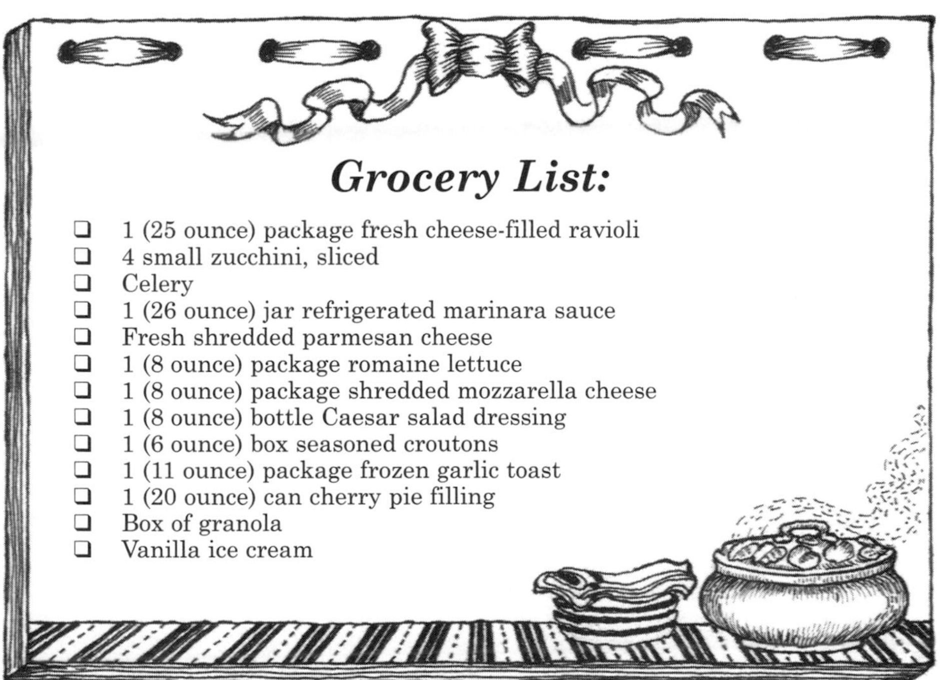

Grocery List:

- ❑ 1 (25 ounce) package fresh cheese-filled ravioli
- ❑ 4 small zucchini, sliced
- ❑ Celery
- ❑ 1 (26 ounce) jar refrigerated marinara sauce
- ❑ Fresh shredded parmesan cheese
- ❑ 1 (8 ounce) package romaine lettuce
- ❑ 1 (8 ounce) package shredded mozzarella cheese
- ❑ 1 (8 ounce) bottle Caesar salad dressing
- ❑ 1 (6 ounce) box seasoned croutons
- ❑ 1 (11 ounce) package frozen garlic toast
- ❑ 1 (20 ounce) can cherry pie filling
- ❑ Box of granola
- ❑ Vanilla ice cream

Buffet Tonight

Scalloped Potatoes
Filet Mignon
Green Salad and Hot Crescent Rolls
Hot Brandied Apples

Scalloped Potatoes

1 (5 ounce) box scalloped potatoes
⅔ cup milk
⅛ cup (¼ stick) butter

- Preheat oven to 425°. Combine all ingredients and cook uncovered for 25 minutes.

Tip: Potatoes need to be started first, so you will need to get them in oven right away. During last 15 minutes of cooking, increase oven temperature to 450° and place steaks in oven. Potatoes and steaks will be done at same time.

Filet Mignon

6 or 8 filet mignon
Italian seasoning
Black pepper

- Preheat oven to 450°. Season each filet with Italian seasoning and pepper.
- In 9 x 13-inch baking pan, bake filets 15 to 20 minutes (may also be broiled or grilled).

Tip: I sometimes buy individual eye of round steaks and place bacon around steaks myself. They are both good steaks!

Green Salad

1 (10 ounce) package chopped romaine lettuce
1 seedless cucumber, sliced
½ cup Craisins® (sweetened dried cranberries)
1 (8 ounce) bottle balsamic vinaigrette salad dressing

◆ In salad bowl, combine romaine, cucumbers and Craisins®. Let each person add their own dressing.

Hot Crescent Rolls

1 or 2 cans refrigerated crescent rolls

◆ Bake rolls according package directions with filets mignon.

Hot Brandied Apples

1 (10 ounce) loaf pound cake
1 (20 ounce) can apple pie filling
½ teaspoon allspice
2 tablespoons brandy

◆ Slice pound cake and place on dessert plates. In saucepan, combine pie filling, allspice and brandy. Heat thoroughly. Place several spoonfuls over cake. Top with scoop vanilla ice cream, if desired.

This extra-special meal is full of good things: choice filet mignon, creamy scalloped potatoes, salad with sweetened, dried cranberries and heavenly brandied apples for dessert!

Grocery List:

- ❑ 1 (5 ounce) box scalloped potatoes
- ❑ Milk
- ❑ Butter
- ❑ 6 or 8 beef filet mignon
- ❑ Italian seasoning
- ❑ 1 (10 ounce) package chopped romaine lettuce
- ❑ 1 seedless cucumber
- ❑ 1 (6 ounce) package Craisins®
- ❑ 1 (8 ounce) bottle balsamic vinaigrette salad dressing
- ❑ 1 or 2 cans refrigerated crescent rolls
- ❑ 1 (10 ounce) loaf pound cake
- ❑ 1 (20 ounce) can apple pie filling
- ❑ Allspice
- ❑ Brandy

Goodness Gracious Good

Family Filet Mignon
Twice-Baked Potatoes
Romaine-Strawberry Salad
Peachy Sundaes

Family Filet Mignon

1½ pounds very lean ground beef
1 (1 ounce) packet dry onion soup mix
½ teaspoon prepared minced garlic
6 slices bacon

- In bowl, combine beef, soup mix and garlic and mix well. Form into 6 thick patties that are flat on top.
- Wrap slice of bacon around each patty and secure with toothpick. Place in shallow baking pan and broil about 10 minutes on each side.

Twice-Baked Potatoes

1 package (6 count) frozen twice-baked potatoes, thawed

- Heat potatoes according to package directions. Place in bottom of oven while filets broil.

Romaine-Strawberry Salad

1 (10 ounce) package chopped romaine lettuce
2 cups broccoli slaw
1½ cups fresh strawberries, quartered
4 fresh green onions, sliced diagonally

◆ In salad bowl, toss ingredients. When ready to serve, use about ½ cup raspberry vinaigrette salad dressing and toss.

Tip: For a nice touch, garnish with about ¼ cup toasted sunflower seeds.

Peachy Sundaes

1 quart vanilla ice cream
1 (12 ounce) jar peach preserves, warmed
½ cup almonds, slivered, toasted

◆ Spoon ice cream into 6 sherbet dishes and top with warmed preserves and almonds.

My kids grew up on this budget-friendly "filet mignon," and were grown before they found out about the real thing! Sometimes I like to heat 1 can of cream of mushroom soup with some milk and pour it over the steak for steak and gravy.

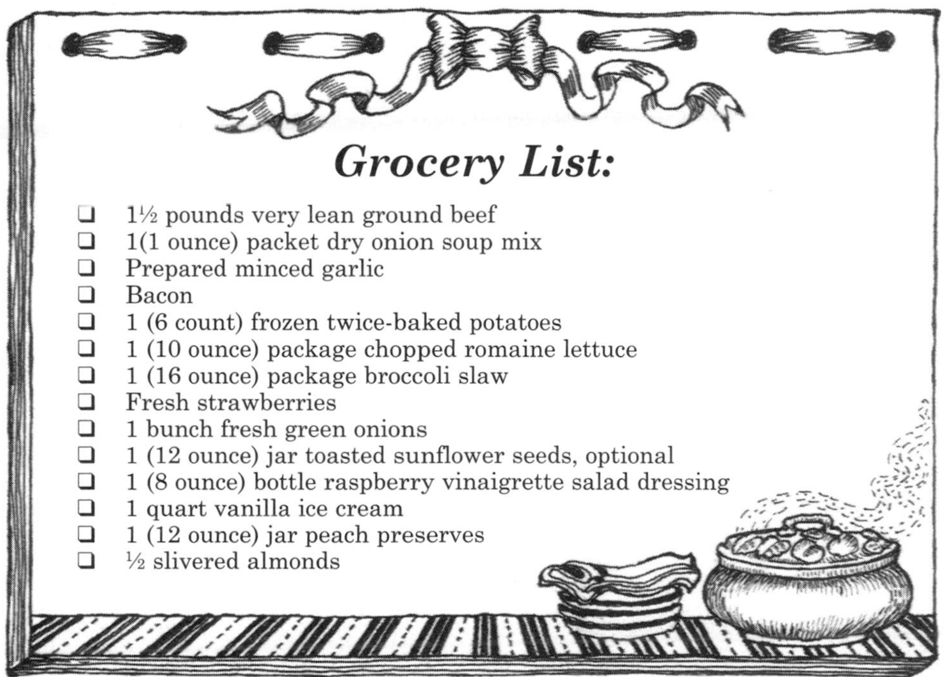

Grocery List:

- ❑ 1½ pounds very lean ground beef
- ❑ 1(1 ounce) packet dry onion soup mix
- ❑ Prepared minced garlic
- ❑ Bacon
- ❑ 1 (6 count) frozen twice-baked potatoes
- ❑ 1 (10 ounce) package chopped romaine lettuce
- ❑ 1 (16 ounce) package broccoli slaw
- ❑ Fresh strawberries
- ❑ 1 bunch fresh green onions
- ❑ 1 (12 ounce) jar toasted sunflower seeds, optional
- ❑ 1 (8 ounce) bottle raspberry vinaigrette salad dressing
- ❑ 1 quart vanilla ice cream
- ❑ 1 (12 ounce) jar peach preserves
- ❑ ½ slivered almonds

High Rollers' Steak Night

Grilled Gorgonzola Tenderloin
Roasted Potato Wedges
Sauteed Pepper Mix
Triple-Chocolate Treat

Grilled Gorgonzola Tenderloin

4 (1½-inch thick) beef tenderloin steaks
Extra-virgin olive oil
Cracked black pepper, seasoned salt
Gorgonzola cheese

- Rub olive oil and sprinkle cracked black pepper and seasoned salt on both sides of steaks. When grill is hot, place steaks on grill over high heat and sear both sides to seal in juices. Move to medium heat and cook about 3 to 5 minutes on each side. Do not overcook.
- Place steaks in baking dish and spread 2 tablespoons gorgonzola cheese on top of each steak. Broil steaks in oven just long enough to melt cheese. Watch carefully.

Roasted Potato Wedges

4 potatoes
Extra-virgin olive oil
Italian dressing
Grated parmesan cheese

- Preheat oven to 350°. Slice potatoes (with skins) into small wedges and rub with olive oil. Place on baking sheet and coat with Italian dressing. Bake for about 18 minutes, remove from oven and turn all potatoes. Sprinkle liberally with grated parmesan cheese. Bake another 10 minutes and serve hot.

Sauteed Pepper Mix

2 green and 2 yellow bell peppers
½ pound button mushrooms
2 sweet onions, peeled
¼ to ½ cup (½ to 1 stick) butter

◆ Remove seeds and membranes from peppers and chop. Clean mushrooms, remove stems and chop into large pieces. Chop onion into similar-size pieces. Melt butter in heavy skillet and saute onion and pepper until onion is translucent. Add mushrooms and saute for 2 to 3 minutes. Sprinkle with salt and serve.

Triple-Chocolate Treat

Bakery brownies
Chocolate ice cream
Hot fudge sauce
1 (8 ounce) carton whipped topping

◆ Cut brownies into squares and place 1 brownie in each serving bowl. Top with 1 to 2 scoops of ice cream. Remove lid from hot fudge sauce jar and microwave according to label directions. Pour hot fudge sauce over ice cream and sprinkle with chopped nuts.

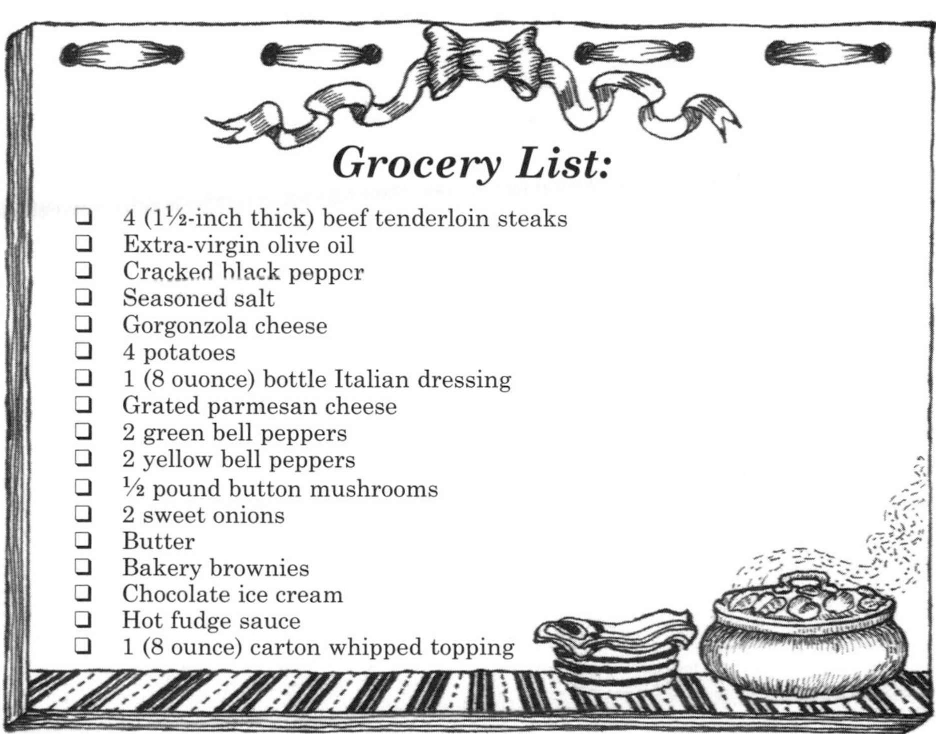

Grocery List:

- ❑ 4 (1½-inch thick) beef tenderloin steaks
- ❑ Extra-virgin olive oil
- ❑ Cracked black pepper
- ❑ Seasoned salt
- ❑ Gorgonzola cheese
- ❑ 4 potatoes
- ❑ 1 (8 ouonce) bottle Italian dressing
- ❑ Grated parmesan cheese
- ❑ 2 green bell peppers
- ❑ 2 yellow bell peppers
- ❑ ½ pound button mushrooms
- ❑ 2 sweet onions
- ❑ Butter
- ❑ Bakery brownies
- ❑ Chocolate ice cream
- ❑ Hot fudge sauce
- ❑ 1 (8 ounce) carton whipped topping

Sirloin in Rich Mushroom Sauce

1 pound boneless beef sirloin, cut into strips
1 (14 ounce) can beef broth
2 teaspoons minced garlic
1 (8 ounce) can sliced mushrooms
1 (10 ounce) can cream of mushroom soup

- In large non-stick skillet with 2 tablespoons oil over medium to high heat, brown steak strips. (Sirloin will be tender with less cooking time than cheaper cuts of meat.)
- Add beef broth, garlic, a generous amount of black pepper and ½ can water. Heat to boiling, reduce heat and simmer 15 minutes.
- Spoon mushroom soup, mushrooms and 1 cup water in saucepan and heat just enough to mix well. Pour over steak and simmer 5 minutes. Serve over angel hair pasta.

Angel Hair Pasta

1 (8 ounce) package uncooked angel hair pasta

- Cook pasta according to package directions. Drain and arrange on serving platter. Spoon steak and mushroom sauce over pasta.

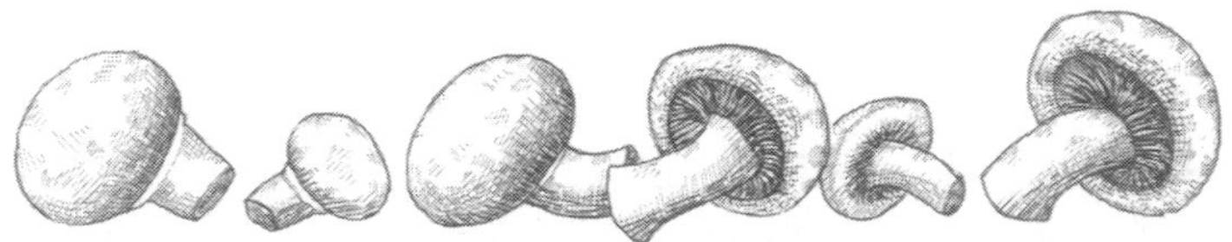

Steamed Broccoli with Cheese

2 (16 ounce) packages frozen broccoli florets, thawed
1 teaspoon seasoned salt and pepper
1 (10 ounce) can cheddar cheese soup
1 (3 ounce) can french-fried onion rings

- Steam broccoli according to package directions and drain well. Sprinkle with seasoned salt and pepper.
- In small saucepan over low heat, stir and heat soup until hot. When ready to serve, place broccoli in serving bowl and spoon cheese soup over broccoli and top with onion rings.

Tip: For spicier flavor, use 1 can fiesta nacho cheese soup instead of cheddar cheese soup.

Carrot Cake

1 (44 ounce) frozen carrot cake, thawed

- Slice and serve on individual dessert plates.

Beef sirloin in rich, creamy sauce is delectable, but the real secret to this meal is the frozen carrot cake for dessert! (Who wants to take time to grate all those carrots?) Just replace the cake box with your own fancy cake plate, sprinkle a little flour around the kitchen and practice the "I've been baking all day!" sigh.

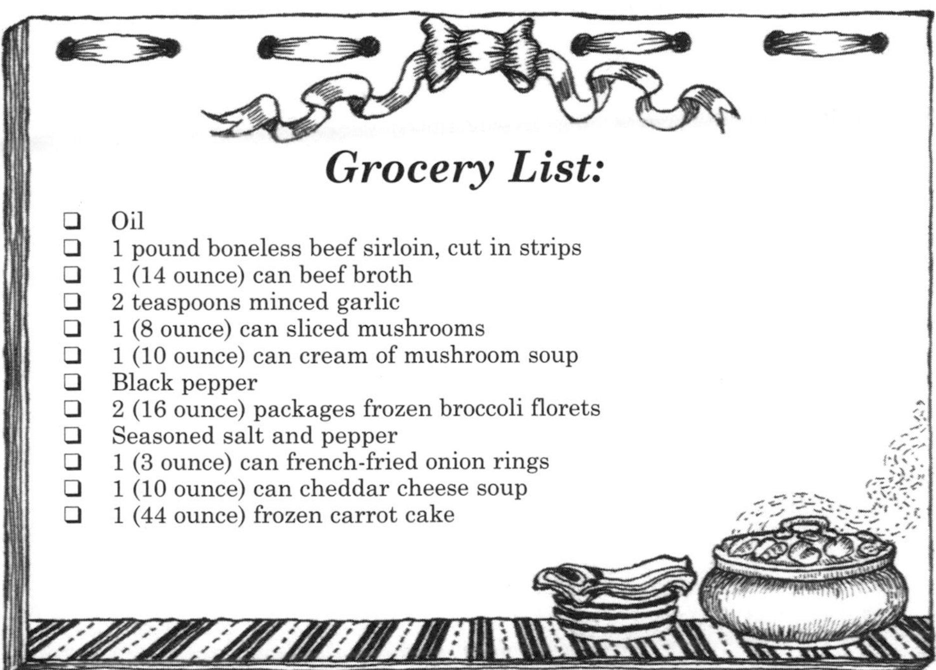

Grocery List:

- ❑ Oil
- ❑ 1 pound boneless beef sirloin, cut in strips
- ❑ 1 (14 ounce) can beef broth
- ❑ 2 teaspoons minced garlic
- ❑ 1 (8 ounce) can sliced mushrooms
- ❑ 1 (10 ounce) can cream of mushroom soup
- ❑ Black pepper
- ❑ 2 (16 ounce) packages frozen broccoli florets
- ❑ Seasoned salt and pepper
- ❑ 1 (3 ounce) can french-fried onion rings
- ❑ 1 (10 ounce) can cheddar cheese soup
- ❑ 1 (44 ounce) frozen carrot cake

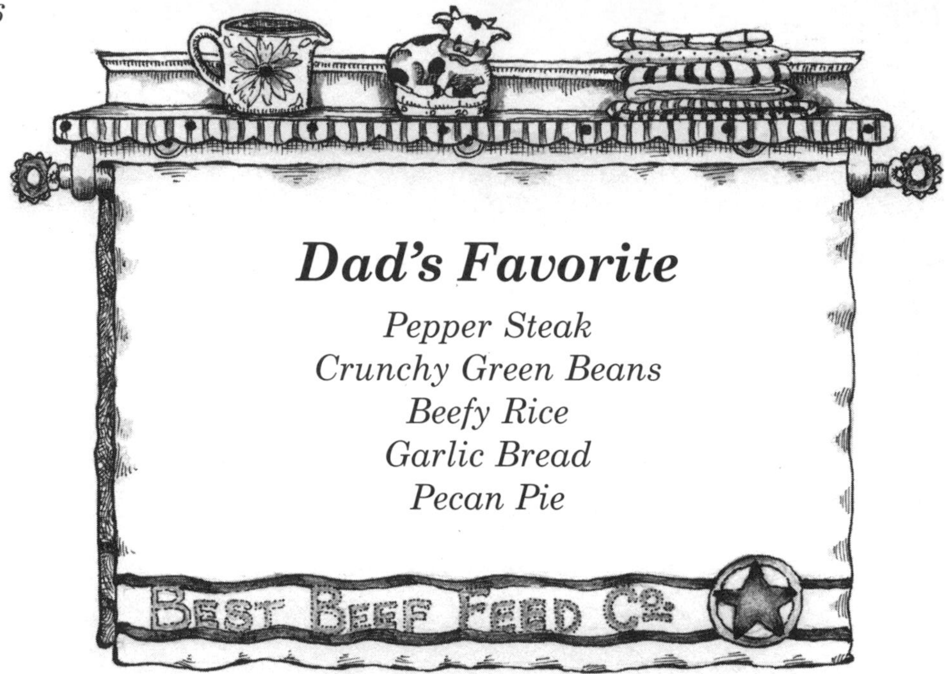

Pepper Steak

1¼ pounds sirloin steak, cut into strips
1 (14 ounce) can beef broth, 1 teaspoon black pepper
1 (16 ounce) package frozen chopped bell peppers and onions, thawed
1 tablespoon seasoned salt
2 tablespoons corn starch

- Sprinkle black pepper over steak strips. In large skillet with a little oil, brown steak strips.
- Pour beef broth over steak and add bell pepper-onion mixture, ¾ cup water and seasoned salt. Bring to boil, reduce heat and simmer 15 minutes.
- In small bowl, combine corn starch and ½ cup water and pour into skillet. Cook and stir over medium heat until mixture thickens. Serve over beef-flavored rice.

Crunchy Green Beans

3 (15 ounce) cans cut green beans
2 (10 ounce) cans cream of mushroom soup
2 (11 ounce) cans water chestnuts, chopped
1 (6 ounce) can french-fried onion rings

- Preheat over to 350°. Combine green beans, soup and water chestnuts and spoon into buttered 9 x 13-inch casserole dish.
- Sprinkle onion rings over casserole and bake 20 minutes or until hot.

Beefy Rice

1 (6 ounce) package beef-flavored rice mix
2 tablespoons butter

- In large skillet, brown rice mixture in butter until rice turns light brown.
- Add 2½ cups hot water and contents of seasoning packet. Bring to boil, reduce heat, cover and simmer 18 to 20 minutes.
- Fluff rice with fork and spoon onto platter. Spoon Pepper Steak over rice to serve.

Garlic Bread

1 (16 ounce) loaf frozen garlic bread

- Heat with green beans according to package directions.

Pecan Pie

1 (32 ounce) frozen pecan pie, thawed

- Slice and serve.

When using steak in one of our 30-minute meals, buy sirloin rather than a cheaper cut, which needs longer simmering time.

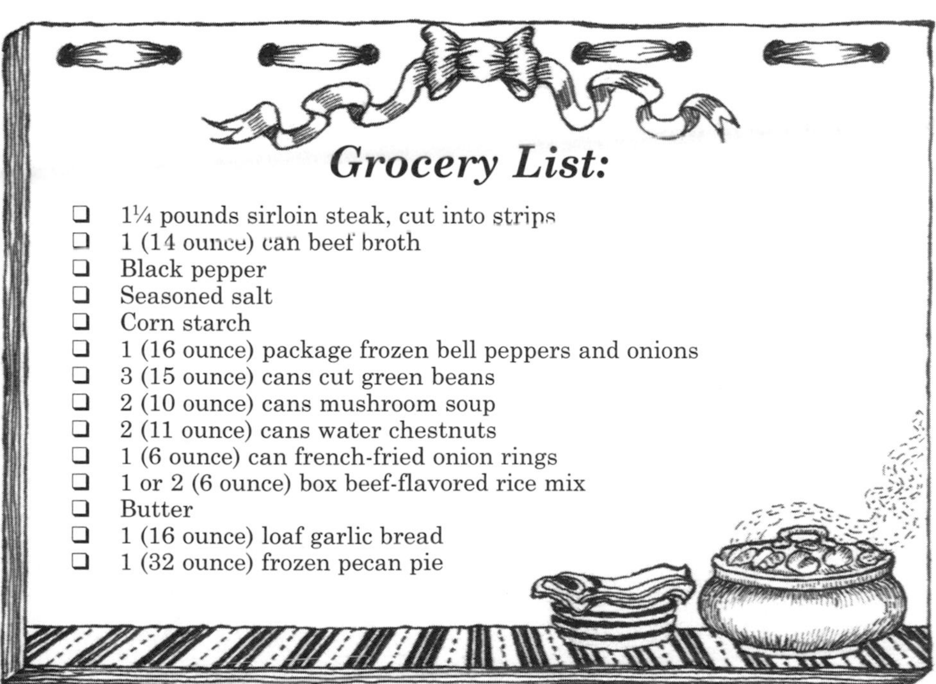

Grocery List:

- ❑ 1¼ pounds sirloin steak, cut into strips
- ❑ 1 (14 ounce) can beef broth
- ❑ Black pepper
- ❑ Seasoned salt
- ❑ Corn starch
- ❑ 1 (16 ounce) package frozen bell peppers and onions
- ❑ 3 (15 ounce) cans cut green beans
- ❑ 2 (10 ounce) cans mushroom soup
- ❑ 2 (11 ounce) cans water chestnuts
- ❑ 1 (6 ounce) can french-fried onion rings
- ❑ 1 or 2 (6 ounce) box beef-flavored rice mix
- ❑ Butter
- ❑ 1 (16 ounce) loaf garlic bread
- ❑ 1 (32 ounce) frozen pecan pie

Meat and Potatoes Night

Easy Smothered Steak
Real Mashed Potatoes
Simple Sliced Vine-Ripened Tomatoes
Strawberry Shortcake

Easy Smothered Steak

Flour
2 pounds round steak, cubed
2 (12 ounce) jars homestyle beef gravy
2 tablespoons oil

- Lightly flour cubed steak on all sides and brown in large skillet with oil. Drain fat, pour gravy over steak, cover and simmer for 15 minutes.

Real Mashed Potatoes

4 medium potatoes
½ cup (1 stick) butter
¼ teaspoon salt
White pepper

- Wash and dice potatoes. Boil in salted water until tender. Drain water and mash with potato masher. Add butter and mash until fluffy. Add white pepper and blend well. (Black pepper is alright if you don't mind black specs.)

Simple Sliced Vine-Ripened Tomatoes

2 to 3 vine-ripened tomatoes

- Arrange slices on serving plate.

Strawberry Shortcake

1 angel food cake
1 (8 ounce) carton whipped topping
1 (16 ounce) carton frozen sweetened strawberries, thawed

◆ Slice cake in 2-inch pieces and place on individual serving plates. Cover cake on each plate with strawberries and whipped topping.

Grocery List:

- ❑ Flour
- ❑ 2 pounds round steak, cubed
- ❑ 2 (12 ounce) jars homestyle beef gravy
- ❑ Oil
- ❑ 4 medium potatoes
- ❑ Butter
- ❑ Salt
- ❑ White pepper
- ❑ 2 to 3 vine-ripened tomatoes
- ❑ 1 angel food cake
- ❑ 1 (8 ounce) carton whipped topping
- ❑ 1 (16 ounce) carton frozen sweetened strawberries

Start-to-Finish Easy

Beef and Broccoli
Potato Souffle
Spring Greens
Cherry-Topped Pound Cake

Beef and Broccoli

1 pound beef sirloin steak
1 onion, chopped
1 (10 ounce) can cream of broccoli soup
1 (10 ounce) package frozen chopped broccoli, thawed

- Slice beef across grain into very thin strips. In large skillet brown steak strips and onion in a little oil and stir several times.
- Reduce heat and simmer 10 minutes. Stir in soup and broccoli and heat. When ready to serve, spoon beef mixture over hot, cooked noodles.

Potato Souffle

2⅔ cups dry instant mashed potatoes
2 eggs, beaten
1 cup shredded cheddar cheese
1 (3 ounce) can french-fried onion rings

- Preheat oven to 350°. Prepare mashed potatoes according to directions. Fold in beaten eggs and cheese and stir well. Spoon into lightly greased 2-quart casserole dish. Sprinkle with onion rings. Bake uncovered for 20 to 25 minutes.

Spring Greens

1 (10 ounce) package spring-mix salad greens
1 seedless cucumber, sliced
1 bunch red radishes, sliced
1 (16 ounce) jar refrigerated honey-mustard salad dressing

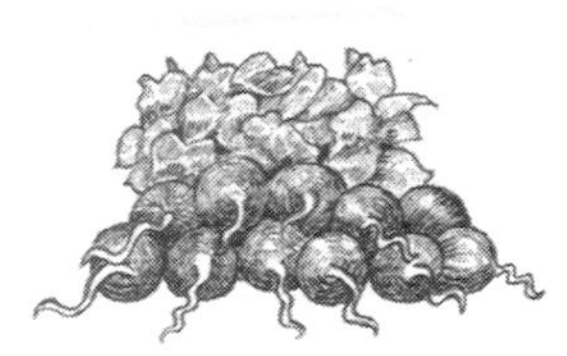

◆ In salad bowl, toss greens, cucumber and radishes. Add dressing.

Cherry-Topped Pound Cake

1 (16 ounce) frozen loaf pound cake
1 (20 ounce) can cherry pie filling
1 (8 ounce) carton whipped topping

◆ Place slices of pound cake on dessert plates and top with generous amount of cherry pie filling and heaping tablespoon whipped topping.

These smothered meatballs are fast, tasty and a regular favorite. Add a frozen pecan cheesecake when company comes.

Grocery List:

- ❑ 1 pound beef sirloin steak
- ❑ 1 onion
- ❑ 1 (10 ounce) can cream of broccoli soup
- ❑ 1 (10 ounce) package frozen chopped broccoli
- ❑ Noodles
- ❑ Instant mashed potatoes
- ❑ 2 eggs
- ❑ 1 (8 ounce) package shredded cheese
- ❑ 1 (3 ounce) can french-fried onion rings
- ❑ 1 (10 ounce) package spring-mix salad greens
- ❑ 1 cucumber
- ❑ 1 bunch red radishes
- ❑ 1 (16 ounce) jar refrigerated honey-mustard salad dressing
- ❑ 1 (16 ounce) frozen pound cake
- ❑ 1 (20 ounce) can cherry pie filling
- ❑ 1 (8 ounce) carton whipped topping

Super Mex

Skillet Fajitas
Mexican Rice and Corn
Quesadilla Rolls
Spinach-Bacon Salad

Skillet Fajitas

1½ pounds boneless beef sirloin steak, cut in thin strips
2 green bell peppers, julienned
1 (14 ounce) jar Pace® Mexican Creations™ sweet roasted onion cooking sauce
12 (8 inch) flour tortillas, warmed

- In large skillet over medium to high heat, place a little oil, cook and stir beef strips 10 minutes until they brown. Add bell pepper, cook and stir constantly another 3 minutes.
- Pour Mexican cooking sauce into skillet with beef and bell pepper. Bring to boil, reduce heat and simmer 10 minutes.
- When ready to serve, spoon equal amounts beef mixture on each tortilla. If desired, add shredded cheddar cheese and roll up. Serve immediately.

Tip: While fajita meat cooks, start heating water for rice, because it has to cook 25 minutes.

Mexican Rice and Corn

1 (8 ounce) package Vigo® Mexican rice with corn
2 tablespoons olive oil
1 (11 ounce) can mexicorn
1 green bell pepper

- Prepare rice according to package directions and stir in vegetables.

Quesadilla Rolls

2 (9 ounce) packages frozen quesadilla rolls

- Heat rolls according to package directions.

Quesadilla rolls are a crispy, crunchy addition to this supper.

Spinach-Bacon Salad

2 quarts fresh spinach, torn into pieces
8 bacon slices, cooked, crumbled
3 eggs, hard-boiled, chopped
Ranch-style dressing

- Combine all ingredients and toss.

I served these skillet fajitas one night and one of the girls was on a diet so instead of rolling the beef mixture in a tortilla, she eliminated the tortilla and spooned the beef mixture over the rice and declared it to be perfect. Either way you serve it, this recipe is a time-saver!

Grocery List:

- ❑ Oil
- ❑ 1½ pounds beef sirloin steak
- ❑ 2 green bell peppers
- ❑ 1 (14 ounce) jar Pace® Mexican Creations™ sweet roasted onion cooking sauce
- ❑ 12 (8 inch) flour tortillas
- ❑ Shredded cheese, optional
- ❑ 1 (8 ounce) package Vigo® Mexican rice with corn (found in the Mexican food section)
- ❑ 1 (11 ounce) can mexicorn
- ❑ 1 green bell pepper
- ❑ 2 (9 ounce) packages frozen quesadilla rolls
- ❑ 2 quarts fresh spinach
- ❑ 8 slices bacon
- ❑ 3 eggs

Pop's Favorites

Savory Cubed Steaks
Mashed Potatoes and Gravy
Buttered Corn
Cookies and Cream

Savory Cubed Steaks

6 beef cubed steaks
2 teaspoons garlic-pepper blend
Oil

- Sprinkle both sides of each cubed steak with garlic-pepper seasoning.
- Spray large skillet with vegetable cooking spray, heat and add steaks and ¼ cup water. Cook on medium-high heat 7 to 9 minutes. Turn once during cooking. Reduce heat, cover and simmer for 10 minutes.

Mashed Potatoes and Gravy

2 cups dry mashed potato flakes
¼ cup (½ stick) butter
¾ cup milk
2 (16 ounce) jars beef gravy

- While steaks cook, prepare mashed potatoes according to package instructions with butter, milk, 2 cups water and salt.
- Open both jars gravy and heat in saucepan. Serve over mashed potatoes and steaks.

Buttered Corn

2 (15 ounce) cans whole kernel corn, drained
2½ tablespoons (⅓ stick) butter
1 teaspoon salt
½ teaspoon white pepper

◆ In saucepan, combine all ingredients and heat until hot.

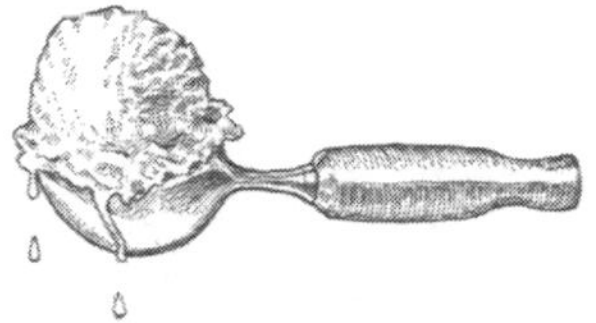

Cookies and Cream

25 Oreo cookies, crushed
½ gallon vanilla ice cream, softened
1 (5 ounce) can chocolate syrup
1 (12 ounce) carton whipped topping

◆ Press crushed cookies in small bowls. Scoop ice cream over cookies. Pour syrup over ice cream, add more cookies and top with whipped topping.

Cubed steak is a traditional family favorite! The other menu items are inexpensive, so you can buy the very best cuts of meat for this recipe.

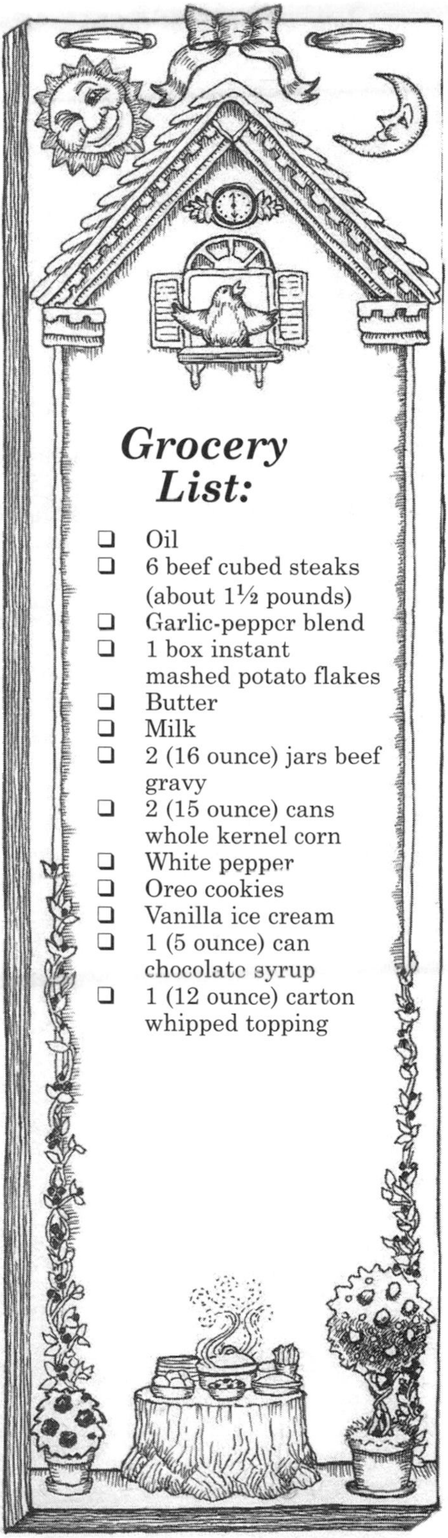

Grocery List:

- ❑ Oil
- ❑ 6 beef cubed steaks (about 1½ pounds)
- ❑ Garlic-pepper blend
- ❑ 1 box instant mashed potato flakes
- ❑ Butter
- ❑ Milk
- ❑ 2 (16 ounce) jars beef gravy
- ❑ 2 (15 ounce) cans whole kernel corn
- ❑ White pepper
- ❑ Oreo cookies
- ❑ Vanilla ice cream
- ❑ 1 (5 ounce) can chocolate syrup
- ❑ 1 (12 ounce) carton whipped topping

Salisbury Steak and Gravy

1½ pounds extra-lean ground beef
1 egg, beaten
½ cup chili sauce
¾ cup seasoned, dry breadcrumbs

Brown Gravy:
2 (14 ounce) cans beef broth
¼ cup dry red wine
2 tablespoons corn starch
1 (8 ounce) can sliced mushrooms, drained

- In medium bowl, combine all steak ingredients and mix well. Shape into 6 or 8 patties about ¾-inch thick.
- In large skillet with a little oil, brown patties about 5 minutes on each side. Set aside in warm oven.
- Add beef broth, wine and corn starch to skillet and stir until corn starch mixture dissolves. Cook and stir over high heat until mixture thickens.
- Add mushrooms and cook until hot and gravy bubbles. Spoon mushroom gravy over steaks to serve.

Salisbury steak is normally made with sirloin or round steak, but this version is more budget-friendly. No one will be able to refuse steak and potatoes covered in rich brown gravy.

Mashed Potatoes

2 cups dry mashed potato flakes
¼ cup (½ stick) butter
¾ cups milk
2 cups water

◆ While steaks cook, prepare mashed potatoes according to package directions.

Green Bean Casserole

2 (15 ounce) cans cut green beans, drained
1 (10 ounce) can cream of mushroom soup
1 cup shredded cheddar cheese
1 (3 ounce) can french-fried onion rings

◆ Preheat oven to 375°. Combine green beans, soup and cheese and spoon into 7 x 11-inch greased baking dish. Top with onion rings and bake 20 minutes.

Strawberries and Cream

1 pint fresh strawberries, washed, sliced
½ cup sugar
1 (8 ounce) carton strawberry whipped topping

◆ In container with lid, combine sugar and strawberries and chill until ready to serve. Spoon strawberries in individual bowls and top generously with whipped topping.

Honest to Goodness

Beef Patties in Creamy Onion Sauce
Hot Biscuits and Fried Okra
Spinach Salad
Butterscotch Peanuts

Beef Patties in Creamy Onion Sauce

1½ pounds lean ground beef
½ cup chunky salsa
1⅓ cups buttery cracker crumbs
2 (10 ounce) cans cream of onion soup

- In large bowl, combine beef, salsa and cracker crumbs and form into 6 or 7 patties. In sprayed skillet over medium heat, brown beef patties. Reduce heat and add ¼ cup water. Cover and simmer 15 minutes.
- In same skillet, combine onion soup, 1 teaspoon black pepper and ½ cup water or milk. Heat and mix well. Pour onion sauce over beef patties and simmer another 5 minutes. Serve over hot biscuits.

Hot Biscuits and Fried Okra

1 (12 ounce) package frozen buttermilk biscuits
1 (24 ounce) package frozen, breaded okra, thawed

- Heat biscuits and okra in oven according to package directions.

Spinach Salad

1 (10 ounce) package fresh baby spinach
1 sweet red bell pepper, julienned
1 bunch fresh green onions, cut in 1-inch slices
1 (12 ounce) bottle raspberry vinaigrette dressing

- In salad bowl, combine spinach, bell pepper and green onions. Let each person add dressing to taste.

Butterscotch Peanuts

1 (12 ounce) package butterscotch morsels
2 cups chow mein noodles
1 cup dry roasted peanuts

- In heavy saucepan, heat and stir butterscotch morsels over very low heat until morsels melt.
- Add noodles and peanuts and stir until each piece is coated. Drop from spoon on wax paper. Cool and store in airtight container.

It would be hard to feed our families without ground beef, which is versatile and inexpensive. These patties have great flavor and a creamy sauce that is wonderful served with hot biscuits. The butterscotch "haystack" dessert is fun and easy to make for all sorts of occasions.

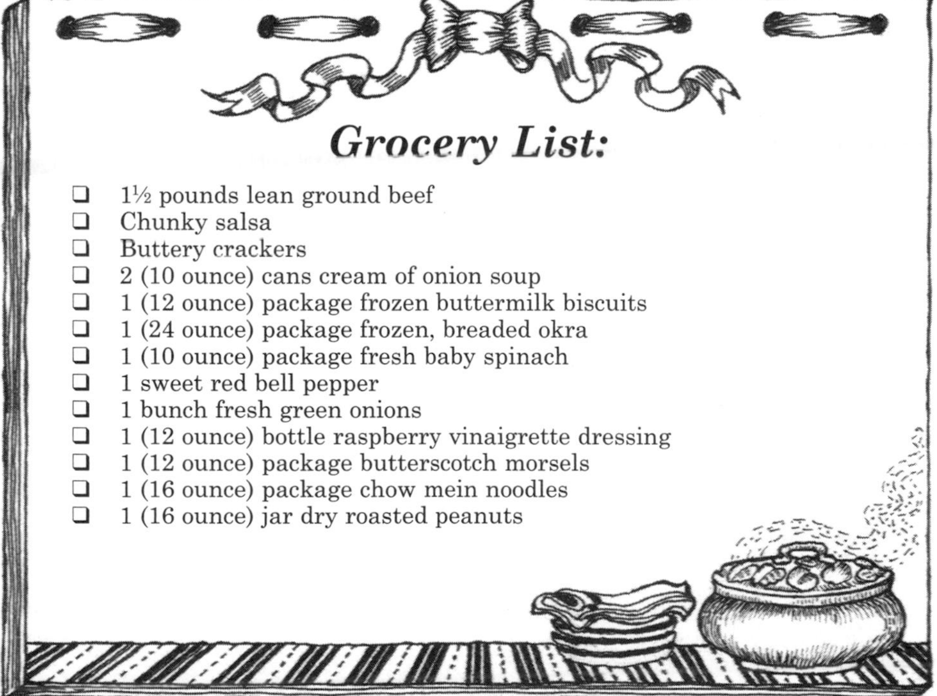

Grocery List:

- ❑ 1½ pounds lean ground beef
- ❑ Chunky salsa
- ❑ Buttery crackers
- ❑ 2 (10 ounce) cans cream of onion soup
- ❑ 1 (12 ounce) package frozen buttermilk biscuits
- ❑ 1 (24 ounce) package frozen, breaded okra
- ❑ 1 (10 ounce) package fresh baby spinach
- ❑ 1 sweet red bell pepper
- ❑ 1 bunch fresh green onions
- ❑ 1 (12 ounce) bottle raspberry vinaigrette dressing
- ❑ 1 (12 ounce) package butterscotch morsels
- ❑ 1 (16 ounce) package chow mein noodles
- ❑ 1 (16 ounce) jar dry roasted peanuts

Pass the Plate

Hi-Ho Meat, Potatoes and Gravy
Scalloped Potatoes
Sliced Tomatoes and Celery Sticks
Fancy Fruit

Hi-Ho Meat, Potatoes and Gravy

1¼ pounds lean ground beef
⅓ cup seasoned dry breadcrumbs
1 egg, beaten
⅓ cup finely minced onion

- In large bowl, combine all ingredients and shape into 6 patties.
- Spray large skillet with cooking spray and cook patties over medium heat 3 to 4 minutes on each side. Transfer patties to glass dish to serve. Keep warm.

Gravy:
2 (12 ounce) jars beef gravy
¼ teaspoon dried thyme
1 (4 ounce) can sliced mushrooms, drained

- Heat gravy, thyme and mushrooms in same skillet patties have been cooked. To serve, pour gravy and mushrooms over patties.

Scalloped Potatoes

1 (5 ounce) package scalloped potatoes
⅔ cup milk
⅛ cup (¼ stick) butter
Water

- Preheat oven to 425°. Prepare potatoes according to package directions and bake 25 minutes.

Sliced Tomatoes and Celery Sticks

3 to 4 vine-ripened tomatoes, sliced
1 stalk celery, ribs cut into 3-inch pieces
1 (16 ounce) carton pimento cheese

- Slice tomatoes on serving plate. Stuff 1 heaping tablespoon pimento cheese on ribs of celery and place on serving plate with tomatoes.

Fancy Fruit

2 (20 ounce) cans peach pie filling, chilled
1 (15 ounce) can pear slices, cut in half, chilled
1 (16 ounce) package frozen sweetened strawberries, thawed
1 (20 ounce) can pineapple tidbits, drained, chilled

- Combine all fruits in pretty, crystal bowl.

Five-minute scalloped potatoes leave you 25 minutes for the rest of this meal. The beef patties are a snap to fix and make a "stick-to-your-ribs" dinner. Gravy is great with or without the mushrooms.

Grocery List:

- ❑ 1¼ pounds lean ground beef
- ❑ Seasoned dry breadcrumbs
- ❑ 1 egg
- ❑ 1 onion
- ❑ 2 (12 ounce) jars beef gravy
- ❑ Dried thyme
- ❑ 1 (4 ounce) can sliced mushrooms
- ❑ 1 (5 ounce) box scalloped potatoes
- ❑ Milk
- ❑ Butter
- ❑ 3 to 4 vine-ripened tomatoes
- ❑ 1 stalk celery
- ❑ 1 (16 ounce) carton pimento cheese
- ❑ 2 (20 ounce) cans peach pie filling
- ❑ 1 (15 ounce) can pear slices
- ❑ 1 (16 ounce) package frozen sweetened strawberries
- ❑ 1 (20 ounce) can pineapple tidbits

Supper's Ready

Quick Skillet
Green Salad Vinaigrette
Poppy Seed Breadsticks
Mixed Fruit

Quick Skillet

1½ pounds lean ground beef
2 (3 ounce) packages Oriental-flavor ramen noodles
⅔ cup stir-fry sauce
1 (16 ounce) package frozen Oriental stir-fry vegetables

- In large skillet, brown and crumble ground beef. Add 2½ cups water, seasoning packets, stir-fry sauce (to taste) and vegetables. Cook and stir on low to medium heat about 5 minutes.
- Break noodles, add to beef-vegetable mixture and cook about 6 minutes. Stir and separate noodles as they soften.

Green Salad Vinaigrette

1 (10 ounce) package mixed salad greens
1 (8 ounce) can water chestnuts, chopped
⅓ cup walnuts, toasted
1 (8 ounce) bottle balsamic vinaigrette dressing

- In salad bowl, combine greens, water chestnuts and walnuts and toss with dressing.

Poppy Seed Breadsticks

1½ cups shredded Monterey Jack cheese
¼ cup poppy seeds
2 tablespoons dry onion soup mix
2 (11 ounce) cans breadstick dough

- Preheat oven to 375°. In large shallow bowl, combine cheese, poppy seeds and soup mix. Separate breadstick dough and stretch slightly until each stick is about 12 inches long.
- Cut dough in pieces 3 to 4 inches long. Dip strips into cheese mixture and turn to coat all sides. Place on greased baking pan and bake about 12 minutes or until breadsticks brown.

Mixed Fruit

1 (24 ounce) package frozen mixed fruit, thawed

- Serve in dessert bowls. Top with frozen whipped topping if desired.

This Oriental-style meal is a good change of pace.

Grocery List:

- ❑ 1½ pounds lean ground beef
- ❑ 2 (3 ounce) packages Oriental-flavored ramen noodles
- ❑ 1 (10 ounce) bottle stir-fry sauce
- ❑ 1 (16 ounce) package frozen Oriental stir-fry vegetables
- ❑ 1 (10 ounce) package mixed salad greens
- ❑ 1 (8 ounce) can water chestnuts
- ❑ Walnuts
- ❑ 1 (8 ounce) bottle balsamic vinaigrette dressing
- ❑ 1 (8 ounce) package shredded Monterey Jack cheese
- ❑ Poppy seeds
- ❑ Dry onion soup mix
- ❑ 2 (11 ounce) cans breadstick dough
- ❑ Butter
- ❑ 1 (24 ounce) package frozen mixed fruit

Down-Home Express

Skillet Beef and Pasta
Green Salad
Onion Biscuits and Butter
Cantaloupe Slices

Skillet Beef and Pasta

1 (8 ounce) package spiral, rotini pasta
1 (14 ounce) can beef broth
1 pound lean ground beef
2 (11 ounce) cans mexicorn, drained
1 (16 ounce) package cubed Mexican processed cheese

- Cook pasta according to package directions and substitute beef broth for 1¾ cups water. (Usually the 8-ounce package pasta will call for 6 cups water, so use 4¼ cups water plus 1¾ cups beef broth.)
- While pasta cooks, brown beef in large skillet and drain.
- Stir in corn and cheese and cook on low heat until cheese melts. Gently stir cooked pasta into beef mixture until pasta coats well. Spoon mixture into serving bowl and garnish with sprigs of parsley, if desired.

Green Salad

1 (10 ounce) package spring mix-salad greens
1 bunch red radishes, sliced
1 small zucchini with peel, sliced
1 cup fresh broccoli florets, stemmed

- In salad bowl, combine salad greens, radishes, zucchini and broccoli florets.
- Toss with honey-mustard vinaigrette dressing.

Onion Biscuits and Butter

2 cups biscuit mix
¼ cup milk
1 (8 ounce) carton French-onion dip

◆ Preheat oven to 375°. Combine all ingredients and mix well. Drop dough by tablespoons in mounds onto greased baking sheet. Bake for 12 minutes.

Cantaloupe Slices

1 cantaloupe, sliced

◆ Arrange cantaloupe slices on serving tray.

Tip: If cantaloupe is not in season, serve refrigerated or frozen mixed fruit.

This 1-dish skillet beef and pasta is ready in a jiffy. Add green salad, breadsticks and fruit and you have a complete meal.

Grocery List:

- ❑ 1 (8 ounce) package spiral, rotini pasta
- ❑ 1 (14 ounce) can beef broth
- ❑ 1 pound lean ground beef
- ❑ 2 (11 ounce) cans mexicorn
- ❑ 1 (12 ounce) package cubed Mexican processed cheese
- ❑ 1 (10 ounce) package spring mix-salad greens
- ❑ 1 bunch red radishes
- ❑ 1 small zucchini
- ❑ 1 cup fresh broccoli florets
- ❑ 1 (8 ounce) bottle honey-mustard vinaigrette dressing
- ❑ Seasoned croutons, optional
- ❑ Cantaloupe or frozen or refrigerated mixed fruit
- ❑ Biscuit mix
- ❑ Milk
- ❑ 1(8 ounce) carton French-onion dip

Lasagna and the Works

Beef Lasagna
Seasoned Green Beans
Spinach-Orange Salad
Quick Pralines

Beef Lasagna

1 (40 ounce) package frozen lasagna, thawed

- Heat lasagna according to package directions and serve from pan.

The frozen lasagnas available in supermarkets are very good and no one will complain about the foil container. It's amazing how many people bring "prepared" lasagna to our church suppers, but the pan is always empty at the end of the evening.

Seasoned Green Beans

5 slices bacon, fried, chopped
1 medium onion, finely diced
1 (16 ounce) package frozen whole green beans
1 teaspoon seasoned salt

- In skillet, saute bacon and onion. With slotted spoon, remove from skillet and drain on paper towels. (Save pan drippings.)
- Place green beans in skillet with bacon drippings and add about ¼ cup water and seasoned salt.
- Cook covered on medium heat 10 to 15 minutes. (Do not overcook. Beans should be crisp-tender.)

Spinach-Orange Salad

1 (10 ounce) package fresh baby spinach
2 (11 ounce) cans mandarin oranges, drained
½ small jacama, peeled, julienned
⅓ cup almonds, slivered, toasted

- In salad bowl, combine all ingredients and toss with vinaigrette dressing.

Quick Pralines

1 (3 ounce) box cook-and-serve butterscotch pudding
1¼ cups sugar
½ cup evaporated milk
2 cups pecan pieces

- In large saucepan, mix pudding, sugar and milk. Bring to boil and stir constantly for 2 minutes. Add pecans, boil another 1½ minutes and stir constantly.
- Remove from heat. Beat until candy begins to cool and drop by tablespoonfuls on wax paper.

Lasagna is always a popular choice with young and old alike. It used to take a long time to make, but with so many good frozen lasagnas available it is OK to take a shortcut on a school night.

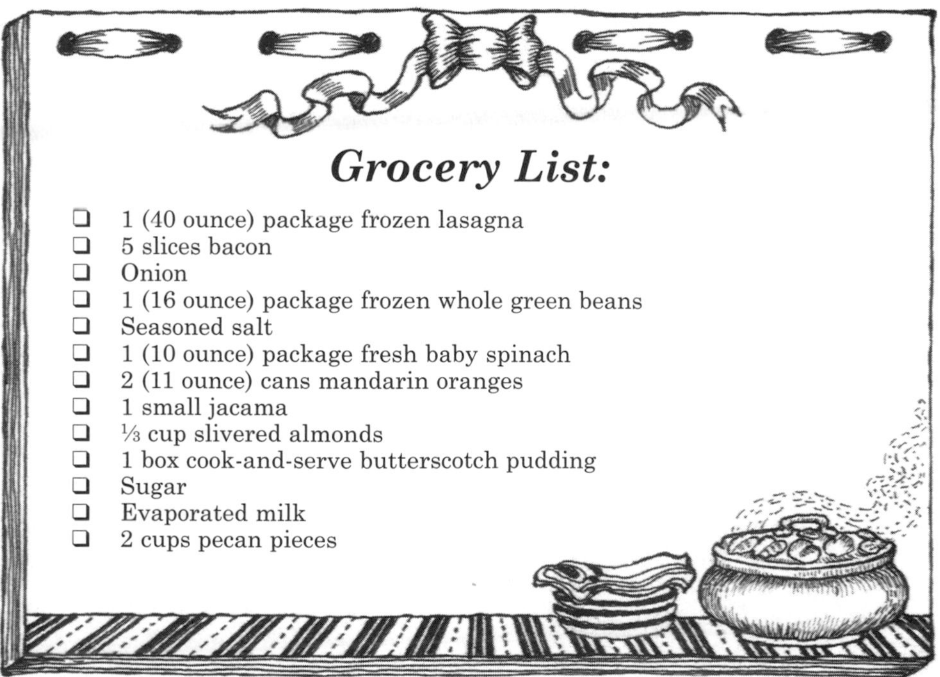

Grocery List:

- ❑ 1 (40 ounce) package frozen lasagna
- ❑ 5 slices bacon
- ❑ Onion
- ❑ 1 (16 ounce) package frozen whole green beans
- ❑ Seasoned salt
- ❑ 1 (10 ounce) package fresh baby spinach
- ❑ 2 (11 ounce) cans mandarin oranges
- ❑ 1 small jacama
- ❑ ⅓ cup slivered almonds
- ❑ 1 box cook-and-serve butterscotch pudding
- ❑ Sugar
- ❑ Evaporated milk
- ❑ 2 cups pecan pieces

Everybody's Favorite

Spaghetti and Meatballs
Italian Green Salad
Hot, Buttered Garlic Bread
Caramel-Apple Delight

Spaghetti and Meatballs

1 (18 ounce) package frozen meatballs, thawed
1 (28 ounce) jar spaghetti sauce
1 (8 ounce) package spaghetti
1 (5 ounce) package fresh shredded parmesan cheese

- In large microwave baking dish, heat meatballs on High for 10 to 12 minutes. Stir twice.
- Cook spaghetti according to package directions and drain well. Pour onto serving plate and spoon meatball sauce over spaghetti. Top with cheese.

This should serve 4 or 5 people, but can easily be doubled.

Italian Green Salad

1 (10 ounce) package Italian-blend salad greens
1 seedless cucumber, sliced
1 small zucchini, unpeeled, sliced
⅓ cup sunflower seeds, roasted

- In salad bowl, combine salad greens, cucumber and zucchini.
- When ready to serve, toss with a creamy Italian dressing and sprinkle sunflower seeds on top. Add croutons, if desired.

Hot, Buttered Garlic Bread

1 (16 ounce) loaf garlic bread
Butter

- Slice bread in 1-inch thick slices. Butter each slice and place back into loaf.
- Cover bread with foil and bake at 350° for 15 to 20 minutes.

If you want to take the easy way out, buy a frozen loaf already buttered.

Caramel-Apple Delight

3 (2 ounce) Snickers candy bars, frozen
2 Granny Smith apples, chilled, chopped
1 (12 ounce) carton whipped topping
1 (3 ounce) package dry, instant vanilla pudding

- Smash frozen candy bars in wrappers with hammer.
- Combine all ingredients in crystal salad bowl and stir very well. Refrigerate. You could also serve in individual sherbet glasses.

Who doesn't like spaghetti and meatballs? Especially with hot crusty bread. The best part of this menu is you can buy meatballs already made and cooked—what a time-saver! I wish I had a quarter for every meatball I've made in my lifetime.

Grocery List:

- ❑ 1 (16 ounce) package frozen meatballs
- ❑ 1 (28 ounce) jar spaghetti sauce
- ❑ 1 (8 ounce) package spaghetti
- ❑ 1 (5 ounce) package shredded parmesan cheese
- ❑ 1 (10 ounce) package Italian salad greens
- ❑ 1 cucumber
- ❑ 1 zucchini
- ❑ 1 (16 ounce) jar roasted sunflower seeds
- ❑ Creamy Italian dressing
- ❑ 1 (16 ounce) loaf garlic bread
- ❑ Butter
- ❑ 3 (2 ounce) Snickers candy bars
- ❑ 2 Granny Smith apples
- ❑ 1 (12 ounce) carton whipped topping
- ❑ 1 (3 ounce) package dry, instant vanilla pudding

Like Mom Used to Make

Meat Loaf with Tomato Sauce
Mary Katherine's Fried Corn
Tator Tots
Butterscotch-Krispie Bars

Meat Loaf with Tomato Sauce

1 (17 ounce) package frozen or refrigerated meat loaf with tomato sauce

- Remove paper sleeve and film from tray. Leave pouch in tray. Cut 3 small slits in pouch and microwave on HIGH 4 minutes. Let stand 4 to 5 minutes.
- Cut end of pouch with scissors and place meat loaf and sauce on serving plate. (2 packages will serve 6 to 7)

Mary Katherine's Fried Corn

1 (16 ounce) package frozen whole kernel corn, thawed
½ cup (1 stick) butter
¾ cup whipping cream
Salt and ¾ teaspoon white pepper

- In large skillet over low heat, combine corn and butter, cook and stir until butter melts.
- Add whipping cream, a little salt and white pepper. Cover and simmer 8 to 10 minutes. (Stir several times during cooking to avoid sticking.) You must stir and cook on low heat or corn will stick to pan.

This recipe originated with folks who had a cornfield and cow that not only gave milk, but heavy cream too—and who counted calories then? My grandkids love this corn, but they don't want me to mention the calories, so I don't.

Tator Tots

1 (16 ounce) package frozen tator tots, thawed
Ketchup or salsa

◆ Heat in oven according to package directions. Serve with ketchup or salsa.

Butterscotch-Krispie Bars

1 (12 ounce) package butterscotch chips
1 cup creamy peanut butter
6 cups crispy rice cereal

◆ Combine butterscotch chips and peanut butter in saucepan. Heat and stir until smooth.

◆ Remove from heat and stir in cereal. Mix until it coats. Press into buttered 9 x 13-inch pan. Chill in freezer so it will firm up quicker. Cut into bars.

There are so many good recipes for meat loaf, but if you're like me, you don't have time to wait for it to cook! This is the best prepared meat loaf that I have found, part of the perfect "Family Night" menu.

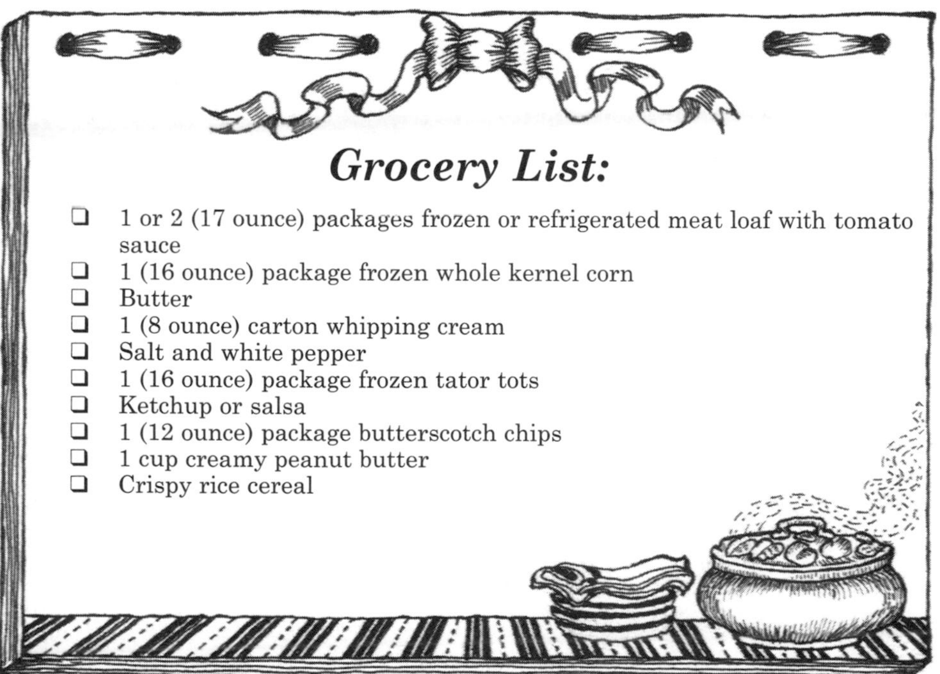

Grocery List:

- ❑ 1 or 2 (17 ounce) packages frozen or refrigerated meat loaf with tomato sauce
- ❑ 1 (16 ounce) package frozen whole kernel corn
- ❑ Butter
- ❑ 1 (8 ounce) carton whipping cream
- ❑ Salt and white pepper
- ❑ 1 (16 ounce) package frozen tator tots
- ❑ Ketchup or salsa
- ❑ 1 (12 ounce) package butterscotch chips
- ❑ 1 cup creamy peanut butter
- ❑ Crispy rice cereal

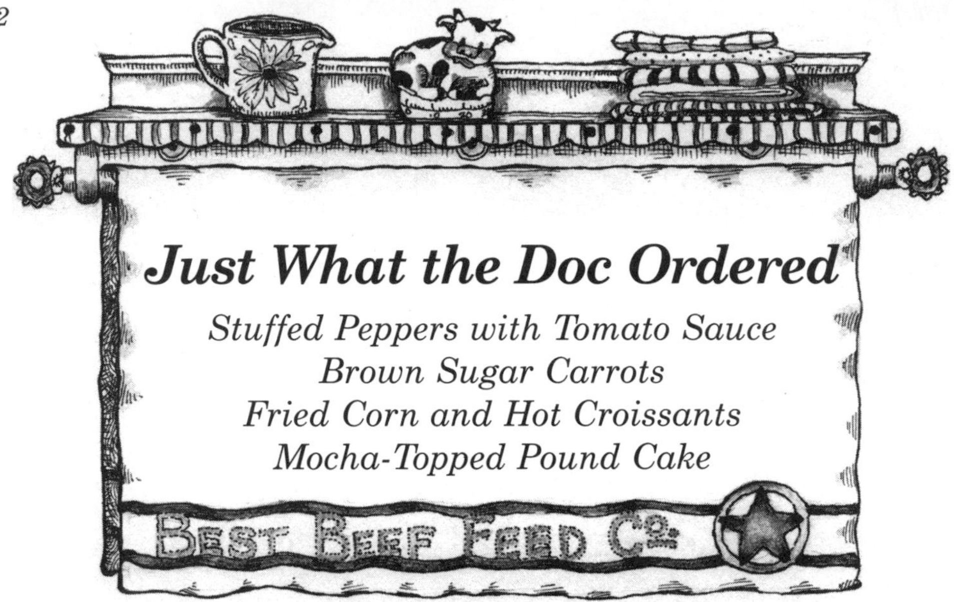

Just What the Doc Ordered

Stuffed Peppers with Tomato Sauce
Brown Sugar Carrots
Fried Corn and Hot Croissants
Mocha-Topped Pound Cake

Stuffed Peppers with Tomato Sauce

1 (32 ounce, 4 count) package frozen or refrigerated stuffed peppers with tomato sauce

◆ Cook peppers in microwave according to package directions (about 8 minutes). Use 2 packages if serving more than 4 people.

Brown Sugar Carrots

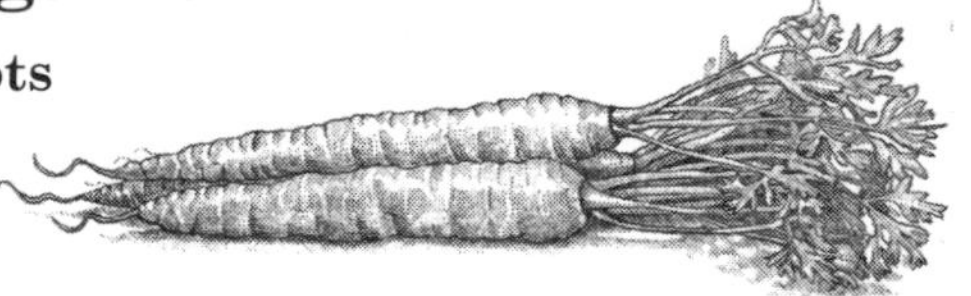

2 (15 ounce) cans sliced carrots
¼ cup (½ stick) butter
¼ cup packed brown sugar
½ teaspoon ground ginger

◆ Reserve 2 tablespoons liquid from carrots and drain remaining liquid. In saucepan, heat carrots and stir in butter, brown sugar and ginger.

Fried Corn

1 (16 ounce) package frozen whole kernel corn
¼ cup (½ stick) butter
½ cup whipping cream
1 teaspoon sugar

◆ In large skillet over medium heat, combine all ingredients with scant teaspoon salt. Cook and stir until liquid absorbs.

The kids will love this rich corn dish.

Hot Croissants

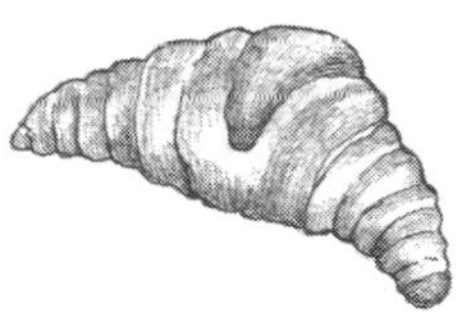

1 (7 ounce, 8 count) package mini-croissants
Butter

◆ Warm croissants at 300° for about 10 minutes.

Mocha-Topped Pound Cake

1 (16 ounce) loaf pound cake
1 (16 ounce) almond candy bar
1 tablespoon instant coffee powder
1 (8 ounce) carton whipped topping

◆ Slice enough pound cake for each person and place on salad plates. Melt candy with coffee powder in double boiler and mix well. Place in freezer for about 10 minutes and stir in whipped topping. Spoon over pound cake.

We've come a long way from traditional TV dinners. Today's frozen entrees are full of flavor and variety. These frozen stuffed peppers are ready from the microwave in just minutes. Macaroni and cheese is always a favorite and this fried corn recipe comes from the good ole' days when we didn't worry about calories!

Grocery List:

- ❑ 1 (32 ounce) package frozen or refrigerated stuffed peppers with tomato sauce
- ❑ 2 (15 ounce) cans sliced carrots
- ❑ Butter
- ❑ Brown sugar
- ❑ Ground ginger
- ❑ 1 (16 ounce) package frozen whole kernel corn
- ❑ 2 (8 ounce) cartons whipping cream
- ❑ Sugar
- ❑ 1 or 2 packages mini-croissants
- ❑ 1 loaf bakery pound cake
- ❑ 1 (16 ounce) almond candy bar
- ❑ Instant coffee powder

No Trouble at All

Texas Chili Pie
Sunshine Salad
Beans, Cheese and Chips
Pecan Pie

Texas Chili Pie

2 (20 ounce) cans chili without beans
1 (13 ounce) package original small corn chips
1 onion, finely chopped
1 (12 ounce) package shredded cheddar cheese

- Preheat oven to 350°. In saucepan, heat and stir chili over low heat.
- In bottom of 9 x 13-inch glass baking dish, layer half corn chips, half chili, half onions and half cheese. Repeat layers except cheese.
- Cover and bake 20 minutes, top with remaining cheese and return to oven until cheese melts. Serve from baking dish.

Sunshine Salad

3 (11 ounce) mexicorn, drained, chilled
1 (15 ounce) can green peas, drained, chilled
1 (15 ounce) can wax beans, rinsed, drained, chilled
1 (8 ounce) bottle Italian dressing, chilled

- In bowl with lid, combine corn, peas and beans. Stir in Italian dressing and toss. Refrigerate.

To have this meal ready in 30 minutes, chill salad in freezer 15 minutes and it will be ready to eat in our 30-minute time limit.

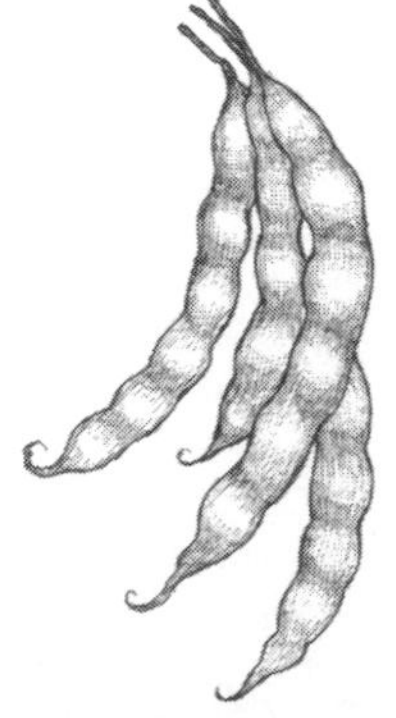

Beans, Cheese and Chips

2 (15 ounce) cans refried beans
1 (10 ounce) can tomatoes and green chilies
1 (8 ounce) package Mexican 4-cheese blend
4 fresh green onions, finely chopped

- Combine beans and tomatoes and green chilies. Spoon into buttered 7 x 11-inch baking dish. Microwave for 2 minutes or until ingredients heat. Cover with half cheese and microwave just until cheese melts.
- Sprinkle with remaining cheese and chopped green onions. Serve as vegetable or with chips.

Pecan Pie

1 (32 ounce) frozen pecan pie, thawed

- Heat according to package directions and serve on dessert plates.
- Transfer pie from freezer to refrigerator the morning of your meal. It can also be served room temperature.

The first time I had this combination of chili, chips, etc. it was called "Frito pie." A small individual package of Fritos® was slit about halfway down the sides. Then the chili, onions and cheese were spooned into the package. Wow! That must have been one of the first "fast foods."

Grocery List:

- ❑ 2 (20 ounce) cans chili without beans
- ❑ 1 (13 ounce) package original small corn chips
- ❑ 1 onion
- ❑ 1 (12 ounce) package shredded cheddar cheese
- ❑ 3 (11 ounce) cans mexicorn
- ❑ 1 (15 ounce) can green peas
- ❑ 1 (15 ounce) can wax beans
- ❑ 1 (8 ounce) bottle Italian dressing
- ❑ 2 (15 ounce) cans refried beans
- ❑ 1 (10 ounce) can tomatoes and green chilies
- ❑ 1 (8 ounce) package Mexican 4-cheese blend
- ❑ 4 fresh green onions
- ❑ 1 (32 ounce) frozen pecan pie

El Paso Olé!

Speedy Gonzales Special
Hot Cheese Dip
Chili Beans
Fresh Avocado Dip
Tropical Coconut Cream Pie

Speedy Gonzales Special

1½ pounds lean ground beef
1 (1.5 ounce) packet taco seasoning
½ teaspoon cayenne pepper, optional
1 (4.5 ounce, 12 count) package tostada shells

- Preheat oven to 300°. In skillet, brown and crumble ground beef. Add 1 cup water and cayenne pepper and heat to boiling. Reduce heat and simmer about 12 minutes.
- While beef cooks, heat 6 to 8 tostada shells on baking sheet at 300°.

Topping:
1 (10 ounce) package shredded lettuce
2 to 3 vine-ripened tomatoes, chopped, drained
1 (8 ounce) package shredded cheddar cheese
1 (16 ounce) bottle chunky salsa

- In serving bowl, combine about 2 cups shredded lettuce, chopped tomatoes and cheese and toss. (Remaining shredded lettuce will be used with guacamole.)
- When ready to serve, place about 2 heaping tablespoons beef on each shell and spread out. Top with heaping spoonfuls lettuce-cheese mixture. Let each person add salsa. Serve immediately.

Hot Cheese Dip

½ cup (1 stick) butter
1 large onion, chopped
2 (10 ounce) cans tomatoes and green chilies
1 (2 pound) package cubed processed cheese

◆ In large saucepan, saute onion in butter, add tomatoes and green chilies and stir while cooking. Add cheese gradually to onion-tomato mixture. Heat and stir on medium until cheese melts. Serve hot with chips.

Chili Beans

2 (15 ounce) cans chili beans

◆ Warm in saucepan and place in serving dish.

Fresh Avocado Dip

3 large ripe avocados, mashed
1 tablespoon lemon juice
1 packet dry onion soup mix
1 (8 ounce) carton sour cream

◆ Mix avocados with lemon juice, soup mix and sour cream. Serve with chips or crackers.

Tropical Coconut Cream Pie

1 (24 ounce) frozen tropical coconut cream pie, thawed

◆ Serve on individual dessert plates.

We have everything for a Mexican fiesta without making reservations! What a great way to get kids to eat lettuce and tomatoes.

Grocery List:

- ❑ 1½ pounds lean ground beef
- ❑ 1 (1.5 ounce) package taco seasoning
- ❑ Cayenne pepper, optional
- ❑ 1 (4.5 ounce) package tostada shells
- ❑ 1 (10 ounce) package shredded lettuce
- ❑ 2 to 3 vine-ripened tomatoes
- ❑ 1 (8 ounce) package shredded cheddar cheese
- ❑ 1 (16 ounce) bottle chunky salsa
- ❑ Butter
- ❑ Onion
- ❑ 2 (10 ounce) cans tomatoes and green chilies
- ❑ 1 (2 pound) package cubed processed cheese
- ❑ 2 (15 ounce) cans Bush's chili beans
- ❑ 3 large, ripe avocados
- ❑ Lemon juice
- ❑ 1 packet dry onion soup mix
- ❑ 1 (8 ounce) carton sour cream
- ❑ 1 bag tortilla chips
- ❑ 1 (24 ounce) frozen tropical coconut cream pie

Super Summer Salad Supreme

Beef, Beans and Greens
Walnut-Cream Sandwiches
Deviled Eggs
Grape Fluff

Beef, Beans and Greens

⅓ pound cooked deli roast beef, julienned
1 (15 ounce) can 3-bean salad, chilled, drained
1 (8 ounce) block mozzarella cheese, cut in chunks
1 (8 ounce) bag mixed-salad greens with Italian dressing

◆ In large salad bowl, lightly toss beef, 3-bean salad and cheese. Pour in just enough dressing to moisten greens.

Tip: Substitute turkey or ham for beef and Swiss cheese for mozzarella.

Walnut-Cream Sandwiches

2 (8 ounce) packages cream cheese, softened
½ cup mayonnaise,
1 teaspoon dijon mustard
6 slices bacon, cooked, crumbled
¾ cup finely chopped walnuts

◆ In mixing bowl, beat cream cheese, mayonnaise and mustard until creamy. Fold in bacon and chopped walnuts and mix well.

◆ Spread on pumpernickel or rye bread and slice in thirds.

Deviled Eggs

6 hard-boiled eggs
3 tablespoons sweet pickle relish
3 tablespoons mayonnaise
½ teaspoon mustard

- Peel eggs and cut in half lengthwise. Take yolks out and mash with fork. Add relish, mayonnaise and mustard to yolks. Place yolk mixture back into egg white halves. Sprinkle with paprika, if you like.

Grape Fluff

1 cup grape juice
2 cups miniature marshmallows
2 tablespoons lemon juice
1 (8 ounce) carton whipping cream

- In saucepan heat grape juice to boiling. Add marshmallows and stir constantly until they melt.
- Add lemon juice and cool.
- Fold in whipped cream and spoon into individual serving dishes. Refrigerate.

Long ago, a salad was simply chopped lettuce and tomatoes with a dab of mayonnaise. (My Dad, a "meat-and-potato" man, called it "rabbit food.") Today salads are full of variety and hearty enough for a main dish.

Grocery List:

- ❑ ⅓ pound cooked deli roast beef
- ❑ 1 (15 ounce) can 3-bean salad
- ❑ 1 (8 ounce) block mozzarella cheese
- ❑ 1 (10 ounce) bag mixed-salad greens
- ❑ Italian salad dressing
- ❑ 2 (8 ounce) packages cream cheese
- ❑ Mayonnaise
- ❑ Dijon mustard
- ❑ 1 pound bacon or precooked bacon
- ❑ Walnuts
- ❑ Pumpernickle or rye bread
- ❑ 6 eggs
- ❑ Sweet pickle relish
- ❑ Mustard
- ❑ Grape juice
- ❑ 2 cups miniature marshmallows
- ❑ Lemon juice
- ❑ 1 (8 ounce) carton whipping cream

Easy Kids' Night

Kids' Chili and Crackers
Grilled-Cheese Sandwiches
Bean Dip and Chips
Peanut Butter Cookies

Kids' Chili and Crackers

1 pound lean ground beef
1 (15 ounce) can pinto beans
1 (15 ounce) can whole kernel corn with liquid
2 (10 ounce) cans tomato soup
1 cup shredded cheddar cheese

- In large skillet, cook and stir ground beef until it browns. Drain.
- Stir in pinto beans, corn, tomato soup and 1 cup water. Bring to boil, reduce heat and simmer about 10 minutes.
- To serve, sprinkle cheddar cheese on top of each bowl. Serve with fish-shaped crackers.

Grilled-Cheese Sandwiches

1 loaf white bread
Butter
1 package American or cheddar cheese slices

- Cut crusts off as many slices of bread as you will need. Butter 3 slices bread and place in large skillet. Top each with 1 slice cheese and another buttered slice of bread.
- Cook sandwiches over medium heat until bottom slice is light brown. With spatula, turn each sandwich over and cook until that slice bread is slightly brown. Repeat for as many sandwiches as you need.

Bean Dip and Chips

1 (15 ounce) can refried beans
1 (8 ounce) package shredded cheese
1 package potato chips

◆ Mix beans and cheese and serve with chips.

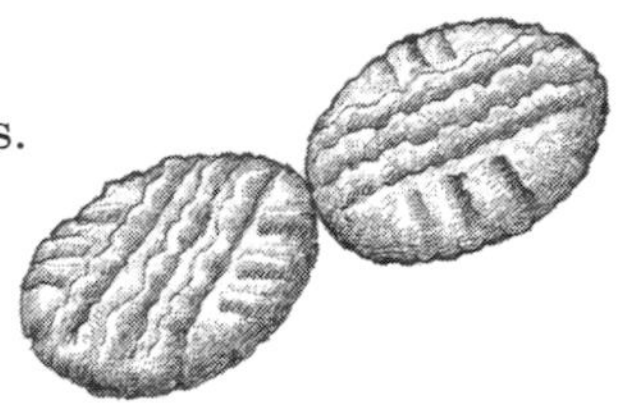

Peanut Butter Cookies

1 package Braum's peanut butter cookies

◆ Arrange cookies on serving tray.

Announce this kid-friendly meal and they'll come running from all over the neighborhood!

Grocery List:

- ❑ 1 pound lean ground beef
- ❑ 1 (15 ounce) can pinto beans
- ❑ 1 (15 ounce) can whole kernel corn
- ❑ 2 (10 ounce) cans tomato soup
- ❑ Shredded cheddar cheese
- ❑ 1 package fish-shaped crackers
- ❑ 1 loaf white bread
- ❑ Butter
- ❑ 1 package American or cheddar cheese slices
- ❑ 1 (15 ounce) can refried beans
- ❑ 1 (8 ounce) package shredded cheese
- ❑ Potato chips
- ❑ Braum's peanut butter cookies

Kids' Soccer Lunch

Cheese-N-Weiner Crescents
Peanutty Grahams
Juicy Apples
Chocolate Bananas

Cheese-N-Weiner Crescents

8 large wieners
4 slices American cheese, cut into 6 strips each
1 (8 ounce) can refrigerated crescent dinner rolls

- Preheat oven to 375°. Split wieners to within ½-inch of edge and insert 3 strips cheese in each slit.
- Separate crescent dough into 8 triangles and roll up wieners inside dough. Place rolls cheese side down on baking sheet and bake 12 to 15 minutes or until golden brown.

Peanutty Grahams

1 (8 ounce) package cream cheese, softened
1¾ cups creamy peanut butter
¾ cup powdered white sugar
1 tablespoon milk
1 box graham crackers

- With mixer, beat cream cheese, peanut butter, sugar and milk. Spread on graham crackers.

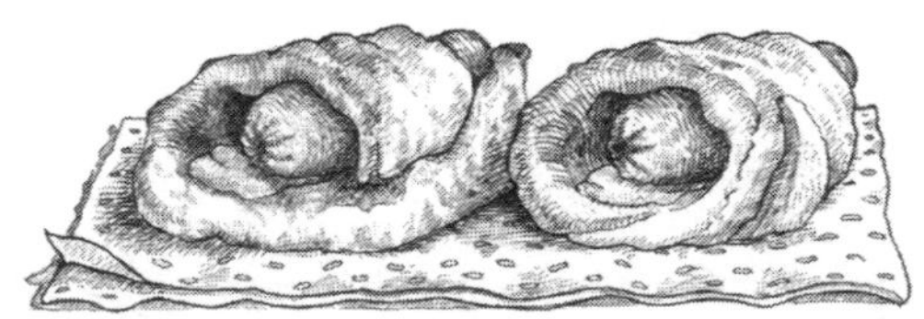

Juicy Apples

1 (8 ounce) package cream cheese, softened
1 (7 ounce) jar marshmallow cream
¼ teaspoon EACH ground ginger and ground cinnamon
2 delicious apples, cut in wedges

◆ With mixer, blend cream cheese, marshmallow creme, ginger and cinnamon. Use apple wedges for dipping.

Chocolate Bananas

Bananas, cut in 1-inch slices
1 or 2 (12 ounce) jars chocolate ice cream topping

◆ Let kids use toothpicks to spear bananas and dip in chocolate.

Whatever their sport, when the kids come in from practice, they're starving! Pick up a prepared cheese dip and extra chips so they can start munching while you get everything on the table.

Grocery List:

- ❑ 1 (8 count) package wieners
- ❑ 1 package American cheese slices
- ❑ 1 (8 count) can refrigerated crescent dinner rolls
- ❑ 2 (8 ounce) packages cream cheese
- ❑ Peanut Butter
- ❑ Powdered white sugar
- ❑ Milk
- ❑ Graham crackers
- ❑ 1 (7 ounce) jar marshmallow cream
- ❑ Ground ginger
- ❑ Ground cinnamon
- ❑ 2 Delicious apples
- ❑ 8 bananas
- ❑ Chocolate ice cream topping

We Love Italy

Italian Sausages and Ravioli
Broccoli Salad
Buttered-Garlic Bread
Lemon Sherbet and Berries

Italian Sausages and Ravioli

1 (16 ounce) package sweet Italian pork sausage, casing removed
1 (28 ounce) jar chunky mushroom and green pepper spaghetti sauce
1 (24 ounce) package frozen cheese-filled ravioli, cooked, drained
Grated parmesan cheese

- In large skillet over medium heat, cook sausage according to package directions. Brown and stir until meat is no longer pink.
- Stir in spaghetti sauce and heat to boiling. Add ravioli and stir gently until it heats through.
- Pour into serving dish and sprinkle with parmesan cheese.

Broccoli Salad

5 cups broccoli florets, stemmed, chilled
1 sweet red bell pepper, julienned, chilled
1 cup diagonally sliced celery, chilled
1 (8 ounce) package Monterey Jack cheese, cubed

- In salad bowl, combine all ingredients and toss with creamy Italian salad dressing.
- Refrigerate or freeze about 15 minutes (no longer). Salad is best served cold.

Buttered-Garlic Bread

1 (12 ounce) loaf frozen garlic bread, thawed

- Heat according to package directions.

Lemon Sherbet and Berries

Lemon sherbet
1 pint raspberries

- Wash raspberries, place in bowl and refrigerate until time to serve dessert.
- Just before serving, spoon lemon sherbet in individual dessert bowls and sprinkle with raspberries.

Enjoy this zesty Italian supper that includes a colorful salad and buttered garlic bread. Top it off with frozen lemon sherbet and you'll have cheers from all around!

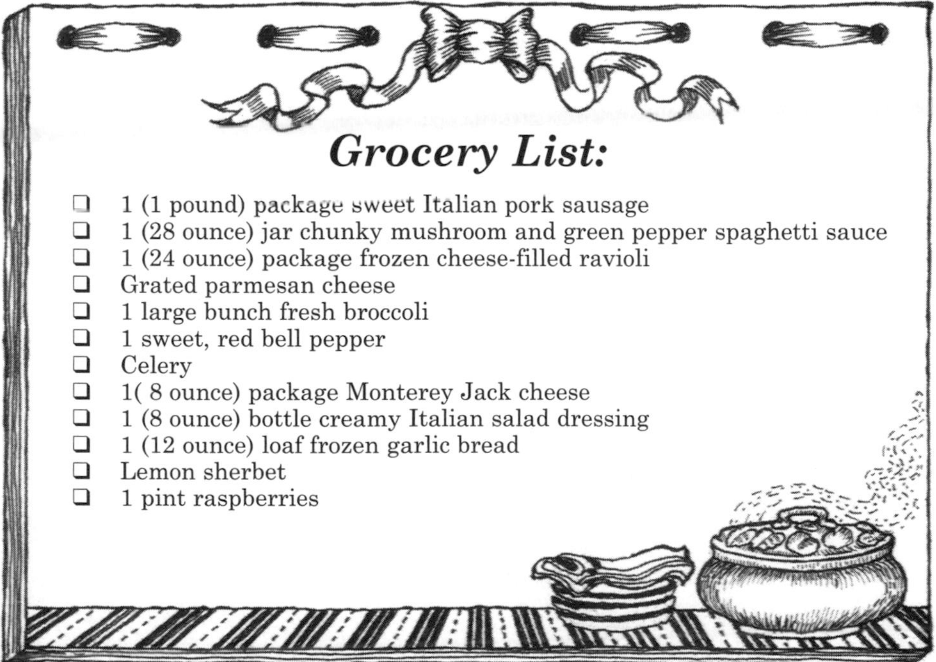

Grocery List:

- ❑ 1 (1 pound) package sweet Italian pork sausage
- ❑ 1 (28 ounce) jar chunky mushroom and green pepper spaghetti sauce
- ❑ 1 (24 ounce) package frozen cheese-filled ravioli
- ❑ Grated parmesan cheese
- ❑ 1 large bunch fresh broccoli
- ❑ 1 sweet, red bell pepper
- ❑ Celery
- ❑ 1(8 ounce) package Monterey Jack cheese
- ❑ 1 (8 ounce) bottle creamy Italian salad dressing
- ❑ 1 (12 ounce) loaf frozen garlic bread
- ❑ Lemon sherbet
- ❑ 1 pint raspberries

Loaded Potatoes

6 large baking potatoes, washed
1 (1 pound) package bulk pork sausage
1 (8 ounce) package cubed processed cheese
1 (10 ounce) can diced tomatoes and green chilies, drained

- Cook potatoes in microwave until done.
- In skillet over medium heat, brown sausage and drain fat. Add cheese and diced tomatoes and stir well.
- With knife, cut potatoes down center and fluff insides with fork. Spoon generous amounts of sausage-cheese mixture on each potato and reheat in microwave 2 to 3 minutes if necessary.

Broccoli-Waldorf Salad

6 to 8 cups fresh broccoli florets, stemmed
1 red and 1 green apple with peel, chopped
½ cup Craisins® or golden raisins
½ cup slightly crushed pecans

- In salad bowl, combine all ingredients and toss with coleslaw dressing. Refrigerate.

Tip: If you don't want to buy a bottle of coleslaw dressing just for this one recipe, make your own by combining 1 cup mayonnaise, ⅓ cup sugar and ¼ cup white vinegar.

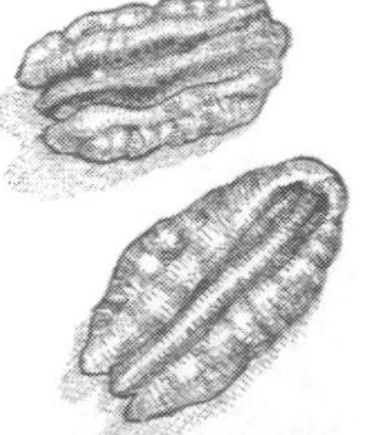

Stuffed Breadsticks

2 (12.5 ounce) boxes frozen stuffed breadsticks.

- Heat according to package directions.

Fruit Salad

1 (14 ounce) can sweetened condensed milk
2 tablespoons lemon juice
2 (15 ounce) cans fruit cocktail, chilled, well drained
1 (20 ounce) can pineapple tidbits, chilled, drained
1 (8 ounce) carton whipped topping

- In large bowl, combine condensed milk and lemon juice. Mix well, add fruit cocktail and pineapple and mix gently. Fold in whipped topping and spoon into crystal bowl.

These potatoes are power-packed and our crunchy salad features a "secret" ingredient. If you haven't tried Craisins® (sweetened dried cranberries), they are wonderful in salads and are a good idea to have on hand for a healthy snack.

Grocery List:

- ❑ 6 large baking potatoes
- ❑ 1 (1 pound) package bulk pork sausage
- ❑ 1 (8 ounce) package cubed processed cheese
- ❑ 1 (10 ounce) can diced tomatoes and green chilies
- ❑ 1 large bunch fresh broccoli
- ❑ 2 apples: 1 red, 1 green
- ❑ 1 package Craisins® (sweetened dried cranberries) or golden raisins
- ❑ ½ cup pecans
- ❑ 1 (8 ounce) bottle coleslaw dressing
- ❑ 2 (12.5 ounce) boxes frozen stuffed breadsticks
- ❑ 1 (14 ounce) can sweetened condensed milk
- ❑ Lemon juice
- ❑ 2 (15 ounce) cans fruit cocktail
- ❑ 1 (20 ounce) can pineapple tidbits
- ❑ 1 (8 ounce) carton whipping topping

Tator-Night Special

Broccoli-Ham-Topped Potatoes
Tossed Green Salad
Breadsticks
Banana Cream Pie

Broccoli-Ham-Topped Potatoes

5 to 6 large baking potatoes
2 cups cooked deli ham, diced
1 (10 ounce) can cream of broccoli soup
1 (8 ounce) package shredded cheddar cheese

- Cook potatoes in microwave until done.
- With knife, cut potatoes down center and fluff insides with fork.
- In saucepan over low heat, combine remaining ingredients, heat and stir until well blended.
- Spoon generous amounts of ham-soup mixture into potatoes and reheat in microwave 2 to 3 minutes if necessary.

Tip: While potatoes cook and before preparing ham-soup mixture, make breadsticks and let them bake while you finish the potatoes.

Tossed Green Salad

1 (10 ounce) package spring-mix salad greens
1 pint cherry tomatoes
1 (8 ounce) bottle ranch-style salad dressing

- In salad bowl, toss greens and tomatoes with dressing to taste.

Breadsticks

1 (8 ounce) package shredded Monterey Jack cheese
¼ cup poppy seeds
2 tablespoons dry onion soup mix
2 (11 ounce) cans breadstick dough

- Preheat oven to 375°. In large shallow bowl, combine cheese, poppy seeds and soup mix. Separate breadstick dough and stretch slightly until each stick is about 12 inches long.
- Cut dough in pieces 3 to 4 inches long. Dip strips into cheese mixture and turn to coat all sides. Place on greased baking pan and bake about 12 minutes or until breadsticks brown.

Banana Cream Pie

1 (32 ounce) frozen banana cream pie, thawed

- Serve on individual dessert plates.

This hearty baked potato is a full meal by itself, but you'll love the easy green salad and crunchy breadsticks on the side. For dessert, savor a piece of banana cream pie. Bananas are good for us, right?

Grocery List:

- ❑ 5 to 6 large baking potatoes
- ❑ ½ pound cooked, sliced deli ham
- ❑ 1 (10 ounce) can cream of broccoli soup
- ❑ 1 (8 ounce) package shredded cheddar cheese
- ❑ 1 (10 or 16 ounce) package spring-mix salad greens
- ❑ 1 pint cherry tomatoes
- ❑ 1 (8 ounce) bottle ranch-style dressing
- ❑ 1 (8 ounce) package shredded Monterey Jack cheese
- ❑ ¼ cup poppy seeds
- ❑ 1 (.2 ounce) packet onion soup mix
- ❑ 2 (11 ounce) cans refrigerated breadstick dough
- ❑ 1 (32 ounce) frozen banana cream pie

Cranberry-Relished Ham

Ham Slices with Cranberry Relish
Vegetable-Stuffed Potatoes
Sliced Tomatoes
Chocolate Oats

Ham Slices with Cranberry Relish

1 (3 pound) boneless, cooked ham

Relish:
1 (16 ounce) can whole cranberry sauce
1 cup orange marmalade
1 (8 ounce) can crushed pineapple, drained
¾ cup coarsely chopped pecans

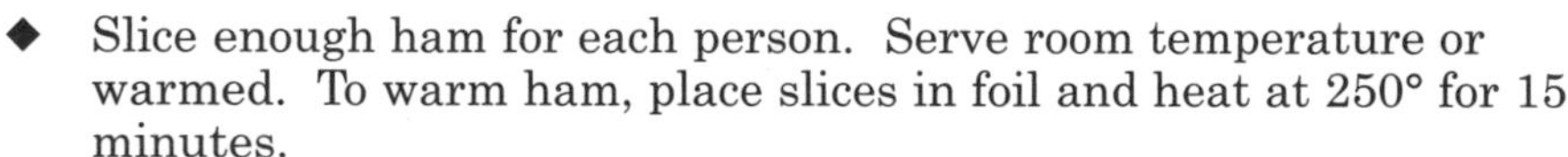

- Slice enough ham for each person. Serve room temperature or warmed. To warm ham, place slices in foil and heat at 250° for 15 minutes.
- In small bowl, combine relish ingredients and place in freezer to chill just until you are ready to serve. This relish can be served cold or warm over ham.

Vegetable-Stuffed Potatoes

2 (10 ounce) cans fiesta nacho cheese soup
1 (16 ounce) package frozen mixed stew vegetables, cooked, drained
8 baking potatoes, washed
Salt and black pepper

- In large saucepan, heat fiesta nacho cheese soup, add cooked vegetables and mix well.
- Prick potatoes with fork and cook in microwave until tender. Slightly mash pulp in each potato and spoon hearty amount of soup-vegetable mixture onto each split potato. If necessary, warm filled potatoes in microwave 1 to 2 minutes.

Sliced Tomatoes

4 to 6 vine-ripened tomatoes

- Slice tomatoes and arrange on serving tray.
  Vine-ripened tomatoes have the best flavor. Sprinkle with seasoned salt if desired.

Chocolate Oats

1 (12 ounce) package chocolate chips
¾ cup crunchy peanut butter
3 cups donut-shaped oat cereal

- In double boiler, melt chocolate chips, remove from heat and stir in peanut butter. Fold in Cheerios, drop by teaspoon on wax paper and refrigerate until firm.

Cranberry relish gives this ham a festive touch and is wonderful with pork roast as well. My stuffed potatoes have everything you need to complete a delicious meal.

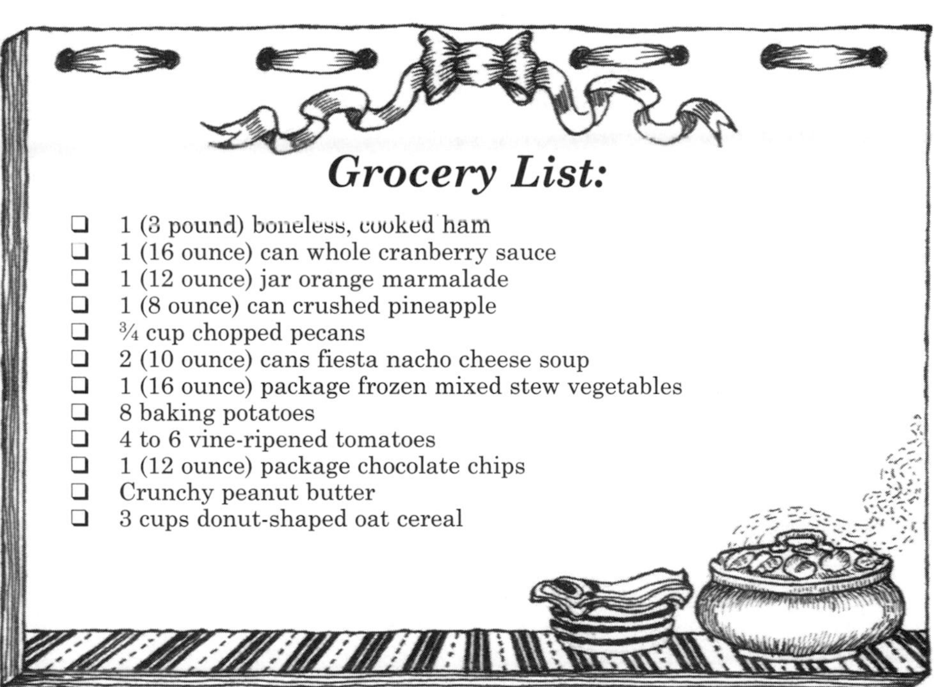

Grocery List:

- ❑ 1 (3 pound) boneless, cooked ham
- ❑ 1 (16 ounce) can whole cranberry sauce
- ❑ 1 (12 ounce) jar orange marmalade
- ❑ 1 (8 ounce) can crushed pineapple
- ❑ ¾ cup chopped pecans
- ❑ 2 (10 ounce) cans fiesta nacho cheese soup
- ❑ 1 (16 ounce) package frozen mixed stew vegetables
- ❑ 8 baking potatoes
- ❑ 4 to 6 vine-ripened tomatoes
- ❑ 1 (12 ounce) package chocolate chips
- ❑ Crunchy peanut butter
- ❑ 3 cups donut-shaped oat cereal

Bow-Tie Pasta, Ham and Veggies

1 (8 ounce) package bow-tie pasta (farfalle)
1 (10 ounce) package each frozen broccoli florets and green peas, thawed
1 (16 ounce) jar alfredo sauce
1 pound cubed, cooked ham

- In large saucepan, cook pasta according to package directions. Add broccoli and peas during last 3 minutes of cooking time. Drain well.
- Add alfredo sauce and ham. (This is a good time to use leftover ham.) Cook and stir gently over very low heat to keep ingredients from sticking to pan. Spoon into serving bowl.

Tip: To substitute deli ham, have butcher cut thick slice and cut ham into chunks.

Garlic Breadsticks

1 package frozen or bakery garlic breadsticks

- Heat breadsticks according to package directions.

Snappy, Spicy Tomato Soup

2 (10 ounce) cans tomato soup
1 (10 ounce) can tomato bisque soup
1 (10 ounce) can tomatoes and green chilies
½ cup sour cream

- In saucepan over medium heat, combine tomato soups, tomatoes and green chilies and ¾ cup water and cook until hot.
- When ready to serve (make sure soup is still very hot), stir in sour cream and pour into cups.

Mini-Lemon Tarts

8 bakery mini-lemon tarts

- Serve on individual dessert plates.

The Italian word farfalle means "little butterflies". It is a classy name for this appealing and versatile pasta that is really showcased in this easy menu. Spicy tomato soup and crunchy breadsticks are hearty and filling and the lemon tarts are a sweet finish!

Grocery List:

- ❑ 1 (8 ounce) package bow-tie pasta (farfalle)
- ❑ 1 (10 ounce) package frozen broccoli florets
- ❑ 1 (10 ounce) package frozen green peas
- ❑ 1 (16 ounce) jar alfredo sauce
- ❑ 1 pound cubed, cooked ham
- ❑ 1 package frozen or bakery garlic breadsticks
- ❑ 2 (10 ounce) cans tomato soup
- ❑ 1 (10 ounce) can tomato bisque soup
- ❑ 1 (10 ounce) can tomatoes and green chilies
- ❑ Sour cream
- ❑ 8 bakery mini-lemon tarts

Hams and Yams I Am

Ham and Yams
Green Beans with Garlic-Butter Sauce
Sliced Vine-Ripened Tomatoes
Tapioca Pudding

Ham

1 (1 pound) fully cooked center-cut ham steak
3 tablespoons frozen orange juice concentrate
3 tablespoons honey or brown sugar
¼ teaspoon ginger

- Place ham steak in large skillet.
- In small bowl, combine orange juice concentrate, honey and ginger. With vegetable brush, spread mixture over ham steak and cook on low to medium heat for 4 minutes.
- Turn steak and brush again with juice mixture. Cook another 4 to 5 minutes over low heat to slightly brown ham.

Yams

1 (28 ounce) can sweet potatoes with liquid
¼ cup (½ stick) butter, melted
1 cup packed brown sugar
2 eggs, beaten

- In mixing bowl, beat yams, butter, brown sugar and eggs until fluffy.
- Cover with paper towel and microwave on HIGH for 5 minutes. Turn once during cooking.
- To serve, place ham on serving platter and spoon yams around ham steak. Garnish with ½ cup chopped pecans.

Tip: If you have to have marshmallow in sweet potatoes, fold them into mixture before microwaving.

Green Beans with Garlic-Butter Sauce

1 (19 ounce) package frozen green beans with garlic-butter sauce

- Heat according to package directions.

Sliced Vine-Ripened Tomatoes

4 to 5 vine-ripened tomatoes, sliced

- Arrange on serving tray.

Tapioca Pudding

4 (1 serving size) tapioca pudding cups (or more as needed), chilled

- Serve in original cups or in dessert cups.

Sweet potatoes are not only delicious, but they are also a great source of vitamin A and beta carotene. To add sparkle to the tomatoes, top with 1 tablespoonful cottage cheese and a dash of seasoned salt and pepper.

Grocery List:

- ❑ 1 (1 pound) fully cooked center-cut ham steak
- ❑ 1 (6 ounce) can frozen orange juice concentrate
- ❑ Honey or brown sugar
- ❑ Dried ginger
- ❑ 1 (28 ounce) can sweet potatoes
- ❑ Butter
- ❑ Brown sugar
- ❑ 2 eggs
- ❑ 1 (10 ounce) package miniature marshmallows, optional
- ❑ ½ cup chopped pecans, optional
- ❑ 1 (19 ounce) package frozen green beans with garlic-butter sauce
- ❑ 4 to 5 vine-ripened tomatoes
- ❑ 4 (1 serving size) tapioca pudding cups, chilled

A Party Dinner

Snappy Ham
Spinach Salad
Toasted Pine-Nut Couscous
Chocolate-Orange Cake

Snappy Ham

1 (¾-inch thick) center-cut ham slice
1 (16 ounce) can whole cranberries
1 cup chopped pecans
1 (12 ounce) jar apricot preserves

- Cook ham according to package directions and place on serving plate.
- In saucepan over medium heat, combine cranberries, pecans and apricot preserves, heat and stir until ingredients mix well.
- Spoon relish into gravy bowl or other small bowl and serve hot or chilled.

Tip: For a complete flavor, add ½ teaspoon cinnamon to relish mixture if you have it in the pantry.

Spinach Salad

1 (8 ounce) package fresh baby spinach
2 hard-boiled eggs, sliced
1 sweet red bell pepper, julienned
½ cup almonds, slivered

- Toast almonds on baking sheet at 275° oven for 10 minutes.
- In salad bowl, combine all ingredients.
- Just before serving, pour about ⅓ bottle raspberry vinaigrette dressing over salad and toss.

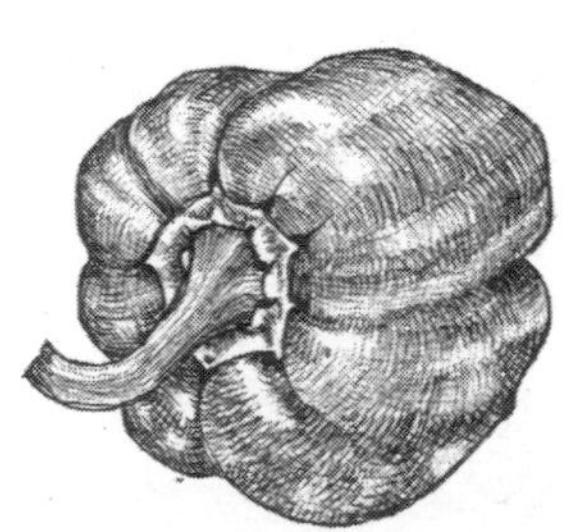

Toasted Pine-Nut Couscous

1 (6 ounce) package toasted pine nut couscous
Butter

- Prepare couscous according to package directions.

Tip: Couscous is a delicious alternative to plain rice.

Chocolate-Orange Cake

1 (16 ounce) loaf frozen pound cake, thawed
1 (12 ounce) jar orange marmalade, chilled
1 (16 ounce) can ready-to-spread chocolate fudge frosting

- Cut cake horizontally to make 3 layers. Place 1 layer on cake platter. Spread with half of marmalade.
- Place second layer over first and spread remaining marmalade. Top with third cake layer and spread frosting liberally on top and sides of cake.

Tip: If you can, bake this cake the night before serving or bake cake before other recipes and place in freezer for at least 30 minutes.

This is an easy dinner for entertaining. To serve more than 4 or 5 people, buy 2 packages of ham. Couscous is a very special favorite of mine and the spinach salad will be a hit with everybody!

Grocery List:

- ❑ 1 (¾-inch thick) center-cut ham slices
- ❑ 1 (16 ounce) can whole cranberries
- ❑ 1 cup chopped pecans
- ❑ 1 (12 ounce) jar apricot preserves
- ❑ Ground cinnamon
- ❑ 1 (6 ounce) package toasted pine nut couscous
- ❑ Butter
- ❑ 1 (8 ounce) package fresh baby spinach
- ❑ 2 eggs
- ❑ 1 sweet red bell pepper
- ❑ Slivered almonds
- ❑ 1 (8 ounce) bottle raspberry vinaigrette dressing
- ❑ 1 (16 ounce) loaf frozen pound
- ❑ 1 (12 ounce) jar orange marmalade
- ❑ 1 (16 ounce) can ready-to-spread chocolate fudge frosting

Love Those Islands

Hawaiian Pork and Rice
Hawaiian Coleslaw
Cheesy Creamy Broccoli
Hawaiian Bread and Butter

Hawaiian Pork

2 (1 pound each) pork tenderloins, sliced
1 (20 ounce) can pineapple tidbits with juice
1 (8 ounce) bottle sweet and sour sauce
1 teaspoon ginger, 1 tablespoon corn starch

- Season pork slices with salt and pepper and place in large skillet with about 2 tablespoons oil. Over medium to high heat, brown slices on both sides and cook about 5 minutes.
- Add pineapple chunks, sweet and sour sauce and ginger and stir well. In small bowl, combine cornstarch and ½ cup water, mix well and add to pork-pineapple mixture.
- Heat to boiling, reduce heat and simmer 25 minutes. Serve over instant rice.

Rice

2 cups uncooked instant white rice

- Cook rice according to package directions.

Hawaiian Coleslaw

1 (16 ounce) package shredded coleslaw mix, chilled
1 (8 ounce) can crushed pineapple, drained, chilled
1 (8 ounce) bottle coleslaw dressing, chilled
¼ cup flaked coconut, optional

- In salad bowl, toss slaw mix, drained pineapple, dressing and coconut to taste.

Cheesy Creamy Broccoli

1 (16 ounce) package frozen broccoli florets, thawed
1 (11 ounce) can water chestnuts, chopped
1 (10 ounce) can fiesta nacho cheese soup
⅓ cup almonds, slivered

- Preheat oven to 325°. Cook broccoli according to package directions and drain well.
- Place broccoli and water chestnuts in greased 9 x 13-inch baking dish and keep warm in oven.
- In small saucepan over low heat, combine soup and ¼ cup water and heat just enough to mix well. Pour over broccoli, sprinkle with almonds and bake 10 minutes.

Tip: If serving 7 or 8, add an extra (10 ounce) box frozen broccoli florets.

Hawaiian Bread and Butter

1 round loaf Hawaiian bread
Butter

- Slice bread into pie wedges. Butter between wedges and heat in oven while broccoli cooks.

The sweet and sour flavors in this Hawaiian-style dinner will have everyone in the "aloha" spirit. In the dining room or by the pool, they'll be dreaming of beautiful beaches!

Grocery List:

- ❑ 2 (1 pound each) pork tenderloins, sliced
- ❑ 1 (20 ounce) can pineapple tidbits
- ❑ 1 (8 ounce) bottle sweet and sour sauce
- ❑ Ginger
- ❑ Corn starch
- ❑ 1 box instant white rice
- ❑ 1 (16 ounce) package shredded coleslaw mix
- ❑ 1 (8 ounce) can crushed pineapple
- ❑ 1 (8 ounce) bottle coleslaw salad dressing
- ❑ 1 (7 ounce) can flaked coconut, optional
- ❑ 1 (16 ounce) package frozen broccoli florets
- ❑ 1 (11 ounce) can water chestnuts
- ❑ 1 (10 ounce) can fiesta nacho cheese soup
- ❑ Slivered almonds
- ❑ 1 round loaf Hawaiian bread
- ❑ Butter

Holiday Every Day

Apricot-Glazed Tenderloin
Crunchy Rice
Spinach-Sprout Salad
Buttered French Bread

Apricot-Glazed Tenderloin

2 (1 pound each) pork tenderloins
1½ cups apricot preserves
⅓ cup chili sauce
2 small onions, sliced

- Cut pork tenderloin crosswise in ¼-inch slices.
- In skillet, heat about 2 tablespoons oil over medium to high heat and add pork slices. Cook and stir about 10 minutes or until pork is no longer pink. Remove from skillet and keep warm.
- Add apricots, chili sauce and onion slices to skillet. Cook about 5 minutes. Return pork slices to skillet and add about ¼ cup water.
- Cover and cook over low to medium heat 10 to 15 minutes. Stir occasionally during cooking. Serve over rice.

Crunchy Rice

1½ cups uncooked instant white rice
Butter
1 (10 ounce) package frozen green peas, thawed

- Cook rice according to package directions. Add half (10 ounce) package frozen green peas and 1 tablespoon butter. Heat on low until rice returns to original temperature. To serve, place rice on platter and top with pork slices and sauce.

Spinach-Sprout Salad

1 (10 ounce) package baby spinach, chilled
1 cup fresh bean sprouts, chilled
8 slices pre-cooked bacon, crumbled, chilled
3 hard-boiled eggs, sliced, chilled

◆ In salad bowl, combine spinach, bean sprouts and crumbled bacon and toss with lime-basil vinaigrette dressing. Place egg slices on top and refrigerate.

Buttered French Bread

1 loaf French bread
Butter
Garlic salt

◆ Preheat oven to 300°. Slice bread in 1-inch slices, butter each slice and sprinkle with garlic salt. Put loaf back together and wrap in large piece of foil. Heat in oven about 20 minutes while tenderloin cooks.

Make any day a holiday with this elegant meal, ready in just 30 minutes. The apricot glaze really complements the pork tenderloin and the spinach salad is to die for! Buttered French bread will always place this menu in top form.

Grocery List:

- ❑ Oil
- ❑ 2 pound pork tenderloins
- ❑ 1 (12 ounce) jar apricot preserves
- ❑ Chili sauce
- ❑ 2 small onions
- ❑ 1 (14 ounce) package uncooked instant white rice
- ❑ Butter
- ❑ 1 (10 ounce) package frozen green peas
- ❑ 1 (10 ounce) package baby spinach
- ❑ 1 cup fresh bean sprouts
- ❑ 1 package pre-cooked bacon
- ❑ 3 eggs
- ❑ 1 (8 ounce) bottle lime-basil vinaigrette dressing
- ❑ 1 loaf French bread
- ❑ Garlic salt

Tenderloin with Orange Sauce

2 (1 pound each) pork tenderloins, cut in thick slices

Orange Sauce:
1 cup orange juice
3 tablespoons soy sauce
2 tablespoons honey mustard
1 tablespoon very finely chopped fresh ginger or ½ teaspoon dried ginger

- ◆ In large skillet over medium heat, brown pork slices in a little oil for 4 to 5 minutes.
- ◆ While pork browns, combine sauce ingredients in small bowl and pour sauce over pork slices in skillet. Bring to boil, reduce heat and simmer uncovered about 10 minutes.
- ◆ Serve tenderloin slices with sauce.

Romaine-Strawberry Salad

1 (10 ounce) package romaine lettuce, torn
1 cup broccoli slaw
1 pint large fresh strawberries, quartered
½ red onion, coarsely chopped

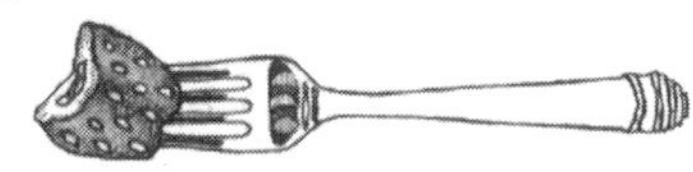

- ◆ In salad bowl, toss all ingredients. When ready to serve, use raspberry vinaigrette salad dressing (not fat-free dressing).

Add extra broccoli slaw to green salad next day.

Roasted-Garlic Couscous

1 (6 ounce) box roasted garlic-couscous
Butter

- Prepare couscous according to package directions. When ready to serve, place in serving bowl and serve with tenderloin.

French Garlic Toast

1 (8 slice) loaf frozen French garlic toast

- Heat according to package directions.

Strawberry-Cream Pie

1 (24 ounce) frozen strawberry cream pie, thawed

- Serve on individual dessert plates.

This recipe calls for common ingredients you probably already have in your pantry: orange juice, soy sauce and tangy mustard. Pork tenderloins are freezer-friendly and can be easily thawed in the microwave. I always keep several boxes Near East® couscous on hand. You could even make a couscous or pasta salad with just some celery, pickles, onions, pimentos and a flavored mayonnaise (see page 268).

Grocery List:

- ❑ 2 (1 pound each) pork tenderloins, cut in thick slices
- ❑ Orange juice
- ❑ Soy sauce
- ❑ 1 (12 ounce) bottle honey mustard
- ❑ Fresh or dried ginger
- ❑ 1 (10 once) package romaine lettuce
- ❑ 1 (16 ounce) package broccoli slaw
- ❑ 1 pint large fresh strawberries
- ❑ 1 red onion
- ❑ Raspberry vinaigrette salad dressing
- ❑ 1 (6 ounce) box roasted-garlic couscous
- ❑ Butter
- ❑ 1 (8 slice) loaf frozen French garlic toast
- ❑ 1 (24 ounce) frozen strawberry cream pie

Fiesta-Tenderloin Verde

2 (1 pound each) pork tenderloins
2 teaspoons ground cumin
1 onion, very finely chopped
1 (14 ounce) jar Pace© Mexican Creations™ verde with tomatillos cooking sauce

- Rub both tenderloins with cumin and a little salt. In large sprayed skillet, place tenderloins over medium to high heat and brown on all sides.
- Add chopped onion, cooking sauce and ¼ cup water and cover. Heat to boiling, reduce heat and simmer 25 minutes. While tenderloin cooks, heat water for Mexican Fiesta Rice and Nopalitos.
- Before serving tenderloin, set aside for about 5 minutes, slice and serve with sauce over rice. This menu will serve 6 to 8.

Mexican Fiesta Rice & Nopalitos

2 (6 ounce) boxes Uncle Ben's® Mexican fiesta rice
1 (15 ounce) bottle nopalitos (prickly pear cactus stems), drained

- Prepare rice according to package directions. Place nopalitos in small serving bowl and serve with rice and tenderloin.

Quesadilla Rolls or Cheese Taquitos

1 (9 ounce) package frozen steak quesadilla rolls
Or 1 (11 ounce) package frozen chicken-cheese taquitos
Or 1 (12 ounce) package frozen beef-cheese tacos

◆ Preheat oven to 425°. Heat quesadillas or taquitos in oven according to package directions. (If you heat in microwave, the rolls and taquitos will not be crispy.)

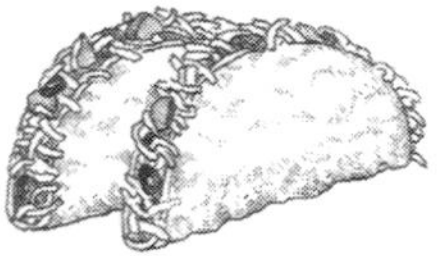

Guacamole and Chips

1 (16 ounce) package frozen guacamole, thawed
Tortilla chips

◆ Serve guacamole in center of serving plate with chips around edges.

Pork is such a versatile meat and the tenderloin is my very favorite cut. This Mexican version is a quick and easy dish full of flavor. Nopalitos are delicious with any Southwestern dish. (My family likes them rolled up in a buttered, heated flour tortilla.) Quesadilla rolls and taquitos add a satisfying crunch to this On-The-Border meal.

Grocery List:

- ❑ 2 (1 pound each) pork tenderloins
- ❑ Ground cumin
- ❑ 1 onion
- ❑ 1 (14 ounce) jar Pace© Mexican Creations™ verde with tomatillos cooking sauce
- ❑ 2 (6 ounce) boxes Uncle Ben's® Mexican fiesta rice
- ❑ 1 (15 ounce) bottle nopalitos
- ❑ 1 (9 ounce) package frozen steak quesadilla rolls
- ❑ 1 (11 ounce) box chicken-cheese taquitos
- ❑ 1 (12 ounce) package frozen beef-cheese tacos
- ❑ 1 (16 ounce) package frozen guacamole
- ❑ Tortilla chips

Lemon-Pepper Pork Chops

6 butterfly pork chops
¾ teaspoon each garlic salt and lemon pepper
½ cup chopped pecans
3 tablespoons lemon juice

- Sprinkle both sides of pork chops with garlic-pepper mixture.
- In large skillet, heat a little oil over medium to high heat. Add chops and cook about 5 minutes on each side until chops brown lightly. Reduce heat, add several tablespoons water, cover and simmer 10 minutes.
- Transfer pork chops to serving plate to keep warm. Top with pecans. Stir lemon juice into pan drippings, heat and stir constantly until they blend. Spoon drippings on pork chops and serve over rice.

Lemon-Herb Rice

1 or 2 (4.5 ounce) boxes Uncle Ben's® lemon-herb rice
Butter

- Cook rice according to package directions.

Mozzarella-Basil Topped Tomatoes

3 to 4 vine-ripened tomatoes
1 (4 to 6 ounce) package soft, white mozzarella cheese, chilled
½ cup chopped fresh basil
Italian salad dressing

- Slice tomatoes and place on serving plate or on individual salad plates.
- Slice mozzarella cheese and place cheese slices on tomatoes. Sprinkle fresh basil on top and drizzle dressing.

Tip: Place cheese in freezer a few minutes for easier slicing.

Fresh Nectarine Slices

5 to 6 nectarines, sliced

- Serve fruit slices in small cereal or custard bowl.

Nectarines are so good that they don't need any sugar, whipped topping or ice cream! Just serve a bowlful and watch them disappear—you don't even have to peel them. If nectarines are not in season, substitute a jar of refrigerated sliced mangoes.

I love to cook with pecans and using them here is a delightful change of pace from traditional pork dishes. This menu is really a healthy, balanced meal that is a colorful feast for family and guests.

Grocery List:

- ❑ 6 butterfly pork chops
- ❑ Garlic salt
- ❑ Lemon-pepper seasoning
- ❑ Chopped pecans
- ❑ Lemon juice
- ❑ 1 or 2 (4.5 ounce) boxes Uncle Ben's® lemon-herb rice
- ❑ Butter
- ❑ 3 to 4 vine-ripened tomatoes
- ❑ 1 (4 to 6 ounce) package soft, white mozzarella cheese
- ❑ Fresh basil
- ❑ 1 (8 ounce) bottle Italian dressing
- ❑ 5 or 6 fresh nectarines

Smoked Pork Chops

1 (4 to 6 count) package thick-sliced, smoked pork chops
1 (8 ounce) jar sweet and sour sauce
¼ cup chipotle salsa

- Place pork chops in skillet with just a little oil. Cook over medium heat and cook about 7 minutes on each side. (Chops do not need to brown. They will dry out if cooked too long.)
- While pork chops cook, combine sweet and sour sauce and salsa. Pour over pork chops in skillet. Heat to boiling, reduce heat, cover and simmer about 10 minutes. Serve over rice.

Tip: You can buy these delicious smoked pork chops thinly sliced if you prefer. To serve 8, double the sauce ingredients.

Herb-Seasoned Vegetables

1 (14 ounce) can seasoned chicken broth with Italian herbs
½ teaspoon garlic powder
1 (16 ounce) package frozen vegetables (broccoli, cauliflower, etc.)
½ cup grated parmesan cheese

- Heat broth, garlic and vegetables to a boil. Cover and cook over low heat for 5 minutes or until tender-crisp. Drain.
- Place in serving dish and sprinkle cheese over vegetables.

Rice and Beans

4 cups cooked rice
1 (15 ounce) can pinto beans with liquid
1 cup shredded cheddar cheese
3 tablespoons butter, melted

- Mix all ingredients in saucepan. Cook over low heat until cheese melts. Serve hot.

Peachy Sundaes

1 pint vanilla ice cream
¾ cup peach preserves, warmed
¼ cup chopped almonds, toasted
¼ cup flaked coconut

- Divide ice cream into 4 sherbet dishes and top with preserves.
- Sprinkle with almonds and coconut.

I have been buying these low-fat "smoked" pork chops since the first time I noticed them in the market. They are full-flavored and cook quickly. Best of all, you can serve them with lots of different sauces. (See Cranberry-Relished Ham on page 160.)

Grocery List:

- ❑ Oil
- ❑ 1 (4 to 6 count) package thick-sliced, smoked pork chops
- ❑ 1 (8 ounce) jar sweet and sour sauce
- ❑ ¼ cup chipotle salsa
- ❑ 1 (14 ounce) can seasoned chicken broth with Italian herbs
- ❑ Garlic powder
- ❑ 1 (16 ounce) package frozen vegetables
- ❑ ½ cup grated parmesan cheese
- ❑ Cooked rice
- ❑ 1 (15 ounce) can pinto beans with liquid
- ❑ 1 (8 ounce) package shredded cheddar cheese
- ❑ Butter
- ❑ 1 pint vanilla ice cream
- ❑ Peach preserves
- ❑ Toasted almonds
- ❑ Flaked Coconut

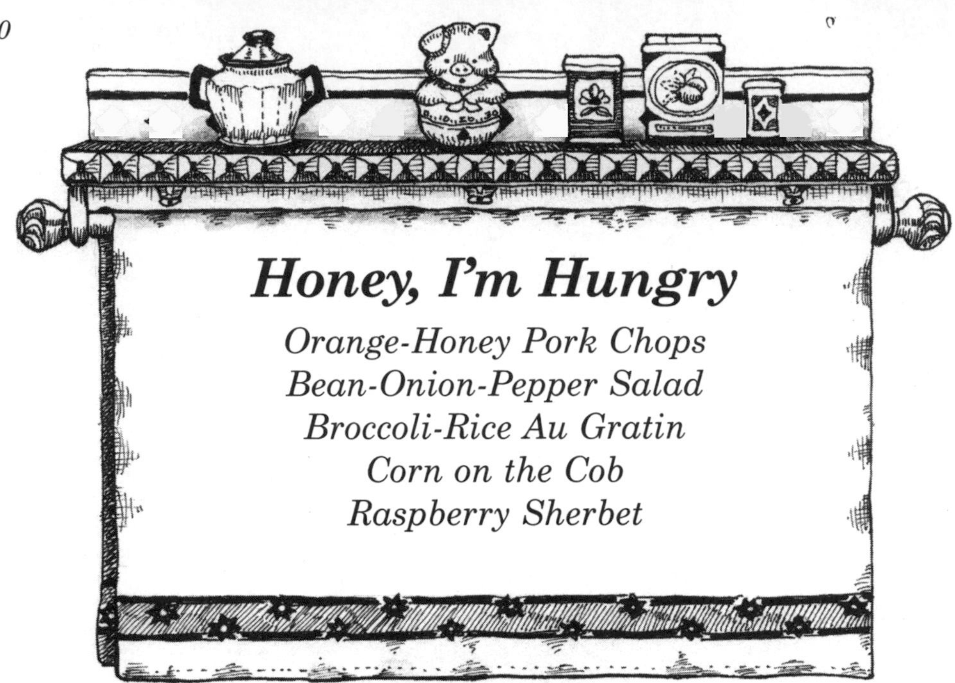

Orange-Honey Pork Chops

6 butterfly-cut pork chops
1½ cups orange juice
½ cup honey
2 teaspoons prepared mustard

- In large skillet over medium to high heat, pour about 2 tablespoons oil and brown pork chops on both sides.
- In bowl, combine orange juice, honey and mustard and pour over pork chops. Heat liquid to boiling, reduce heat and simmer about 20 minutes.
- Boil water for rice and cook according to package directions. Rice should be ready when pork chops are done.

Bean-Onion-Pepper Salad

2 (15 ounce) cans cut green beans, drained, chilled
1 (15 ounce) can yellow wax beans, drained, chilled
1 small red onion, chopped, chilled
1 orange bell pepper, julienned, chilled

- In container with lid, combine green beans, wax beans, onion and bell pepper. Pour Italian dressing over vegetables just to cover.

Tip: This salad is best made a few hours before serving and refrigerated. If this is not possible, chill in freezer about 20 minutes.

Broccoli-Rice Au Gratin

1 (6 ounce) package broccoli rice au gratin

◆ To serve, spoon rice onto serving plate and place pork chops over rice. Serve orange sauce in gravy boat to serve over pork chops and rice.

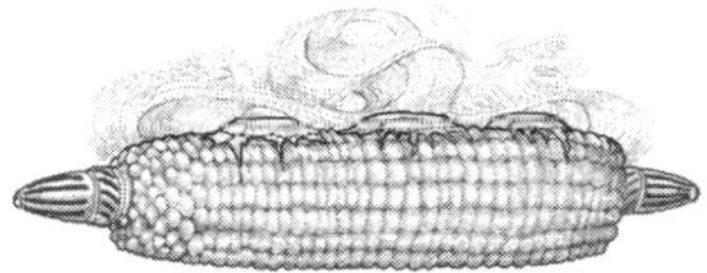

Corn-on-the-Cob

4 to 8 ears fresh or frozen corn-on-the-cob
Butter

◆ Boil corn until tender. Serve with butter.

Raspberry Sherbet

1 quart raspberry sherbet
Raspberries or strawberries

◆ Serve in individual dessert bowls garnished with fresh raspberries or strawberries, if desired.

When the dinner bell rings for this meal, everyone will come running and ready to eat. Ingredients are so easy to put together and the orange juice and honey give the pork chops a special flavor.

Grocery List:

- ❑ Oil
- ❑ 6 butterfly-cut pork chops
- ❑ Orange juice
- ❑ Honey
- ❑ 2 (15 ounce) cans cut green beans
- ❑ 1 (15 ounce) can yellow wax beans
- ❑ 1 small red onion
- ❑ 1 orange bell pepper, julienned
- ❑ 1 (8 ounce) bottle Italian dressing
- ❑ Prepared mustard
- ❑ 1 (6 ounce) package broccoli rice au gratin
- ❑ Fresh or frozen corn-on-the-cob
- ❑ Butter
- ❑ 1 quart raspberry sherbet
- ❑ Fresh raspberries or fresh strawberries

Delicious Pork Chops

¾ cup biscuit mix, 1 teaspoon paprika
¾ cup Italian dressing
1 cup garlic herb-seasoned breadcrumbs
6 (½ inch thick) boneless pork chops

- In 3 shallow bowls, place biscuit mix and paprika, Italian dressing and breadcrumbs. Dip pork chops in biscuit mix, then in salad dressing and last in breadcrumbs.
- In skillet, heat about 3 tablespoons oil and cook pork chops 5 to 8 minutes or until both sides brown lightly. Reduce heat to low, cover and cook about 15 minutes longer. Drain on paper towels.

Tangy Carrot Coins

2 (15 ounce) cans sliced carrots
2 tablespoons (¼ stick) butter
2 tablespoons brown sugar
1 tablespoon dijon mustard

- Place all ingredients in a saucepan. Cook and stir over medium heat for about 2 minutes. Serve hot.

Mushrooms and Corn

4 ounces fresh mushrooms, sliced
3 chopped green onions and tops
2 tablespoons butter
1 (15 ounce) package frozen whole kernel corn

◆ Place all ingredients in 2-quart saucepan and cook on medium heat for 5 to 10 minutes. Add salt and pepper to taste.

Strawberry Ice Cream and Cookies

1 quart strawberry
1 package sugar cookies

◆ Scoop ice cream into individual dessert bowls and serve with cookies.

Let the kids get into the act tonight. They will love dipping and breading these pork chops, which have a "fried" taste without all the fat. Round out the meal with quick and easy side dishes of tangy carrot coins and mushrooms and corn. Strawberry ice cream and sugar cookies complete the meal, which is sure to become a family favorite.

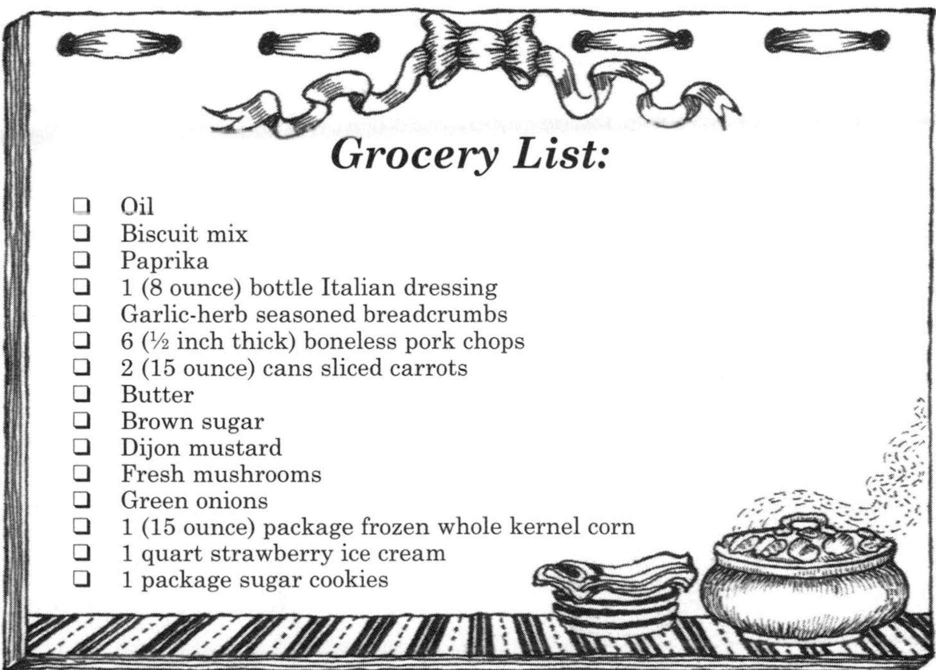

Grocery List:

- ❑ Oil
- ❑ Biscuit mix
- ❑ Paprika
- ❑ 1 (8 ounce) bottle Italian dressing
- ❑ Garlic-herb seasoned breadcrumbs
- ❑ 6 (½ inch thick) boneless pork chops
- ❑ 2 (15 ounce) cans sliced carrots
- ❑ Butter
- ❑ Brown sugar
- ❑ Dijon mustard
- ❑ Fresh mushrooms
- ❑ Green onions
- ❑ 1 (15 ounce) package frozen whole kernel corn
- ❑ 1 quart strawberry ice cream
- ❑ 1 package sugar cookies

Quick Wonders with Fish

Crispy Oven Fish
Fruit Salsa
Potato Casserole
Corn-on-the-Cob

Crispy Oven Fish

¾ cup biscuit mix
⅓ cup yellow cornmeal
1½ teaspoons chili powder
1 egg, beaten
1¼ pounds orange roughy filets

- Preheat oven at 425°. Pour several tablespoons oil into 9 x 13-inch baking pan and place in oven to heat oil.
- In shallow bowl, combine biscuit mix, cornmeal and chili powder. Add 1 tablespoon water to egg and mix well.
- Dip each piece of fish in egg and in biscuit-cornmeal mixture to coat well. Place in heated pan.
- Bake 20 to 25 minutes or until fish flakes easily with fork.

Fruit Salsa

1 mango, 2 kiwifruit, peeled, chopped
1 (15 ounce) can pineapple tidbits, drained
1 tablespoon lime juice
1 tablespoon fresh, chopped cilantro

- While orange roughy bakes, combine all fruit salsa ingredients and refrigerate.
- To serve, top each serving of fish with heaping tablespoon fruit salsa.

  Tip: If you would like to spice up the salsa a little, add 1 seeded, chopped jalapeno pepper.

Potato Casserole

5 potatoes, peeled, sliced
1 (10½ ounce) can golden cream of mushroom soup
1 cup grated cheddar cheese
Milk

◆ Preheat oven at 400°. Place sliced potatoes in greased 2-quart casserole dish. Dilute soup with ½ cup milk or water and mix well. Pour over potatoes. Bake covered 45 minutes. Uncover and top with cheese and bake 15 minutes longer.

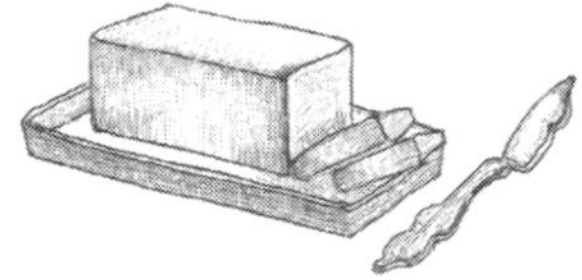

Corn-on-the-Cob

1 (12 count) package frozen corn-on-the-cob halves
Butter
Garlic salt

◆ Heat corn according to package directions. Spread with butter and sprinkle with garlic salt.

This Fruit Salsa is a little different twist on seafood, but it really perks up the orange roughy and would be great if you just wanted to bake your fish. It would also be good on roast pork or baked pork chops.

Grocery List:

- ❑ Oil
- ❑ Biscuit mix
- ❑ Yellow cornmeal
- ❑ Chili powder
- ❑ 1 egg
- ❑ 1½ pounds orange roughy filets
- ❑ 1 mango or 1 (15 ounce) can mango slices
- ❑ 2 kiwifruit
- ❑ 1 (15 ounce) can pineapple tidbits
- ❑ Lime juice
- ❑ Fresh cilantro
- ❑ 5 potatoes
- ❑ 1 (10.5 ounce) can golden cream of mushroom soup
- ❑ 1 (8 ounce) package shredded cheddar cheese
- ❑ Milk
- ❑ 1 (12 count) package frozen corn-on-the-cob halves
- ❑ Butter
- ❑ Garlic salt

Beer-Battered Fish

1 cup biscuit mix
1 (12 ounce) can beer
1 pound flounder filets
Oil

- In large saucepan or fish cooker, heat 1 to 2 inches oil. (If filets are particularly large, you may need to cut them in half.)
- In mixing bowl, combine biscuit mix and just enough beer to make a batter (not too thin). Use tongs to dip 1 filet at a time in batter.
- Place battered filets in hot oil and cook. Drain on paper towels and continue frying remaining filets.

Tip: If needed, add a little more biscuit mix to thicken or little more beer to thin. In case you use all the batter, just mix up a little more.

Crunchy Broccoli

2 (10 ounce) packages frozen broccoli florets
1 (8 ounce) can sliced water chestnuts, drained, chopped
½ cup (1 stick) butter, melted
1 (1 ounce) envelope dry onion soup mix

- Place broccoli in microwave-safe dish, cover and microwave on HIGH for 5 minutes. Turn dish and cook another 4 minutes.
- Add water chestnuts. Combine melted butter and soup mix and blend well. Toss with cooked broccoli.

Garden Vegetable Rice-A-Roni®

2 (4.3 ounce) packages garden vegetable Rice-A-Roni®
Butter

- Cook rice according to package directions.

Million Dollar Pie

24 Ritz crackers, crumbled
1 cup chopped pecans
4 egg whites (absolutely no yolks at all)
1 cup sugar

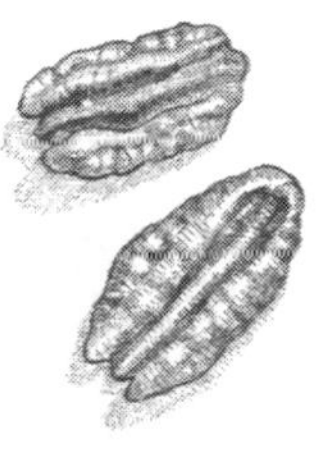

- Preheat oven at 350°. Mix cracker crumbs with pecans. In separate mixing bowl, beat egg whites until stiff and slowly add sugar while mixing. Gently fold in crumbs and pecan mixture. Pour in pie tin and bake 20 minutes. Cool before serving.

My Dad grew up on the North Carolina coast and he loved flounder. We always went back to North Carolina every summer and my Aunt Repsie would cook flounder for my Dad. Today we can get wonderful flounder in our supermarkets and I try my best to make it taste just like hers did.

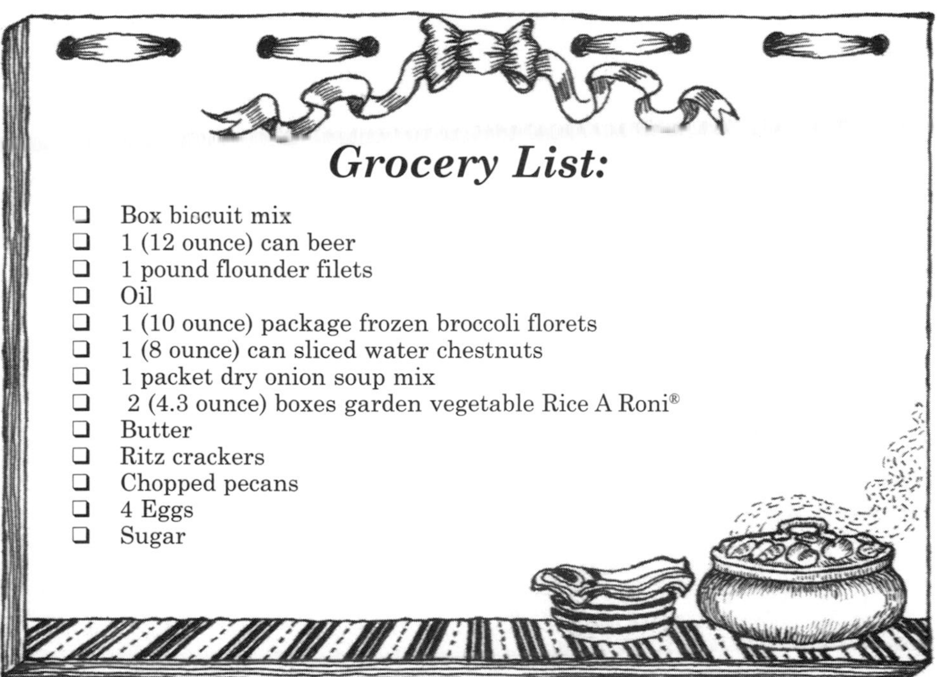

Grocery List:

- ❑ Box biscuit mix
- ❑ 1 (12 ounce) can beer
- ❑ 1 pound flounder filets
- ❑ Oil
- ❑ 1 (10 ounce) package frozen broccoli florets
- ❑ 1 (8 ounce) can sliced water chestnuts
- ❑ 1 packet dry onion soup mix
- ❑ 2 (4.3 ounce) boxes garden vegetable Rice A Roni®
- ❑ Butter
- ❑ Ritz crackers
- ❑ Chopped pecans
- ❑ 4 Eggs
- ❑ Sugar

Spicy Catfish Amandine

¼ cup (½ stick) butter, melted
6 to 8 catfish filets
1½ teaspoons Creole seasoning
½ cup almonds, sliced, toasted

◆ Preheat oven to 350°. Dip each filet in butter and arrange filets in 9 x 13-inch baking dish. Sprinkle with Creole seasoning and almonds. Bake for 20 to 25 minutes or until fish flakes easily when tested with fork.

Lickety-Split Macaroni and Cheese

2 cups elbow macaroni, uncooked
1 (8 ounce) package cubed processed cheese
2 tablespoons (¼ stick) butter
2 tablespoons milk

◆ Add macaroni to 1½ quarts boiling water and cook until al dente. Drain well. Add cheese, butter and milk to macaroni and stir until well blended. Cover and simmer for 5 minutes until cheese melts.

Red and Green Salad

1 (12 ounce) package mixed salad greens
3 fresh green onions with tops, chopped
2 medium red apples, unpeeled, diced
½ cup poppy seed salad dressing

- In mixing bowl, toss salad greens, onions and fruit. Drizzle with dressing and toss.

Sweet Strawberries and Cream

2 pints fresh strawberries, sliced
Sugar
1 (8 ounce) carton whipping cream
1 cup almonds, chopped

- Divide sliced strawberries in serving bowls and sprinkle sugar liberally on top. Beat whipping cream with 1 tablespoon sugar until peaks form. Sprinkle almonds over strawberries and top with whipped cream.

Grocery List:

- ❑ Butter
- ❑ 6 to 8 catfish filets
- ❑ Creole seasoning
- ❑ ½ cup sliced almonds
- ❑ Uncooked elbow macaroni
- ❑ 1 (8 ounce) package cubed processed cheese
- ❑ Milk
- ❑ 1 (12 ounce) package mixed salad greens
- ❑ 3 fresh green onions
- ❑ 2 medium red apples
- ❑ 1 bottle poppy seed salad dressing
- ❑ 2 pints fresh strawberries
- ❑ Sugar
- ❑ 1 (8 ounce) carton whipping cream
- ❑ 1 cup chopped almonds

Crunchy Baked Fish

1 cup mayonnaise
2 tablespoons fresh lime juice
1 to 1½ pounds haddock filets
2 cups finely crushed corn chips

- Preheat oven to 425°. In small bowl, mix mayonnaise and lime juice. Spread on both sides of fish filets.
- Place crushed corn chips on wax paper and dredge both sides of fish in chips. Place filets on foil-covered baking sheet and bake 15 minutes or until fish flakes easily.

Pasta Salad and Sliced Tomatoes

1 (7.5 ounce) package pasta salad mix
½ cup mayonnaise (not fat free)
3 or 4 vine-ripened tomatoes

- Cook pasta according to package directions. Drain and rinse with cold water. Combine seasoning mix and mayonnaise, add pasta and toss. Place in salad bowl and refrigerate.
- Serve with sliced tomatoes.

Baked-Onion French Fries

1 (1 ounce) envelope dry onion soup mix
3 teaspoons canola oil
1 (24 ounce) package french-fried potatoes

◆ In large bowl, combine soup mix and oil. Add potatoes and stir until coated with soup mixture. Bake according to directions on potatoes and stir as needed.

Surprise Chocolates

2 pounds white chocolate or almond bark
2 cups Spanish peanuts
2 cups small pretzel sticks, broken

◆ Mix chocolate in double boiler. Stir in peanuts and pretzels. Drop by teaspoonfuls on wax paper. (Work fast because mixture hardens quickly.) Place in freezer to chill before serving and store at room temperature.

It will just take 15 minutes to cook these filets, so start pasta first. You can use crushed corn flakes if you prefer, though the fish will be crispier using the crushed corn chips.

Grocery List:

- ❑ Mayonnaise
- ❑ Lime juice
- ❑ 1 to 1½ pounds fresh or frozen haddock filets or orange roughy
- ❑ 1 (10 ounce) bag corn chips
- ❑ 1 (7.5 ounce) package pasta salad mix
- ❑ 3 or 4 vine-ripened tomatoes
- ❑ 1 (1 ounce) envelope onion soup mix
- ❑ Canola oil
- ❑ 1 (24 ounce) package french-fried potatoes
- ❑ 2 pounds white chocolate
- ❑ 2 cups Spanish peanuts
- ❑ 2 cups pretzel sticks

Fish Sticks or Breaded Fish Filets

1 (16 ounce) package frozen fish sticks or breaded fish filets, thawed
1 (11 ounce) bottle tartar sauce
1 (8 ounce) bottle ketchup

- Preheat oven to 350°. Heat fish according to package directions. For best crispness, do not heat in microwave.
- Serve with tartar sauce and/or ketchup.

Broccoli-Cheese Dip

½ cup (1 stick) butter, softened
1 (16 ounce) package cubed processed cheese
1 (10 ounce) package frozen chopped broccoli, partially thawed

- Combine butter and cheese in saucepan on lowest heat until cheese melts. Cook broccoli according to package directions and drain. Stir in cheese-soup mixture and heat until broccoli is hot. Dip with your favorite vegetables.

Hush Puppies

1 (16 ounce) package frozen hush puppies

- Heat according to package directions. (You can heat hush puppies at the same time you are heating fish. For best crispness, do not heat in microwave.)

Strawberry-Banana Pudding

8 (4 ounce) strawberry-banana or chocolate-vanilla pudding cups

- Serve in containers or transfer to serving bowl.

They aren't especially nutritious, but I understand the lure of those fish sticks and mashed potatoes after the grandkids have spent an hour in the pool. If you can fool them, buy breaded flounder or tilapia.

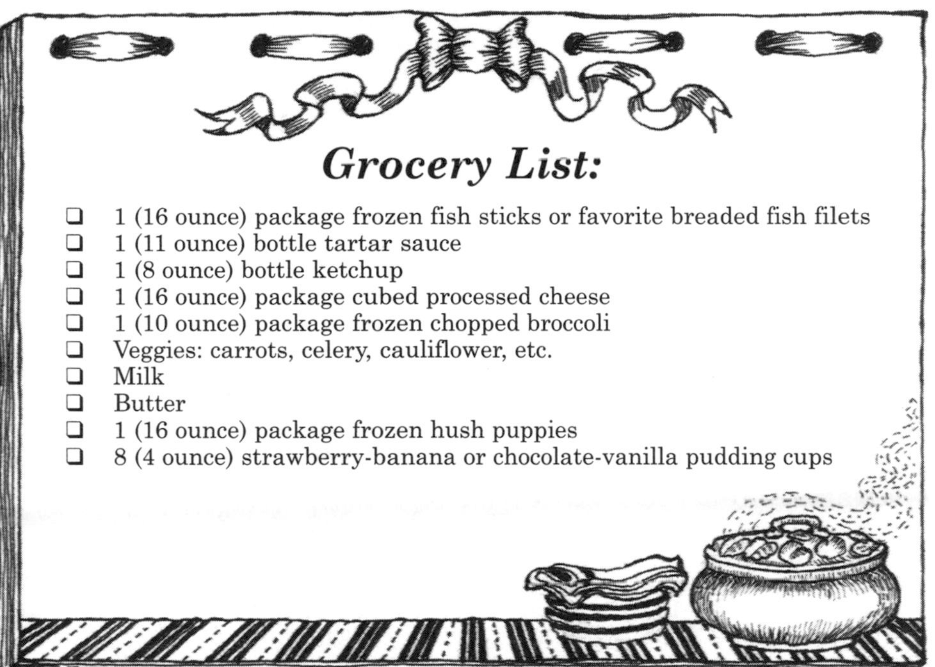

Grocery List:

- ❑ 1 (16 ounce) package frozen fish sticks or favorite breaded fish filets
- ❑ 1 (11 ounce) bottle tartar sauce
- ❑ 1 (8 ounce) bottle ketchup
- ❑ 1 (16 ounce) package cubed processed cheese
- ❑ 1 (10 ounce) package frozen chopped broccoli
- ❑ Veggies: carrots, celery, cauliflower, etc.
- ❑ Milk
- ❑ Butter
- ❑ 1 (16 ounce) package frozen hush puppies
- ❑ 8 (4 ounce) strawberry-banana or chocolate-vanilla pudding cups

Chipper Fish

1½ to 2 pounds sole or orange roughy
½ cup Caesar salad dressing
1½ cups seasoned breadcrumbs
1 cup crushed potato chips

- Preheat oven to 375°. Pour dressing in shallow bowl and breadcrumbs in second shallow bowl. Dip fish in dressing and breadcrumbs and coat lightly. Place coated fish in large, sprayed baking dish.
- Sprinkle fish lightly with crushed potato chips and bake 20 to 25 minutes or until fish flakes easily with fork.

Broccoli-Waldorf Salad

6 cups very small fresh broccoli florets, chilled
1 large red apple, unpeeled, chopped, chilled
¾ cup slightly chopped pecans, chilled
½ cup prepared coleslaw dressing

- In bowl with lid, combine broccoli, chopped apple and pecans.
- Drizzle with dressing and toss to coat. Use more dressing if ingredients are not coated well. Refrigerate.

Tip: Add some golden raisins if desired.

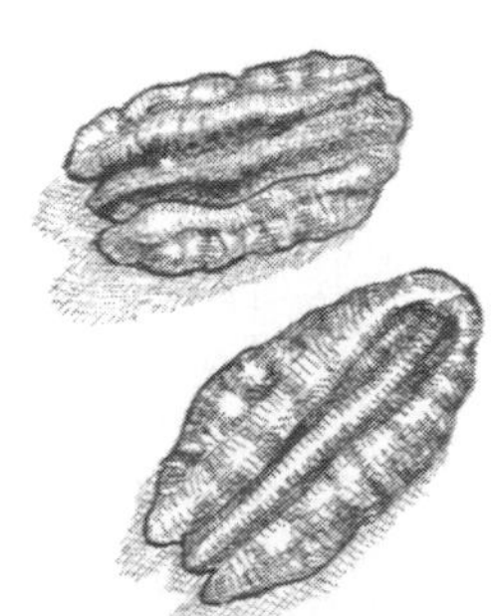

Chili-Baked Beans

2 (16 ounce) cans pork and beans
1 (15 ounce) can chili with beans
¼ cup molasses
1 teaspoon chili powder

- Drain pork and beans. In 2-quart casserole combine beans, molasses and chili powder. Heat until bubbly.

Scotch Crunchies

½ cup crunchy peanut butter
1 (6 ounce) package butterscotch bits
2½ cups frosted flakes
½ cup peanuts

- Combine peanut butter and butterscotch bits in large saucepan and melt over low heat. Stir until butterscotch bits melt. Stir in cereal and peanuts.
- Drop by teaspoonfuls on wax paper. Refrigerate until firm. Store in airtight container.

Try this crispy, melt-in-your mouth fish. You won't believe it's oven-fried! When you add this absolutely delightful salad and good ole baked beans, you have a top-notch supper. And who can turn down Scotch Crunchies?

Grocery List:

- ❑ 1½ to 2 pounds sole or orange roughy
- ❑ 1 (8 ounce) bottle Caesar salad dressing
- ❑ 1 (15 ounce) carton seasoned breadcrumbs
- ❑ 1 small bag potato chips
- ❑ 1 large bunch fresh broccoli
- ❑ 1 large red apple
- ❑ Pecans
- ❑ 1 (8 ounce) bottle coleslaw dressing
- ❑ 2 (16 ounce) cans pork and beans
- ❑ 1 (15 ounce) can chili with beans
- ❑ Molasses
- ❑ Chili powder
- ❑ Crunchy peanut butter
- ❑ 1 (6 ounce) package butterscotch bits
- ❑ Frosted flakes
- ❑ ½ cup peanuts

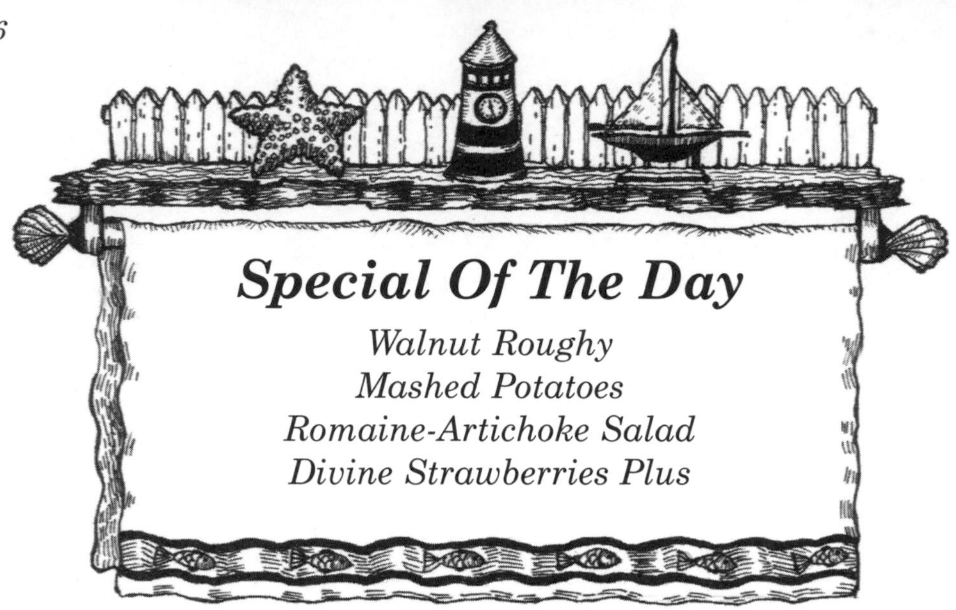

Walnut Roughy

1½ pounds fresh or frozen orange roughy
3 tablespoons grated parmesan cheese
1 teaspoon dried basil
½ cup mayonnaise
⅓ cup chopped walnuts

- Preheat oven to 425°. Cut orange roughy into serving-size pieces and place in greased baking pan. Do not let pieces touch.
- In bowl, combine mayonnaise, parmesan cheese and dried basil and spread over fish. Sprinkle with chopped walnuts.
- Bake uncovered 14 to 15 minutes or until fish flakes easily.

Tip: Just a little spicy touch excites the flavors. Try ½ teaspoon ancho chile pepper or chili powder for kicks.

Mashed Potatoes

1 (7 ounce) box home-style, creamy butter mashed potatoes

- Heat according to package directions. You will need a little milk, butter and water.

Romaine-Artichoke Salad

1 (10 ounce) package romaine lettuce
1 (6 ounce) jar artichoke hearts, drained, chopped, chilled
1 sweet red bell pepper, julienned, chilled
⅓ cup toasted sunflower seeds, toasted

- In salad bowl, combine romaine, artichoke hearts and bell pepper.
- Add about ½ (8-ounce) bottle garlic-vinaigrette dressing (more if needed) and toss. Sprinkle sunflower seeds over top of salad.

Divine Strawberries Plus

1 quart fresh strawberries, washed, well drained, chilled
1 (20 ounce) can pineapple chunks, well drained, chilled
2 bananas, sliced, chilled
1 (18 ounce) carton strawberry glaze, chilled

- Cut strawberries in half or in quarters if strawberries are very large. Add pineapple chunks and bananas.
- Fold in strawberry glaze and chill.

This is a beautiful and absolutely delicious dessert. Serve in sherbet glass with dollop of frozen whipped topping, if desired. It is also a fabulous topping for slices of pound cake.

Orange roughy is a mild fish that goes well with light sauces. This recipe has all the taste that you would find in an elegant seafood restaurant. The vegetables and salad complete a delicious seafood dinner and the dessert is five-star.

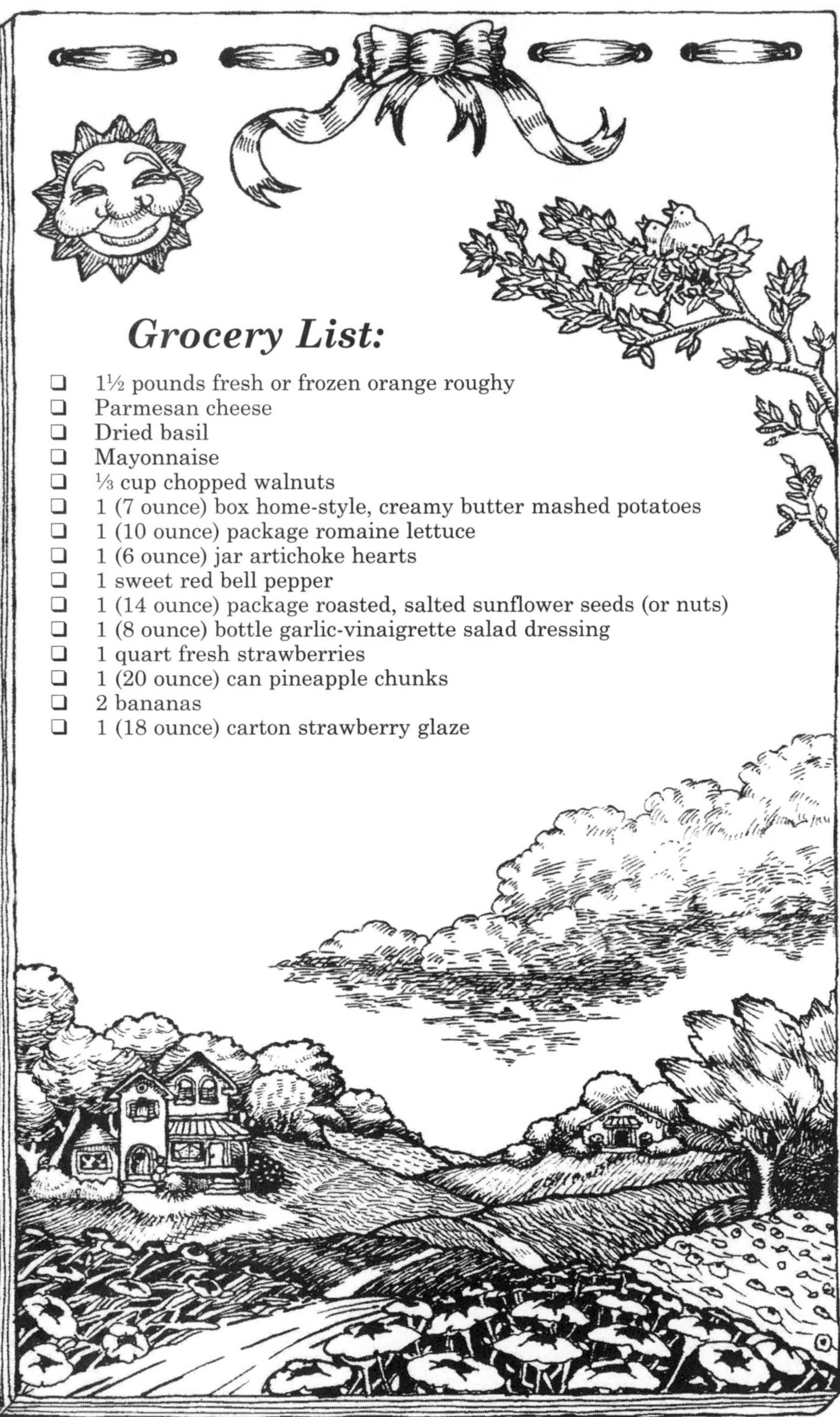

Grocery List:

- ❑ 1½ pounds fresh or frozen orange roughy
- ❑ Parmesan cheese
- ❑ Dried basil
- ❑ Mayonnaise
- ❑ ⅓ cup chopped walnuts
- ❑ 1 (7 ounce) box home-style, creamy butter mashed potatoes
- ❑ 1 (10 ounce) package romaine lettuce
- ❑ 1 (6 ounce) jar artichoke hearts
- ❑ 1 sweet red bell pepper
- ❑ 1 (14 ounce) package roasted, salted sunflower seeds (or nuts)
- ❑ 1 (8 ounce) bottle garlic-vinaigrette salad dressing
- ❑ 1 quart fresh strawberries
- ❑ 1 (20 ounce) can pineapple chunks
- ❑ 2 bananas
- ❑ 1 (18 ounce) carton strawberry glaze

Buttered Flounder

4 to 6 (about 2 pounds) flounder filets
⅔ cup butter
3 tablespoons fresh cilantro leaves
1 tablespoon lime juice

- Preheat broiler. Spray large broiler pan with cooking spray and place filets in pan.
- Broil about 3 to 4 minutes and carefully turn filets over (with tongs and not with fork).
- Broil 3 minutes more or until fish flakes easily when tested with fork.
- In saucepan, heat and stir butter, cilantro leaves and lime juice. Just before serving, spoon mixture over flounder.

Microwave Potato Skins

4 baked potatoes
1 cup shredded cheddar cheese
4 to 6 slices bacon, fried crisp, drained, crumbled

- Slice potatoes lengthwise and microwave for 3 minutes. Scoop out potato, leaving ¼-inch thick potato on skins. Fill each potato skin with cheese and bacon. Place on plate. Cover with paper towel or plastic wrap and microwave for 30 seconds or until cheese melts.

Stuffed Celery

3 large ribs celery
1 (16 ounce) carton pimento cheese

- Cut ribs in 3-inch pieces. Stuff with pimento cheese and place on serving plate with cucumber slices.

Stuffed Cucumber Slices

2 cucumbers, peeled
1 (8 ounce) package cream cheese, softened
½ cup stuffed green olives, finely chopped, drained
½ teaspoon seasoned salt

- Halve cucumbers lengthwise and scoop out seeds. (Use grapefruit spoon to scrape down middle of cucumbers to leave hollow in each half.)
- In mixing bowl with mixer, beat cream cheese until creamy. Fold in olives and seasoned salt and mix well.
- Fill cucumber hollows to top with cream cheese mixture. Press halves together, wrap tightly in plastic wrap and chill. Cut crosswise in ⅓-inch slices to serve.

Tip: Place on serving plate with stuffed celery and you have a crunchy good salad.

Iced-Chocolate Pudding Cake

Oreo cookies
1 bakery iced chocolate pudding cake

- Crumble oreo cookies on bottom of dessert plate. Add slice of cake on top and sprinkle with more crumbled Oreo cookies.

Flounder is my favorite of all varieties of fish. The best thing about fish in general is that it is nutritionally healthy for us, high in protein, low in saturated fat and can be baked, broiled or grilled.

Grocery List:

- ❑ 4 to 6 (about 2 pounds) flounder filets
- ❑ Butter
- ❑ Fresh cilantro leaves
- ❑ Lime juice
- ❑ 4 baked potatoes
- ❑ 1 cup (8 ounce) package shredded cheese
- ❑ Bacon
- ❑ Large celery ribs
- ❑ 1 (16 ounce) carton pimento cheese
- ❑ 2 cucumbers
- ❑ 1 (8 ounce) package cream cheese
- ❑ 1 (8 ounce) bottle stuffed green olives
- ❑ Seasoned salt
- ❑ Oreo cookies
- ❑ 1 bakery iced-chocolate pudding cake

Simple Flounder Delight

Flounder Au Gratin
Herbed New Potatoes
Toasty Garlic Bread
Broccoli-Stuffed Tomatoes
Ice Cream Chambord

Flounder Au Gratin

½ cup fine dry breadcrumbs
¼ cup grated parmesan cheese
1 pound flounder
⅓ cup mayonnaise

- Preheat oven to 350°. In shallow dish, combine crumbs and cheese. Brush both sides of fish with mayonnaise and coat with crumb mixture.
- Arrange fish in single layer in shallow pan and bake for 20 to 25 minutes or until fish flakes easily when tested with fork.

Herbed New Potatoes

1½ pounds new potatoes
½ cup (1 stick) butter, sliced
½ cup chopped fresh parsley
½ teaspoon rosemary

- Scrub potatoes and cut in halves but do not peel. In medium saucepan, boil in lightly salted water. Cook until potatoes are tender, about 20 minutes and drain. Add butter, parsley and rosemary and toss gently until butter melts. Serve hot.

Toasty Garlic Bread

1 loaf French bread, sliced
Butter
Garlic salt

- Separate slices of bread, spread butter on both sides and sprinkle with garlic salt. Wrap in foil and warm in oven at 350° for 15 minutes.

Broccoli-Stuffed Tomatoes

4 medium tomatoes
1 (10 ounce) package frozen chopped broccoli
1 (6 ounce) roll garlic cheese, softened
½ teaspoon garlic salt

- Preheat oven to 350°. Cut tomato tops off and scoop out pulp. Cook frozen broccoli in microwave according to package directions and drain well.
- Combine broccoli, cheese and garlic salt. Heat just until cheese melts, stuff broccoli mixture into tomatoes and place on baking sheet. Bake for about 10 minutes.

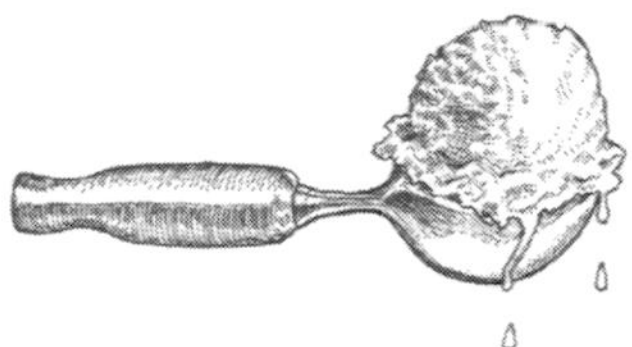

Ice Cream Chambord

Vanilla ice cream
Chambord liqueur
Fresh raspberries or chopped nuts
Whipped topping

- Place several scoops of vanilla ice cream in serving bowls and pour chambord over top. Sprinkle raspberries and chopped nuts over ice cream and top with whipped cream.

Tip: Chambord is a delicious raspberry liqueur that can be found in most liquor stores.

Grocery List:

- ❑ 1 box fine dry breadcrumbs
- ❑ ¼ cup grated parmesan cheese
- ❑ 1 pound flounder
- ❑ Mayonnaise
- ❑ 1½ pounds new potatoes
- ❑ Butter
- ❑ Fresh parsley
- ❑ Rosemary
- ❑ Garlic salt
- ❑ 1 loaf French bread, sliced
- ❑ 4 medium tomatoes
- ❑ 1 (10 ounce) package frozen chopped broccoli
- ❑ 1 (6 ounce) roll garlic cheese, softened
- ❑ Vanilla ice cream
- ❑ Chambord liqueur
- ❑ Fresh raspberries
- ❑ Chopped nuts
- ❑ 1 (8 ounce) carton whipped topping

Salmon Fiesta

Southwest Salmon
Basil-Buttered Corn
Cucumber-Jicama Salad
Chocolate-Almond Pie

Southwest Salmon

1 to 1½ pounds salmon filet or pieces, cut into 4 equal pieces
3 tablespoons fresh lime juice
½ teaspoon each cumin, chili powder, oregano
2 tablespoons (¼ stick) butter, melted

- Preheat oven to 400°. Place salmon skin side down in sprayed 9 x 13-inch baking dish.
- Rub lime juice over filets and marinate at room temperature about 10 minutes.
- In small bowl, combine cumin, chili powder, oregano and salt and pepper. Pat salmon lightly with paper towel and rub cumin mixture on tops and sides of salmon.
- Roast salmon in baking pan between 5 to 10 minutes or until salmon is opaque and flakes easily. Do not overcook!

Basil-Buttered Corn

4 to 6 fresh or frozen ears of corn
3 tablespoons butter, melted
½ teaspoon basil flakes

- Cook corn in boiling water for 5 to 10 minutes.
- In salad bowl, combine butter, basil and ½ teaspoon salt. When ready to serve, brush each ear of corn with basil-butter.

Cucumber-Jicama Salad

1 (1 pound) jicama
1 small cucumber, sliced
½ cup red onion, slivered
Shredded lettuce

- With sharp knife, peel jicama, cut lengthwise into wedges and cut crosswise into thin sticks.
- In bowl, combine jicama, cucumber and red onion. Toss with lemon-vinaigrette dressing and spoon into salad bowl lined with shredded lettuce.

Chocolate-Almond Pie

1 (8 ounce) chocolate almond bar
1 (8 ounce) carton whipped topping
1 (8-inch) graham cracker piecrust

- Melt chocolate bar in top of double broiler. Remove from heat and cool. Stir whipped topping into chocolate, fill piecrust and chill.

Tip: Garnish, if desired, by using a potato peeler to shave chocolate curls off an additional chocolate candy bar.

On wonderful trips to Canada, salmon was always on the top of our list of favorites, but I learned one very important tidbit: don't overcook salmon. I also love this salad. We discovered jicama on a visit to friends in the Dominican Republic. They prepared jicama in many different ways, but my favorite is the crunchy jicama with a lemon vinaigrette dressing.

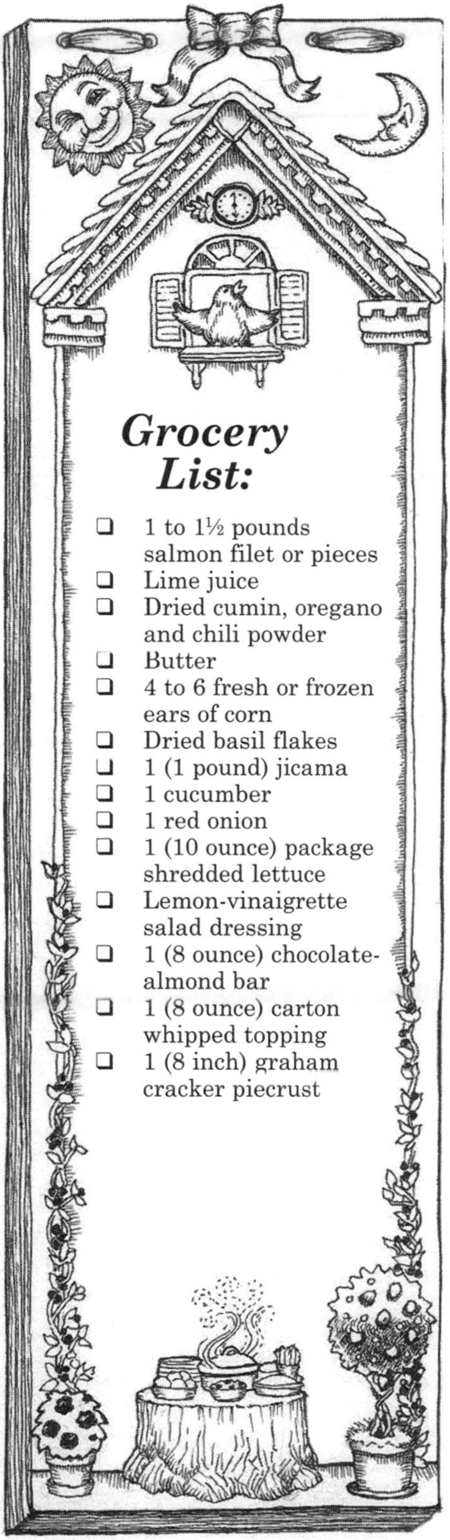

Grocery List:

- ❑ 1 to 1½ pounds salmon filet or pieces
- ❑ Lime juice
- ❑ Dried cumin, oregano and chili powder
- ❑ Butter
- ❑ 4 to 6 fresh or frozen ears of corn
- ❑ Dried basil flakes
- ❑ 1 (1 pound) jicama
- ❑ 1 cucumber
- ❑ 1 red onion
- ❑ 1 (10 ounce) package shredded lettuce
- ❑ Lemon-vinaigrette salad dressing
- ❑ 1 (8 ounce) chocolate-almond bar
- ❑ 1 (8 ounce) carton whipped topping
- ❑ 1 (8 inch) graham cracker piecrust

Bless My Sole

1½ pounds fresh or frozen sole or cod
1 egg, beaten
2 tablespoons milk
2 cups crushed corn flakes

- Cut fish into serving-size pieces and sprinkle with salt and pepper.
- In shallow bowl, combine egg and milk or water and place corn flake crumbs in second bowl.
- Dip fish in egg mixture and coat well on both sides with crushed flakes. Fry in thin layer of oil in skillet until brown on both sides, about 5 to 8 minutes on each side.

Tip: Serve with prepared tartar sauce or ketchup or even twist of lemon or lime juice.

Potato Salad Extra

1 (24 ounce) carton deli potato salad
3 fresh green onions, chopped
1 (4 ounce) jar chopped pimento
1 (10 ounce) jar stuffed green olives

- In serving bowl, combine potato salad, onions and pimentos.

Tip: Spice up deli potato salad by adding celery or red bell pepper.

Onion Rings

1 (20 ounce) package frozen, breaded onion rings, thawed

◆ For maximum crispness, heat onion rings in oven according to package directions.

Potato Dinner Rolls, optional

1 (14 ounce) package potato dinner rolls

◆ Heat rolls in 300° oven 10 to 15 minutes.

Mocha Pudding

1 (16 ounce) almond candy bar
1 tablespoon instant coffee powder
1 (12 ounce) carton whipped topping

◆ Melt candy with coffee powder in double boiler over boiling water and stir often. Remove from heat and cool completely. Stir in whipped topping and serve in dessert dish as pudding or pour into graham cracker crust to serve as pie. Refrigerate until firm.

This fish is unmistakably juicy and tender with a crispy, crunchy exterior. Add your own flair to deli potato salad with additions like chopped celery and red bell pepper.

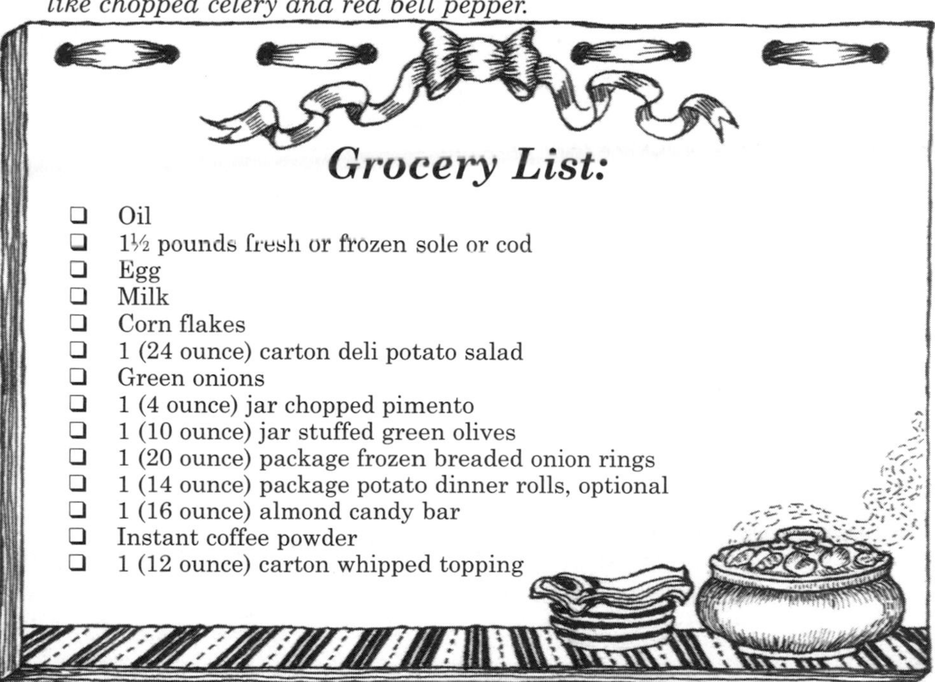

Grocery List:

- ❑ Oil
- ❑ 1½ pounds fresh or frozen sole or cod
- ❑ Egg
- ❑ Milk
- ❑ Corn flakes
- ❑ 1 (24 ounce) carton deli potato salad
- ❑ Green onions
- ❑ 1 (4 ounce) jar chopped pimento
- ❑ 1 (10 ounce) jar stuffed green olives
- ❑ 1 (20 ounce) package frozen breaded onion rings
- ❑ 1 (14 ounce) package potato dinner rolls, optional
- ❑ 1 (16 ounce) almond candy bar
- ❑ Instant coffee powder
- ❑ 1 (12 ounce) carton whipped topping

Tuna Melts On the Table

Tuna Melts
Buttermilk Biscuits
Cottage Cheese-Topped Tomato Slices
Fast-Action Fudge

Tuna Melts

1 (12 ounce) can chunk light tuna packed in water, drained
¾ cup chopped celery
½ cup sweet pickle relish
⅓ cup refrigerated honey-mustard salad dressing

- In large bowl, combine tuna, celery, pickle relish and dressing to taste.
- Divide tuna mixture among split biscuits and place ½ slice cheese over top of tuna. Bake 6 to 7 minutes or until filling is hot and cheese melts.

Buttermilk Biscuits

1 (10 ounce, 5 count) can refrigerated buttermilk biscuits
5 slices Swiss cheese

- Preheat oven to 375°. Bake biscuits according to can directions and cool slightly. Set aside cheese slices for topping on tuna.
- Split biscuits and arrange cut side up on same baking pan used to cook biscuits.

I have not used canned biscuits in other recipes and have suggested frozen buttermilk biscuits for all occasions, but canned biscuits will work in this recipe (mainly because you only need 5), but I strongly urge you to keep a package of frozen biscuits on hand.

Cottage Cheese-Topped Tomato Slices

3 to 4 vine-ripened tomatoes
1 (16 ounce) carton small-curd cottage cheese, drained
Seasoned salt
Lettuce leaves or shredded lettuce

- Slice tomatoes and place on individual salad plates lined with lettuce leaves or shredded lettuce.
- Top with 2 heaping tablespoons cottage cheese and sprinkle with seasoned salt.

Fast-Action Fudge

1 pound powdered sugar
½ cup cocoa
¼ cup milk
½ cup (1 stick) butter
1 tablespoon vanilla
½ cup chopped nuts

- Blend sugar and cocoa then add milk and butter, but do not stir. Microwave on HIGH for 2 minutes. Remove from microwave and stir well to mix.
- Add vanilla and nuts and stir until they blend. Pour into sprayed dish and freeze for 20 minutes. Cut into squares and serve.

What would we do without canned tuna? It has a distinctively rich flavor, is flaky, tender and wonderful eaten right from the can, in a casserole or our version of a tuna-melt sandwich. Be sure to buy the best grade of tuna, the solid or large pieces of white meat packed in water.

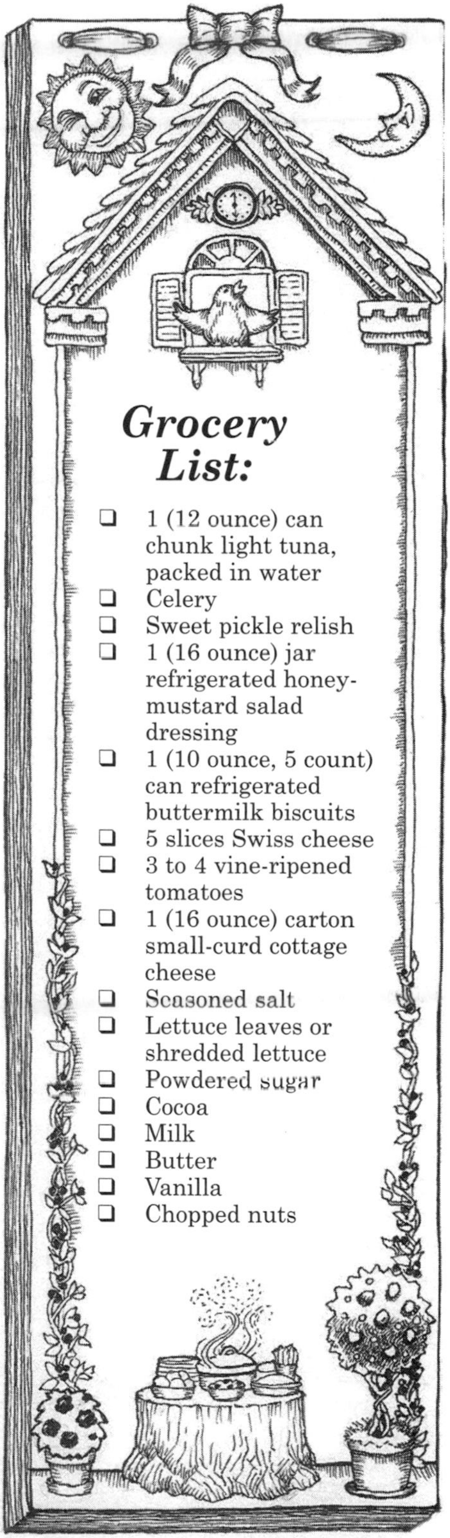

Grocery List:

- ❑ 1 (12 ounce) can chunk light tuna, packed in water
- ❑ Celery
- ❑ Sweet pickle relish
- ❑ 1 (16 ounce) jar refrigerated honey-mustard salad dressing
- ❑ 1 (10 ounce, 5 count) can refrigerated buttermilk biscuits
- ❑ 5 slices Swiss cheese
- ❑ 3 to 4 vine-ripened tomatoes
- ❑ 1 (16 ounce) carton small-curd cottage cheese
- ❑ Seasoned salt
- ❑ Lettuce leaves or shredded lettuce
- ❑ Powdered sugar
- ❑ Cocoa
- ❑ Milk
- ❑ Butter
- ❑ Vanilla
- ❑ Chopped nuts

Tuna Twisters

2 (3 ounce) packages tuna
⅓ cup sweet pickle relish, drained
½ cup chipotle mayonnaise
1 (8 ounce) package finely shredded mozzarella cheese
6 to 8 flour tortillas

- In small bowl, place tuna and break up chunks with fork to shred. Add pickle relish and mayonnaise and mix well.
- Lay all tortillas out flat and spread tuna mixture over tortillas. Top with about ⅓ cup shredded cheese. Mash down ingredients to make rolling tortillas easier. (You will probably not need all of cheese.) Roll up tortilla.
- Place tortillas seam side down on microwave-safe tray and microwave on HIGH about 15 to 20 seconds or until cheese melts.

Tip: To make twisters easier to eat, cut them in half diagonally before heating.

Calypso Coleslaw

1 (16 ounce) package finely shredded coleslaw mix
1 bunch fresh green onions, sliced
1 (8 ounce) package shredded cheddar cheese
1 (11 ounce) can mexicorn, drained

- In large bowl, combine all ingredients with about 1 teaspoon salt. Toss and add about one-half bottle coleslaw dressing.

Five-Minute Dip

1 (8 ounce) package cream cheese, softened
1 cup mayonnaise
1 package dry ranch-style salad dressing mix
½ onion, finely minced

◆ Combine cream cheese and mayonnaise and beat until creamy. Stir in dressing mix and onion. Chill and serve with fresh vegetables.

Peanut Butter Fudge

12 ounces chunky peanut butter
12 ounces milk chocolate chips
1 (14 ounce) can sweetened condensed milk
1 cup chopped pecans

◆ In saucepan, combine peanut butter, chocolate chips and condensed milk. Heat on low, stirring constantly until chocolate melts. Add pecans and mix well. Pour into 9 x 9-inch buttered dish.

Tuna in a vacuum-sealed pouch needs no refrigeration until it is opened and it's great. This tuna sandwich wrapped in a flour tortilla is a sure winner—fun to make and fun to eat! Add zip to ordinary coleslaw with a handful of toasted almonds or sunflower seeds.

Grocery List:

- ❑ 2 (3 ounce) packages tuna
- ❑ Sweet pickle relish
- ❑ French's® GourMayo™ chipotle mayonnaise
- ❑ 1 (8 ounce) package finely shredded mozzarella cheese
- ❑ 6 to 8 flour tortillas
- ❑ 1 (16 ounce) package finely shredded coleslaw mix
- ❑ 1 bunch fresh green onions
- ❑ 1 (8 ounce) package shredded cheddar cheese
- ❑ 1 (11 ounce) can mexicorn
- ❑ 1 (8 ounce) bottle coleslaw dressing
- ❑ 1 (8 ounce) package cream cheese
- ❑ Mayonnaise
- ❑ 1 package dry french-style salad dressing mix
- ❑ 1 onion
- ❑ Veggies
- ❑ 12 ounces chunky peanut butter
- ❑ 12 ounces milk chocolate chips
- ❑ 1 (14 ounce) can sweetened condensed milk
- ❑ Chopped pecans

Family Night

Tuna Toast
French Fry-Cheese Melt
Niblet Corn in Butter Sauce
Blueberry Tarts

Tuna Toast

1 (10 ounce) can cream of chicken soup
1 (6 ounce) can white tuna in water, drained
3 slices frozen thick Texas toast, toasted on both sides
3 fresh green onions, chopped

- ◆ In saucepan over low heat, combine soup, tuna, dash black pepper and about ¼ cup milk or water. Heat and stir until hot.
- ◆ Place each slice Texas toast on individual plates and spoon one-third tuna mixture on top of toast. Sprinkle chopped green onion over tuna mixture.

Tip: This recipe will provide only 3 generous servings, so double recipe if you need more servings.

French Fry-Cheese Melt

1 large bag frozen french fries
1 (12 ounce) package shredded cheddar cheese

- ◆ Preheat oven to 375°. Place 1 serving fries on large baking sheet and bake according to package directions. Salt and pepper fries and bunch fries together in individual servings. Sprinkle cheese on top. Return to oven and bake just until cheese melts.

Tip: Most kids prefer crinkle-cut fries for their extra crispness.

Niblet Corn in Butter Sauce

1 (19 ounce) package frozen niblet corn in butter sauce

- Heat according to package directions.

Blueberry Tarts

1 (8 count) package graham cracker tart shells, chilled
1 (20 ounce) can blueberry pie filling, chilled
1 (8 ounce) carton whipped topping

- Fill tart shells with blueberry pie filling and top with whipped topping.

You may be surprised at what you can create with tuna, but this is a menu you can get on the table in far less than 30 minutes. Everything in this menu can be kept in your pantry, except maybe the Texas toast. Use what you have on hand, like Uncle Ben's® rice or Near East® couscous. Or heat a can of green beans with butter and seasoned salt. Top with french-fried onion rings.

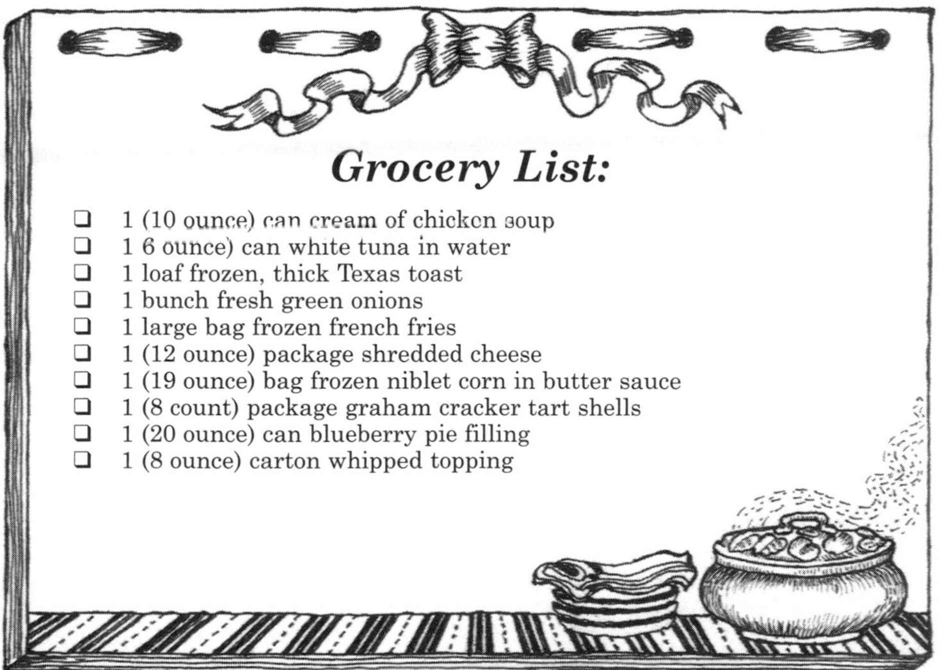

Grocery List:

- ❑ 1 (10 ounce) can cream of chicken soup
- ❑ 1 6 ounce) can white tuna in water
- ❑ 1 loaf frozen, thick Texas toast
- ❑ 1 bunch fresh green onions
- ❑ 1 large bag frozen french fries
- ❑ 1 (12 ounce) package shredded cheese
- ❑ 1 (19 ounce) bag frozen niblet corn in butter sauce
- ❑ 1 (8 count) package graham cracker tart shells
- ❑ 1 (20 ounce) can blueberry pie filling
- ❑ 1 (8 ounce) carton whipped topping

Tuna Noodles

1 (8 ounce) package wide noodles, cooked, drained
2 (6 ounce) cans white tuna, drained
1 (10 ounce) can cream of chicken soup
¾ cup milk

- Preheat oven to 300°. Place half noodles in 2-quart buttered casserole dish. In saucepan, combine tuna, soup and milk and heat just enough to mix well.
- Pour half soup mixture over noodles and repeat layers. Cover and bake for 20 minutes.

Tip: It is not necessary, but ¾ cup chopped black olives are great in this recipe.

Baked Tomatoes with Basil

3 large tomatoes
1½ cups seasoned, dry breadcrumbs
4 tablespoons butter
Dried basil

- Preheat oven to 350°. Cut tomatoes in half or slice tomatoes in ½ to 1-inch thick slices and place on baking sheet.
- Sprinkle generously with breadcrumbs and top with butter and basil. Bake for 10 to 15 minutes or until light brown on top.

Parmesan-Bread Deluxe

1 (16 ounce) loaf Italian bread, unsliced
½ cup refrigerated creamy Caesar dressing and dip
⅓ cup grated parmesan cheese
3 tablespoons finely chopped green onions

◆ Cut 24 (½-inch thick) slices from bread. In small bowl, combine dressing, cheese and onion and spread 1 teaspoon dressing mixture onto each bread slice. Place bread on baking sheet and broil 4-inches from heat until golden brown. Serve warm.

Pink Lady Pie

1 (6 ounce) concentrated pink lemonade, frozen
1 (14 ounce) can sweetened condensed milk
1 (8 ounce) package whipped topping
1 (9 inch) graham cracker piecrust

◆ Combine lemonade and condensed milk and blend well.

◆ Fold in whipped topping, pour into piecrust and freeze until ready to serve.

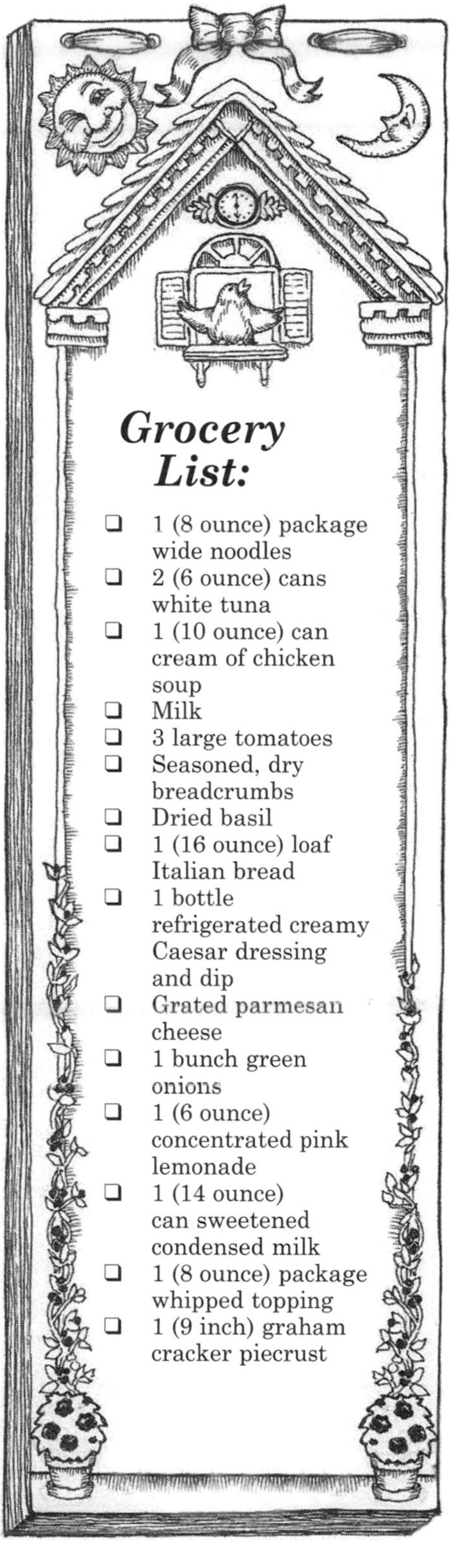

Grocery List:

- ❑ 1 (8 ounce) package wide noodles
- ❑ 2 (6 ounce) cans white tuna
- ❑ 1 (10 ounce) can cream of chicken soup
- ❑ Milk
- ❑ 3 large tomatoes
- ❑ Seasoned, dry breadcrumbs
- ❑ Dried basil
- ❑ 1 (16 ounce) loaf Italian bread
- ❑ 1 bottle refrigerated creamy Caesar dressing and dip
- ❑ Grated parmesan cheese
- ❑ 1 bunch green onions
- ❑ 1 (6 ounce) concentrated pink lemonade
- ❑ 1 (14 ounce) can sweetened condensed milk
- ❑ 1 (8 ounce) package whipped topping
- ❑ 1 (9 inch) graham cracker piecrust

Downtown Express

Skillet Shrimp
Special Spinach Salad
Stuffed Breadsticks
Apricot-Topped Pound Cake

Skillet Shrimp

2 teaspoons olive oil
2 pounds uncooked shrimp, peeled, veined
⅔ cup herb-garlic marinade with lemon juice
¼ cup finely chopped green onion with tops

◆ In large nonstick skillet, heat oil and add shrimp and marinade. Cook, stirring often, until shrimp turns pink. Stir in green onions. Serve over hot, cooked rice or your favorite pasta.

Special Spinach Salad

1 (10 ounce) package fresh spinach
1 (16 ounce) can bean sprouts, drained
8 slices bacon, cooked crisp
1 (11 ounce) can water chestnuts, chopped

◆ Combine spinach and bean sprouts. When ready to serve, add crumbled bacon and water chestnuts. Toss with vinaigrette salad dressing made from 3 parts olive oil and 1 part red wine vinegar.

Stuffed Breadsticks

1 (12.5 ounce) package frozen stuffed breadsticks, thawed

◆ Heat according to package directions.

Apricot-Topped Pound Cake

1 loaf bakery pound cake
1 (20 ounce) can apricot pie filling, chilled
1 (8 ounce) carton whipped topping

- Place slices of pound cake on dessert plates with heaping spoon of apricot pie filling.
- Top with a dollop of whipped topping.

I'm not one to minimize the benefit of frozen entrees and this stir-fry shrimp is a real winner. There are several different types of egg rolls (pork, shrimp, etc.) so try them all to find your favorite. They add a great crunch to the meal and you may like them better than the breadsticks. My dessert is so easy you will want to try it with other pie fillings.

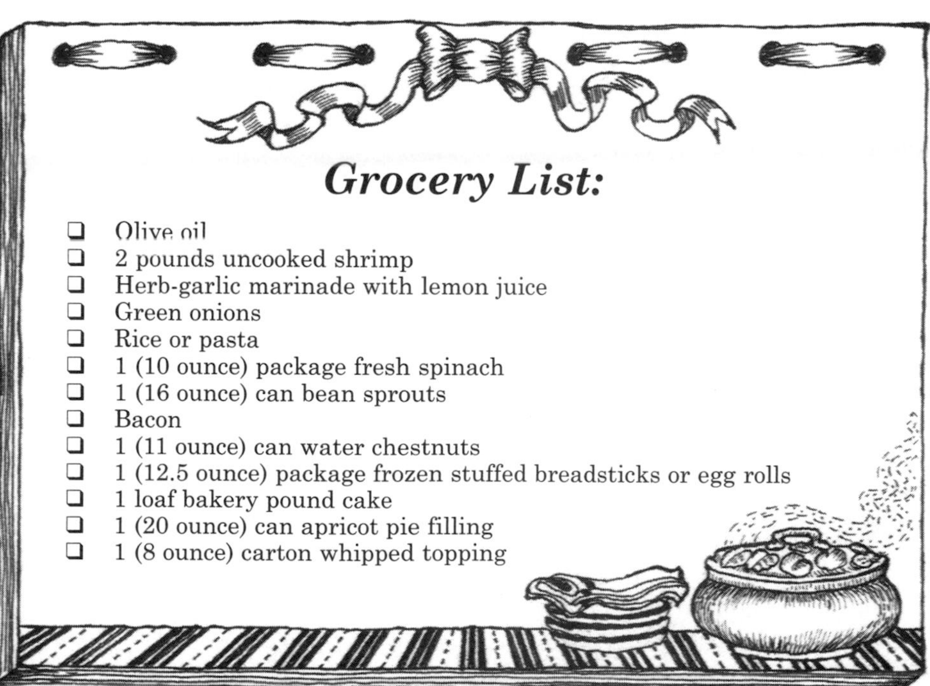

Shrimp Marinara

1½ pounds shelled, veined, uncooked medium-sized shrimp, tails removed
1 (16 ounce) jar refrigerated marinara sauce
1 tablespoon lime juice
1 teaspoon minced garlic

- In large skillet with a little oil, cook shrimp over medium heat 2 to 3 minutes or until shrimp turn pink.
- Stir in marinara sauce, lime juice and minced garlic. (It is really good with a dash of cayenne pepper.) Simmer 5 minutes or until sauce heats through. Serve over angel hair pasta.

Angel Hair Pasta

1 (8 ounce) package angel hair pasta
2 tablespoons butter
2 tablespoons cream
Salt

- Cook pasta according to package directions. Drain well and stir in butter, cream and a little salt.
- Pour onto serving platter and spoon marinara shrimp on top of pasta.

Green Spring Salad Mix

1 (10 ounce) bag green, spring salad mix
Fresh green onions, sliced
Creamy Italian salad dressing
1 (16 ounce) box seasoned croutons

- In salad bowl, toss salad, onion and dressing. Top with croutons.

Hot Buttered Garlic Toast

1 (11 ounce, 8 count) package frozen Texas garlic toast, thawed
Butter

- Heat according to package directions.

Chocolate Ice Cream with Raspberries

Chocolate ice cream
1 (10 ounce) package frozen raspberries in syrup
6 tablespoons chocolate syrup

- Place 1 large scoop of ice cream in each of 4 dessert bowl. Pour half of raspberries into blender and blend until pureed. Combine with remaining half package berries. Pour chocolate sauce over ice cream. Drizzle raspberry mixture over top.

Shrimp is a favorite of many of us and it is so easy to buy fresh or frozen—and certainly so easy to cook. One time my 6-year-old granddaughter was telling me how much she liked seafood and I ask her what "seafood" she liked best. Her quick answer was "just shrimp and more shrimp!"

Grocery List:

- ❑ 1½ pounds shelled, veined, uncooked medium size shrimp, tails removed
- ❑ 1 (16 ounce) jar refrigerated marinara sauce
- ❑ Lime juice
- ❑ Minced garlic and cayenne pepper
- ❑ 1 (8 ounce) package angel hair pasta
- ❑ Cream and butter
- ❑ 1 (10 ounce) bag green, spring salad mix
- ❑ 1 bunch fresh green onions
- ❑ 1 (8 ounce) bottle creamy Italian dressing
- ❑ 1 (6 ounce) box seasoned croutons
- ❑ 1 (11 ounce) package frozen Texas garlic toast
- ❑ Chocolate ice cream
- ❑ 1 (10 ounce) package frozen raspberries in syrup
- ❑ Chocolate syrup

Lobster Boat Special

Easy Steamed Lobster Tails
Cajun Squash
Tomato-Mozzarella Salad
Bacon Breadsticks
Choco-Banana Cream Pie

Easy Steamed Lobster Tails

4 (4 ounce) lobster tails
3 lemons, halved
Salt
Butter

- Arrange lobster tails (meat facing outward) in baking dish. Pour 1½ cups water, juice of ¼ lemon and a little salt in baking dish. Microwave on HIGH for 5 minutes.
- Turn dish and microwave an additional 5 minutes or until shells are bright pink. Loosen meat from shell with knife and serve with melted butter and lemon halves.

Cajun Squash

3 yellow squash
3 zucchini
1 (12 ounce) bottle squeeze butter
Cajun seasoning

- Slice squash and zucchini diagonally and arrange in glass pie plate. Cover with plastic wrap and open small vent. Microwave on HIGH for 3 minutes, turn and cook additional 1 minute or until squash are slightly tender.
- Remove plastic wrap and squeeze butter over squash. Sprinkle liberally with Cajun seasoning. Serve hot.

Tomato-Mozzarella Salad

3 vine-ripened tomatoes
6 ounces fresh mozzarella
Fresh basil, minced
Italian salad dressing

- Slice tomatoes and mozzarella about ¼-inch thick. Place slice of tomato on serving plate and top with mozzarella slice. Sprinkle basil and drizzle dressing over each.

Bacon Breadsticks

3 slices bacon
9 breadsticks

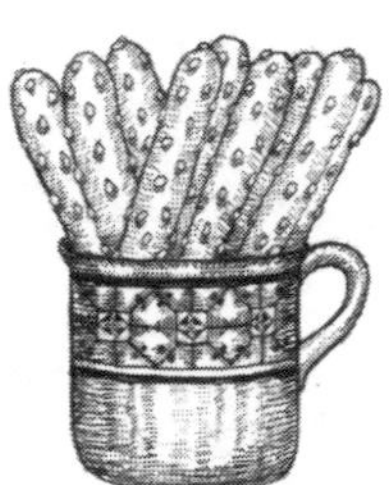

- Cut each bacon slice with kitchen shears lengthwise in 3 pieces. Wrap each piece at an angle around 1 breadstick.
- Place breadsticks on paper towel and cover with extra paper towel. Microwave on HIGH for about 2 minutes. Dry breadsticks with paper towels and serve.

Choco-Banana Cream Pie

1 (3.9 ounce) package instant chocolate pudding
2 bananas
1 (9-inch) ready shortbread piecrust
1 (7 ounce) can Reddi-Whip topping

- Prepare chocolate pudding according to package directions. Slice bananas about ¼ inch thick and line bottom of piecrust.
- Pour chocolate pudding over bananas. Place remaining banana slices around edges of piecrust. Spread or squirt whipped topping over pudding.

Grocery List:

- ❑ 4 (4 ounce) lobster tails
- ❑ 3 lemons
- ❑ Salt
- ❑ Butter
- ❑ 3 yellow squash
- ❑ 3 zucchini
- ❑ 1 (12 ounce) bottle squeeze butter
- ❑ Cajun seasoning
- ❑ 3 vine-ripened tomatoes
- ❑ 6 ounces fresh mozzarella
- ❑ Fresh basil
- ❑ 1 bottle Italian salad dressing
- ❑ Bacon
- ❑ Breadsticks
- ❑ 1 (3.9 ounce) package instant chocolate pudding
- ❑ 2 bananas
- ❑ 1 (9-inch) ready shortbread piecrust
- ❑ 1 (7 ounce) can Reddi-Whip topping

Lunch for Success

Stand-Up Shrimp Salad
Millionaire Sandwiches
Glazed-Fruit Salad
Tapioca Pudding with Fresh Blueberries

Stand-Up Shrimp Salad

1 (12 ounce) package frozen, cooked salad shrimp, thawed, drained
1 (32 ounce) carton deli potato salad
1 bunch fresh green onions with tops, chopped
1½ teaspoons dried thyme leaves

- In large bowl, combine well drained shrimp and potato salad and mix well.
- Add white parts of onions and thyme leaves and toss lightly. Add a little seasoned black pepper, if desired.
- Serve in pretty salad bowl and garnish with reserved chopped green tops.

Millionaire Sandwiches

¾ pound bacon, cooked, crumbled
1 (4 ounce) can chopped ripe olives
½ cup chopped pecans
1½ cups mayonnaise

- In bowl, combine all ingredients and blend well. Spread on crust-trimmed white or whole wheat bread and cut sandwiches into 3 strips.

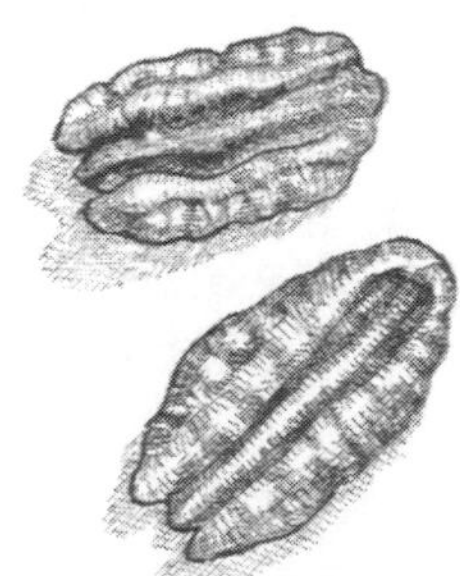

Glazed-Fruit Salad

1 (20 ounce) can apricot pie filling, chilled
1 (15 ounce) can pineapple chunks, drained, chilled
2 (11 ounce) cans mandarin oranges, drained, chilled
2 or 3 bananas, sliced, chilled

- In large bowl, combine apricot pie filling, pineapple chunks and mandarin oranges. Mix gently and carefully to keep fruit intact.
- Fold in bananas and spoon into pretty crystal bowl. Cover with plastic wrap and refrigerate until ready to serve.

Tapioca Pudding with Fresh Blueberries

1 or 2 (16 ounce) cartons tapioca pudding
1 small carton fresh blueberries, washed, drained

- Spoon serving-size amount of tapioca pudding into sherbet glasses. Garnish with several blueberries in each glass.

Company coming for lunch? Three different recipes to make in 30 minutes seems like you might need roller-skates to get this all done. In fact, there are only 5 cans and 2 packages to open, green onions to chop, bananas to slice and bacon to fry. Use crystal bowls, sherbet glasses, cloth napkins and you have a "gourmet" lunch.

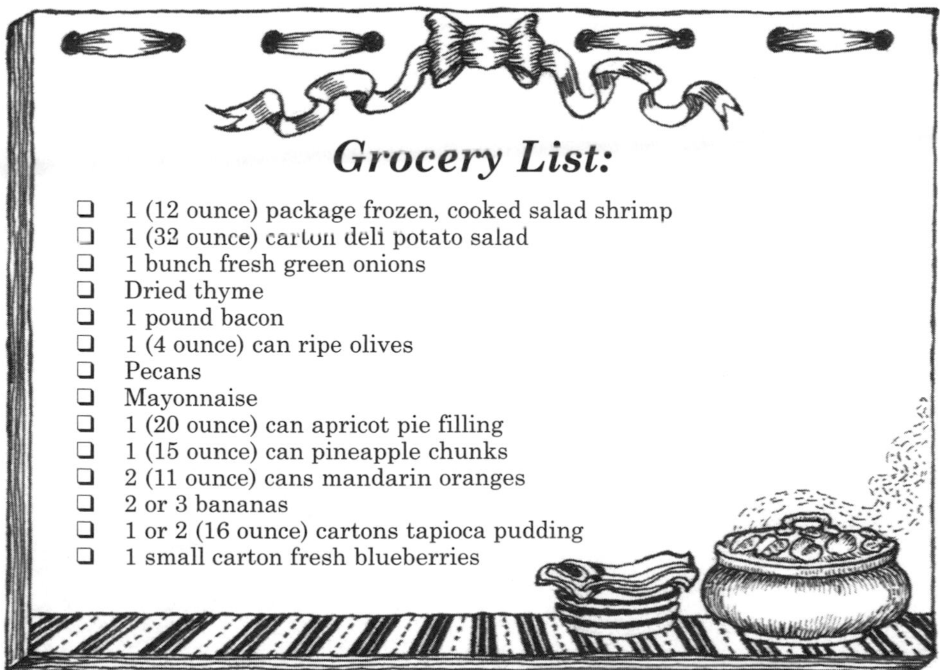

Grocery List:

- ❑ 1 (12 ounce) package frozen, cooked salad shrimp
- ❑ 1 (32 ounce) carton deli potato salad
- ❑ 1 bunch fresh green onions
- ❑ Dried thyme
- ❑ 1 pound bacon
- ❑ 1 (4 ounce) can ripe olives
- ❑ Pecans
- ❑ Mayonnaise
- ❑ 1 (20 ounce) can apricot pie filling
- ❑ 1 (15 ounce) can pineapple chunks
- ❑ 2 (11 ounce) cans mandarin oranges
- ❑ 2 or 3 bananas
- ❑ 1 or 2 (16 ounce) cartons tapioca pudding
- ❑ 1 small carton fresh blueberries

Down by the Dock

Seafood Delight
Swiss Salad With Vinaigrette Dressing
Carrots and Peas
Banana Splits

Seafood Delight

2 (6 ounce) cans small, veined shrimp, drained
1 (6 ounce) can crabmeat, drained, flaked
2 (10 ounce) cans corn chowder
2 cups seasoned dry breadcrumbs, divided

- ◆ Preheat oven to 375°. In bowl, combine shrimp, crab, chowder and ¾ cup breadcrumbs. Spoon into greased, glass pie plate.
- ◆ Sprinkle remaining breadcrumbs over top of casserole and bake 25 minutes.

Swiss Salad

1 large head romaine lettuce
1 bunch fresh green onions with tops, chopped
1 (8 ounce) package shredded Swiss cheese
½ cup toasted sunflower seeds

- ◆ Tear lettuce into bite-size pieces. Add onions, cheese, sunflower seeds and toss. Serve with vinaigrette dressing.

Vinaigrette Dressing:
⅔ cup oil
⅓ cup red wine vinegar
1 tablespoon seasoned salt

- ◆ Mix all ingredients and refrigerate.

Carrots and Peas

1 (15 ounce) can sliced carrots, drained
1 (15 ounce) can green peas, drained
¼ cup (½ stick) butter
⅓ cup chopped cashew nuts

◆ In saucepan, combine carrots, peas, butter and cashew nuts. Heat until butter melts and mix well. Serve hot.

Banana Splits

Bananas
Ice cream: chocolate, vanilla, strawberry or selected favorites
Dessert toppings: fudge sauce, butterscotch sauce, cherries, chopped nuts
1 (7 ounce) can Reddi-Whip cream topping

◆ This is a "make-your-own dessert!" Give each person a bowl or the traditional boat-shaped dishes and a banana.

◆ Place ice cream in middle of table with your favorite toppings and WOW, everybody's having fun!

Here's a hot, delicious seafood casserole prepared simply by opening cans. The great flavors in the rice make a fantastic side dish and the crunch of the cucumbers and celery give zip to this speedy menu. But wait—the fun really starts when the crew realizes Banana Splits are on the way.

Grocery List:

- ❑ 2 (6 ounce) cans small, veined shrimp
- ❑ 1 (6 ounce) can crabmeat
- ❑ 2 (10 ounce) cans corn chowder
- ❑ 1 (15 ounce) can seasoned breadcrumbs
- ❑ 1 head romaine lettuce
- ❑ Green onions
- ❑ 1 (8 ounce) package shredded Swiss cheese
- ❑ Toasted sunflower seeds
- ❑ Oil
- ❑ Red wine vinegar
- ❑ Seasoned salt
- ❑ 1 (15 ounce) can sliced carrots
- ❑ 1 (15 ounce) can green peas
- ❑ Butter
- ❑ ⅓ cup chopped cashew nuts
- ❑ Bananas
- ❑ Ice cream, assorted flavors
- ❑ Dessert toppings, assorted favorites
- ❑ 1 (7 ounce) can Reddi-Whip cream topping

Shrimp Alfredo

12 ounces fresh asparagus spears, trimmed
1 sweet red bell pepper, julienned
1 (12 ounce) package frozen, shelled, veined, uncooked shrimp, tails removed, thawed
1 (16 ounce) jar alfredo sauce

- Cut asparagus in 1½-inch pieces. Combine asparagus and bell pepper in skillet with ¼ cup water. Bring to boil, reduce heat, cover and simmer about 5 minutes.
- Add shrimp, cook and stir about 4 minutes or until shrimp turns pink.
- Stir in alfredo sauce and a little black pepper. Simmer for 3 to 4 minutes or until mixture heats through.

Buttered Linguine

8 ounces uncooked linguine
1 green bell pepper, seeded, chopped
¼ cup (½ stick) butter
2 tablespoons chopped fresh chives

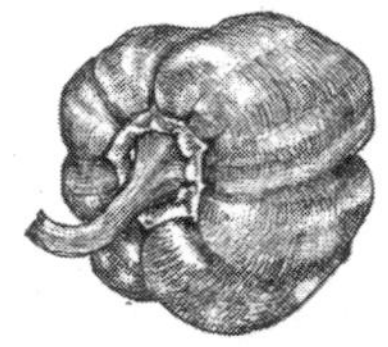

- Cook linguine according to package directions. Drain, cover and keep warm.
- In skillet, saute bell pepper in butter until crisp-tender. Add bell pepper and chives to linguine and mix well.
- Spoon linguine mixture into serving bowl and pour shrimp alfredo over pasta.
- Garnish shrimp with fresh, shredded parmesan cheese, if desired.

Broccoli Salad

5 to 6 cups broccoli florets (no stems)
1 sweet orange bell pepper, julienned
1 (8 ounce) package cubed mozzarella cheese
1 teaspoon seasoned salt

◆ Combine all ingredients and mix well. Toss with creamy Italian salad dressing. Salad needs to be chilled. If you can't get it made that morning, place in sealed freezer bag for 15 minutes (not longer). It will be chilled and be ready to serve in about 30 minutes.

Strawberry Ice Cream and Cookies

Strawberry ice cream
Powdered sugar wedding cookies
1 (10 ounce) box frozen strawberries

◆ Serve strawberry ice cream in sherbet dishes and top with sweetened strawberries. Serve with cookies.

Alfredo sauce is a wonderful, rich, creamy cheese sauce that tickles the taste buds in seafood, asparagus and pasta for this supper by the sea. Other vegetables can be added to the shrimp mixture, such as 1 cup fresh mushrooms or 1 cup sugar snap peas. They will cook along with the asparagus and bell pepper in the same amount of time. What a colorful dish along with lots of nutrition and good eats!

Grocery List:

- ❑ 1 bunch fresh asparagus
- ❑ 1 green and 1 red bell pepper
- ❑ 1 (12 ounce) package frozen shrimp, veined, uncooked shrimp, tails removed
- ❑ 1 (16 ounce) jar alfredo sauce
- ❑ 8 ounces uncooked linguine
- ❑ Butter
- ❑ Fresh chives
- ❑ Broccoli flowerets
- ❑ Orange bell pepper
- ❑ 1 (8 ounce) package cubed mozzarella
- ❑ Seasoned salt
- ❑ Strawberry ice cream
- ❑ Powdered sugar wedding cookies
- ❑ 1 (10 ounce) carton frozen, sweetened strawberries

Scrumptious Shrimp Dinner

Shrimp Newburg over White Rice
Italian Green Beans
Pistachio Salad

Shrimp Newburg

1 (10½ ounce) can condensed cream of shrimp soup
¼ cup water
1 teaspoon seafood seasoning
1 (1 pound) package frozen cooked salad shrimp, thawed

◆ In saucepan, combine soup, water and seafood seasoning and bring to boil. Reduce heat and stir in shrimp. Heat thoroughly.

White Rice

2 cups uncooked, instant white rice

◆ Prepare white rice according to package directions.

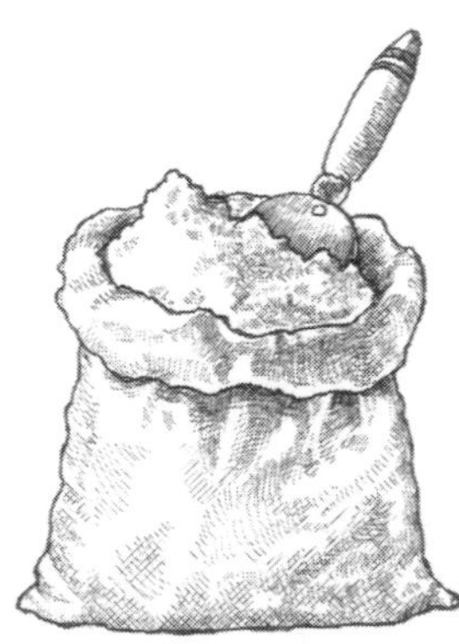

Italian Green Beans

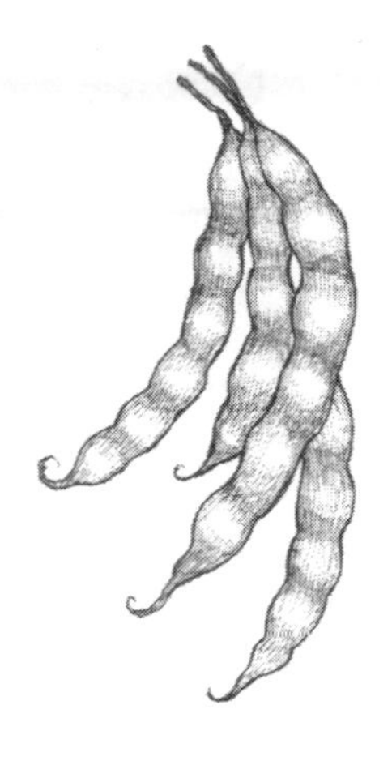

1 (16 ounce) package frozen Italian green beans
3 green onions and tops, chopped
2 tablespoons (¼ stick) butter
1 teaspoon mixed Italian seasoning

◆ Mix all ingredients in 2-quart saucepan and cook in microwave according to frozen package directions.

Pistachio Salad

1 (4 ounce) package instant pistachio pudding
1 (15½ ounce) can crushed pineapple
1 (8 ounce) carton whipped topping

◆ Stir instant pudding and pineapple together and fold in whipped topping. Place in freezer until ready to serve.

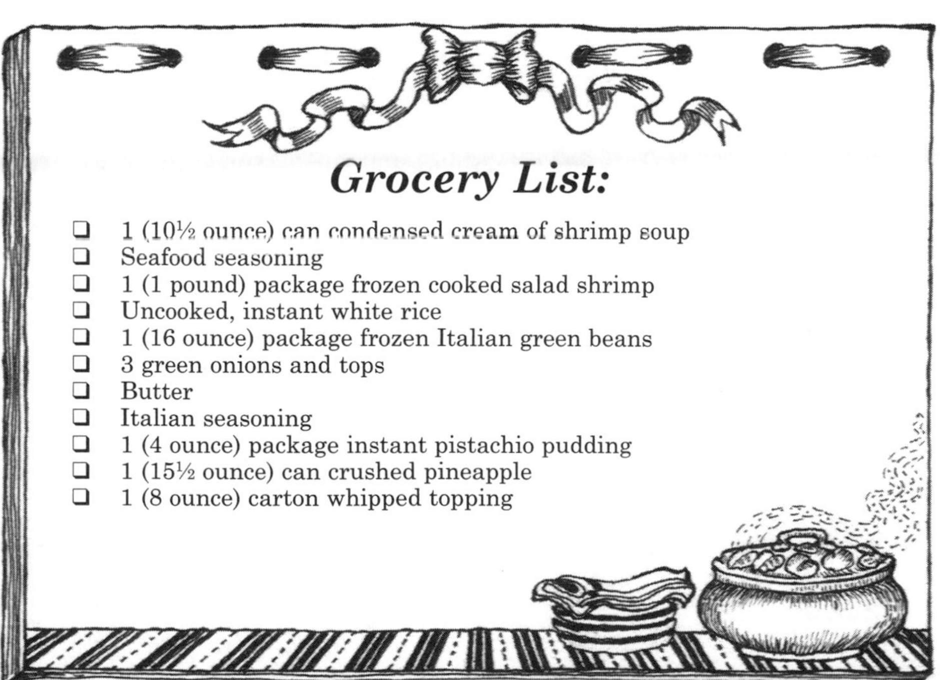

Grocery List:

- ❑ 1 (10½ ounce) can condensed cream of shrimp soup
- ❑ Seafood seasoning
- ❑ 1 (1 pound) package frozen cooked salad shrimp
- ❑ Uncooked, instant white rice
- ❑ 1 (16 ounce) package frozen Italian green beans
- ❑ 3 green onions and tops
- ❑ Butter
- ❑ Italian seasoning
- ❑ 1 (4 ounce) package instant pistachio pudding
- ❑ 1 (15½ ounce) can crushed pineapple
- ❑ 1 (8 ounce) carton whipped topping

Sunset on the Patio

Apricot-Glazed Chicken
Crunchy Salad
Twice-Baked Potatoes
Blueberry Crunch

Apricot-Glazed Chicken

½ cup prepared teriyaki baste and glaze
⅔ teaspoon dried ginger
1 cup apricot preserves
8 boneless, skinless chicken breast halves, thawed

- In small bowl, combine teriyaki glaze, ginger and apricot preserves. Mix well and set aside.
- Salt and pepper all chicken breast halves and place on grill over medium heat. Grill 18 to 22 minutes (depending on size of chicken breasts) or until chicken is fork-tender.
- Turn chicken once on grill. When chicken has 5 to 10 minutes remaining in cooking time, brush liberally with teriyaki-apricot mixture.

Crunchy Salad

¼ cup sesame seeds
½ cup sunflower seeds
½ cup almonds, sliced
1 head red leaf lettuce

- Toast sesame seeds, sunflower seeds and almonds at 300° for about 15 minutes or until light brown. Tear lettuce into bite-size pieces and add seed mixture. Toss with creamy Italian salad dressing.

Twice-Baked Potatoes

1 (16 ounce) package twice-baked potatoes, thawed
Butter
Shredded cheese

- Heat according to package directions or warm on grill with chicken. Add butter and top with shredded cheese.

Blueberry Crunch

1 (20 ounce) can blueberry pie filling, chilled
1 (14 ounce) package pecan-shortbread cookies
1 (8 ounce) carton whipped topping or vanilla ice cream

- Spoon blueberry pie filling into 6 dessert dishes and break up, not crush, several cookies over blueberries.
- Top with large spoonful whipped topping or ice cream.

Time your dinner so you can watch the day drift into night while dining on delicious Apricot-Glazed Chicken. When day is done, you can feast on blueberry crunch, a super speedy, super delicious dessert.

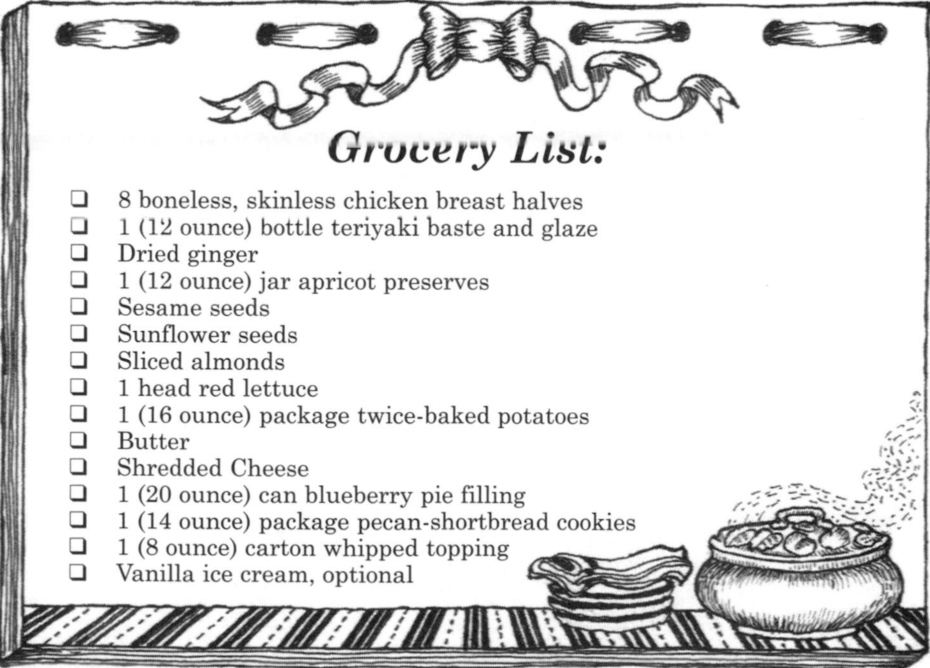

Grocery List:

- ❑ 8 boneless, skinless chicken breast halves
- ❑ 1 (12 ounce) bottle teriyaki baste and glaze
- ❑ Dried ginger
- ❑ 1 (12 ounce) jar apricot preserves
- ❑ Sesame seeds
- ❑ Sunflower seeds
- ❑ Sliced almonds
- ❑ 1 head red lettuce
- ❑ 1 (16 ounce) package twice-baked potatoes
- ❑ Butter
- ❑ Shredded Cheese
- ❑ 1 (20 ounce) can blueberry pie filling
- ❑ 1 (14 ounce) package pecan-shortbread cookies
- ❑ 1 (8 ounce) carton whipped topping
- ❑ Vanilla ice cream, optional

Chicken Grill

Grilled-Lemon Chicken
Summer Salad
Hard Rolls and Relish Plate
Frosted Sugar Cookies

Grilled-Lemon Chicken

6 boneless, skinless chicken breast halves
2 teaspoons garlic salt
1 tablespoon freshly grated lemon peel
2 teaspoons dried thyme leaves

- In small bowl, combine garlic salt, lemon peel, thyme leaves and a little black pepper.
- Heat coals and spray grill with cooking spray. Sprinkle seasoning mixture over chicken breasts.
- Grill chicken 20 to 25 minutes or until chicken is no longer pink and juices run clear. Turn once during cooking.

Summer Salad

1 (16 ounce) package frozen green peas, thawed, drained
1 small head cauliflower, cut into bite-size pieces
1 (8 ounce) carton sour cream, ⅓ cup mayonnaise
1 (1 ounce) packet dry ranch-style salad dressing mix

- In large bowl with lid, combine peas and cauliflower. In separate bowl, combine sour cream, mayonnaise and dressing mix and toss with vegetables.

Hard Rolls

1 package bakery hard rolls or garlic bread

- Wrap rolls or bread in foil and warm on grill away from direct flame.

Tip: Bakery hard rolls are very good and even better with a big dab of butter. Crusty, buttered garlic bread is also a favorite with grilled meats.

Relish Plate

Ripe olives
Green olives
Pickles
Fresh green onions

- Arrange relish ingredients on serving tray.

Tip: These condiments, as well as radishes, pickled green okra, celery and a few hot peppers are great additions to this summer supper.

Frosted Sugar Cookies

1 package bakery sugar cookies

Icing for Sugar Cookies:
1 (3 ounce) package cream cheese, softened
1 teaspoon vanilla
1 cup powdered sugar

- Blend all ingredients, mix well and ice cookies.

Grocery List:

- ❑ 6 boneless, skinless chicken breast halves
- ❑ Garlic salt
- ❑ 2 lemons
- ❑ Dried thyme leaves
- ❑ 1 (16 ounce) package frozen green peas
- ❑ 1 small head cauliflower
- ❑ 1 (8 ounce) carton sour cream
- ❑ Mayonnaise
- ❑ 1 (1 ounce) packet dry ranch-style salad dressing mix
- ❑ Bakery hard rolls or 1 loaf garlic bread
- ❑ Green or ripe olives, dill pickles, pickled green okra, fresh green onions, radishes, celery or hot peppers
- ❑ Butter
- ❑ 1 package bakery sugar cookies
- ❑ 1 (3 ounce) package cream cheese
- ❑ Vanilla
- ❑ Powdered sugar

On the Patio

Jam-Glazed Pork Tenderloins
Fresh Broccoli
Pasta Salad and Sliced Tomatoes
Brandied Cherries Over Ice Cream

Jam-Glazed Pork Tenderloins

4 pork tenderloins (about 2 pounds)

Jam Glaze:
1¼ cups grape or plum jam
¼ cup dry sherry, ¼ cup oil
2 teaspoons chopped fresh rosemary leaves
1 small onion, finely chopped

- In saucepan over low heat, combine jam, oil, rosemary leaves and chopped onion. Heat and stir just until ingredients mix well.
- Place pork in resealable plastic bag and pour half jam mixture over pork. Seal and marinate 15 minutes, turning once.
- Remove pork from marinade and grill over unheated side of grill about 20 minutes. Turn, brush with reserved basting marinade and continue to cook until pork is no longer pink. Discard any remaining marinade.
- When ready to serve, heat reserved jam mixture and slice pork tenderloins. Serve heated jam mixture over sliced pork.

Fresh Broccoli

4 cups broccoli florets
Butter, melted
Tony Chachere's Creole Seasoning

- Place broccoli in microwave-safe bowl, cover with plastic wrap and vent corner. Microwave on HIGH for 2 minutes and turn. Microwave another 1 to 2 minutes or until slightly tender. Season with butter and Creole seasoning.

Pasta Salad and Sliced Tomatoes

1 (24 ounce) carton deli pasta salad
1 (4 ounce) can chopped pimento, drained
1 or 2 dill pickles, chopped
4 or 5 vine-ripened tomatoes, quartered

- In salad bowl, combine pasta salad, pimento and pickles. Place quartered tomatoes around edges.

Brandied Cherries over Ice Cream

1 (15 ounce) can pitted sweet bing cherries
Orange juice
⅓ cup sugar
2 tablespoons corn starch
2 tablespoons brandy, optional

- Drain cherry liquid into 1-cup measuring cup and add orange juice or cranberry juice to equal 1 cup liquid. Set cherries aside.
- In saucepan, combine cherry-liquid mixture, sugar and corn starch and mix well. Cook and stir over medium to high heat just until liquid thickens. Stir in brandy and cherries.
- Place 2 scoops vanilla ice cream in sherbet dishes and pour sauce over ice cream.

There is something about eating on the patio that makes everything taste better. Since pork tenderloin is such a popular menu item, this meal will be a big hit outside or in. Its tender, juicy flavor is complemented by rich side dishes and fabulous dessert.

Grocery List:

- ❑ 4 pork tenderloins (about 2 pounds)
- ❑ Grape or plum jam
- ❑ Dry sherry
- ❑ Oil
- ❑ Fresh rosemary leaves
- ❑ 1 small onion
- ❑ 4 cups broccoli florets
- ❑ Butter
- ❑ Tony Chachere's Creole seasoning
- ❑ 1 (24 ounce) carton deli pasta salad
- ❑ 1 (4 ounce) can ❑ chopped pimento
- ❑ 1 or 2 dill pickles
- ❑ 4 to 5 vine-ripened tomatoes
- ❑ 1 (15 ounce) can pitted sweet bing cherries
- ❑ Orange juice
- ❑ Sugar
- ❑ Corn starch
- ❑ Brandy, optional
- ❑ Vanilla ice cream

I Flip Over Burgers

Turkey Burgers
Tortilla Chips and Hot Dill Pickles
Refried Beans and Cheese
Chocolate-Cherry Drops

Turkey Burgers

2 pounds ground turkey
1 (16 ounce) jar hot chipotle salsa, divided
8 slices Monterey Jack cheese
Sesame seed hamburger buns

- In large mixing bowl, combine ground turkey with 1 cup salsa. Mix well and shape into 8 patties.
- Place patties on broiler pan and broil 12 to 15 minutes. Turn once during cooking. Top each patty with cheese slice and grill just long enough to melt cheese.
- Place burgers on buns, spoon heaping tablespoon salsa over cheese and top with half of bun.

Tip: Some salsas are a little thinner than others, therefore if ground turkey and salsa seem a little too soupy, add about ¼ cup breadcrumbs or cracker crumbs to make patties firmer.

Tortilla Chips and Hot Dill Pickles

Chips
Hot dill pickles

- Arrange on serving tray.

Refried Beans and Cheese

2 (15 ounce) cans refried beans
¾ to 1 cup hot chipotle salsa
1 (8 ounce) package shredded cheddar cheese
3 fresh green onions, chopped

- Preheat oven to 350°. Spoon refried beans into glass pie plate and cover with chipotle salsa. (Use 3 cans if you need to serve more than 5 or 6.) Cover with foil and heat about 10 minutes.
- When ready to serve burgers, sprinkle shredded cheese over refried beans and return to oven for a few minutes to let cheese barely melt.
- Sprinkle chopped green onions over top for garnish.

Chocolate-Cherry Drops

1 (6 ounce) package chocolate chips
2 tablespoons milk
1 (8 ounce) jar maraschino cherries, drained, patted dry, sliced

- In top of double boiler over hot water, melt chocolate chips. Add milk and stir constantly to make thick sauce. Add cherries and mix well. Drop by teaspoonfuls on wax paper and cool until firm.

Who needs takeout when you can grill (or broil) these healthier burgers. Hot salsa and chopped green onions add pizzaz to refried beans.

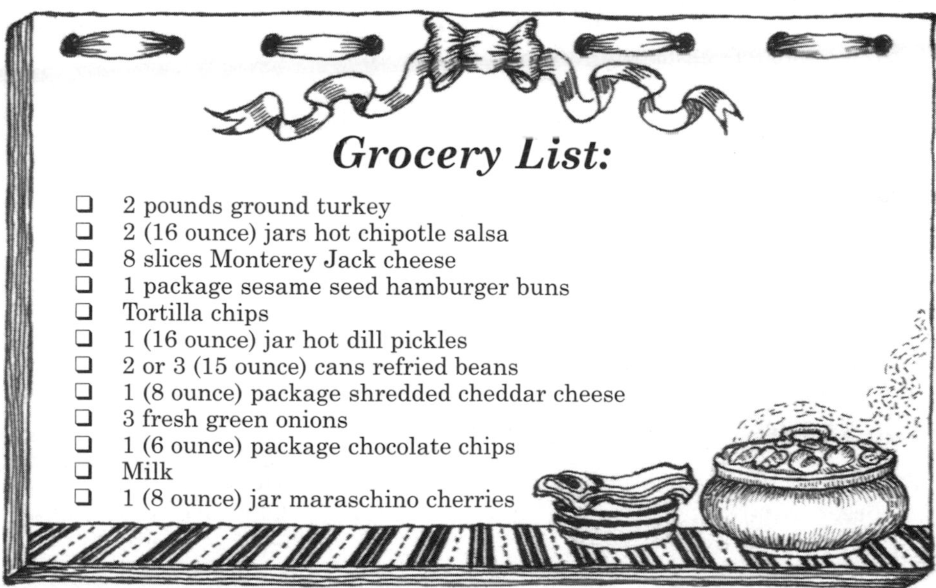

Grocery List:

- ❑ 2 pounds ground turkey
- ❑ 2 (16 ounce) jars hot chipotle salsa
- ❑ 8 slices Monterey Jack cheese
- ❑ 1 package sesame seed hamburger buns
- ❑ Tortilla chips
- ❑ 1 (16 ounce) jar hot dill pickles
- ❑ 2 or 3 (15 ounce) cans refried beans
- ❑ 1 (8 ounce) package shredded cheddar cheese
- ❑ 3 fresh green onions
- ❑ 1 (6 ounce) package chocolate chips
- ❑ Milk
- ❑ 1 (8 ounce) jar maraschino cherries

Sassy Burger Supper

Sassy Burgers
Potato Pancakes
Stuffed Tomatoes
Honeydew Melon Slices

Sassy Burgers

You need 8 kaiser buns for these Sassy Burgers.

2 pounds lean ground beef
1 packet taco seasoning mix
1 cup regular or hot chipotle salsa
8 slices hot pepper-jack cheese

- In large mixing bowl, combine beef, taco seasoning and ¼ cup salsa. Shape mixture into 8 patties.
- If you are grilling, cook patties about 12 minutes or until thoroughly cooked, turning once. To broil in oven, place patties on broiler pan 4 to 5 inches from heat and broil until thoroughly cooked. Turn once during cooking.
- When patties are almost done, place buns cut side down on grill and heat 1 or 2 minutes. Place 8 patties on bottom half of buns, top with cheese and cook an additional 1 minute or until cheese melts. Top with heaping tablespoon salsa, then with top half of bun.

Potato Pancakes

3 pounds white potatoes, peeled, grated
1 onion, finely minced
3 eggs, beaten
½ cup seasoned, dry breadcrumbs

- In large bowl, combine potatoes, onions, eggs, little salt and pepper and breadcrumbs and mix well. In skillet, drop by spoonfuls in hot oil and brown on both sides.

Stuffed Tomatoes

6 large vine-ripened tomatoes
1 (16 ounce) carton small-curd cottage cheese, drained
1 bunch fresh green onions, chopped
½ cup mayonnaise, ½ teaspoon Tony Chachere's Creole seasoning

- Cut very thin slice on bottom of each tomato so it will sit upright. Cut 6 wedges in each tomato about two-thirds of way down. Turn tomatoes upside down and drain on paper towels.
- In mixing bowl, combine cottage cheese, onions and mayonnaise with a little salt and pepper. Turn each tomato upright and fill space in center with cottage cheese mixture.
- Place tomatoes on individual salad plates or one serving plate.

Honeydew Melon Slices

2 honeydew melons or refrigerated seasonal fruit

- Peel and slice melons and place on serving plate.

A burger is a burger right? Not true! Salsa adds sizzle to the ground beef in this recipe. For extra flavor, use hot chipotle salsa.

Grocery List:

- ❑ 2 pounds lean ground beef
- ❑ 1 packet taco seasoning
- ❑ 1 (12 ounce) jar regular or hot chipotle salsa
- ❑ 1 (8 count) package kaiser or regular hamburger buns
- ❑ 8 slices hot pepper-jack cheese
- ❑ 6 large vine-ripened tomatoes
- ❑ 1 (16 ounce) carton small-curd cottage cheese
- ❑ 1 bunch fresh green onions
- ❑ Mayonnaise
- ❑ Tony Chachere's Creole seasoning
- ❑ 3 pounds white potatoes
- ❑ 1 onion
- ❑ 3 eggs
- ❑ Seasoned, dry breadcrumbs
- ❑ Honeydew melons or frozen or refrigerated seasonal fruit

Southwest Grilled Burgers

You need 6 hamburger buns for these burgers.

1½ pounds lean ground beef
¾ cup hot chipotle salsa, divided
¼ cup seasoned dry breadcrumbs
6 slices pepper-jack cheese

- Heat grill. In large bowl, combine ground beef, 4 tablespoons salsa and seasoned dry breadcrumbs and mix well.
- Shape mixture into 6 (½-inch thick) patties and grill patties about 14 minutes or broil in oven about 12 minutes. Turn once during cooking.
- Place buns cut side down on grill and cook about 2 minutes or until buns toast lightly. Place 1 slice cheese on each cooked patty and cook just long enough for cheese to begin to melt.
- Move patties and cheese to bottom halves of buns, add 1 tablespoon salsa to each and top bun.

Deviled Eggs

6 to 8 hard-boiled eggs, halved lengthwise
2 heaping tablespoons sweet pickle relish, drained
½ cup mayonnaise, salt to taste
2 tablespoons salsa

- Remove yolks from egg whites and set whites aside. Mash egg yolks and combine with pickle relish, mayonnaise and salsa. Spoon mixture into egg whites, using all mixture.
- Place stuffed eggs around edge of serving platter.

Jazzy Beans

3 (15 ounce) cans pinto beans, drained
¾ cup hot chipotle salsa
½ cup packed light brown sugar

◆ In saucepan over medium heat, combine beans, salsa and brown sugar until hot.

Potato Chips or Tortilla Chips

1 large bag potato or tortilla chips

◆ Select your favorite chips and pile them high in center of serving platter lined with deviled eggs.

Hot Fudge Sundaes

Chocolate ice cream sauce
Vanilla ice cream
Chopped nuts
Maraschino cherries

◆ Microwave jar of chocolate sauce on HIGH according to label directions. Stir and cook until desired temperature. Pour over scoops of ice cream in bowls and top with nuts and cherries.

Give the predictable grilled burger a sassy Southwest makeover! The salsa gives the burger a nice change of pace. Prepare beans and eggs before grilling and you will have plenty of time left in your 30 minutes to grill.

Grocery List:

- ❑ 1½ pounds lean ground beef
- ❑ 1 (16 ounce) jar hot chipotle salsa
- ❑ ¼ cup seasoned dry breadcrumbs
- ❑ 6 slices pepper-jack cheese
- ❑ 6 hamburger buns with sesame seeds
- ❑ 6 or 8 large eggs
- ❑ Sweet pickle relish
- ❑ Mayonnaise
- ❑ 3 (15 ounce) cans pinto beans
- ❑ Brown sugar
- ❑ Potato chips or tortilla chips
- ❑ Chocolate ice cream sauce
- ❑ Vanilla ice cream
- ❑ Chopped nuts
- ❑ Maraschino cherries

Special Grilling Tonight

Orange-Dijon Chops
Romaine-Almond Salad
Broccoli-Rice Au Gratin
Scotch Shortbread

Orange-Dijon Chops

1 cup orange marmalade
3 tablespoons dijon-style mustard
3 tablespoons soy sauce
8 (¾-inch thick) pork loin chops

- In small saucepan over low heat, stir marmalade, dijon-style mustard and soy sauce until preserves melt.
- When ready to grill, sprinkle both sides of pork chops with salt and pepper. Place chops on grill about 5 inches from heat.
- Cook about 15 minutes or until pork is no longer pink in center. Turn once during cooking and brush with preserve mixture last 2 minutes of cooking time.
- When ready to serve, heat preserves mixture to boiling and serve hot with pork chops.

Romaine-Almond Salad

1 bunch romaine lettuce, torn into pieces
2 (11 ounce) cans mandarin oranges, well drained
½ cup almonds, sliced, toasted
1 (8 ounce) bottle poppy seed dressing

- In salad bowl, combine lettuce, oranges and toasted almonds. Toss with enough dressing to moisten salad.

Tip: To toast almonds, put nuts in small pan and heat at 275° about 12 minutes. Do this while you are putting the rice together.

Broccoli-Rice Au Gratin

2 (6 ounce) boxes broccoli-rice au gratin mix
Butter

- Cook according to package directions.

Scotch Shortbread

½ cup (1 stick) unsalted butter, softened
⅓ cup sugar
1¼ cups flour
Powdered sugar

- Preheat oven to 325°. Cream butter and sugar until light and fluffy. Add flour and pinch of salt and mix well. Spread dough in 8-inch square pan and bake for 20 minutes or until light brown. Let shortbread cool in pan, dust with powdered sugar and cut into squares.

The combination of orange marmalade, dijon-style mustard and soy sauce really puts some spirit in these pork chops and they are so good and so easy! Combine them with broccoli, rice and our fantastic salad to create a winner.

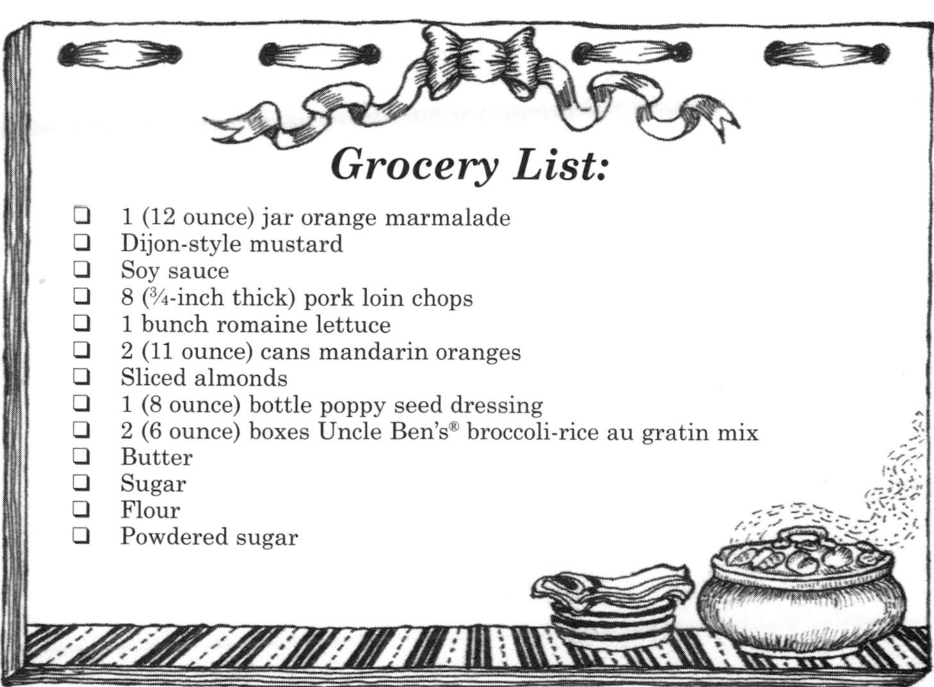

Grocery List:

- ❑ 1 (12 ounce) jar orange marmalade
- ❑ Dijon-style mustard
- ❑ Soy sauce
- ❑ 8 (¾-inch thick) pork loin chops
- ❑ 1 bunch romaine lettuce
- ❑ 2 (11 ounce) cans mandarin oranges
- ❑ Sliced almonds
- ❑ 1 (8 ounce) bottle poppy seed dressing
- ❑ 2 (6 ounce) boxes Uncle Ben's® broccoli-rice au gratin mix
- ❑ Butter
- ❑ Sugar
- ❑ Flour
- ❑ Powdered sugar

Grilled Swordfish Steaks With Mango Salsa

4 (6 to 8 ounce) swordfish steaks
Extra-virgin olive oil
1 lime, halved
Garlic salt

- Rinse and dry swordfish steaks. Rub olive oil over surface, drizzle juice of ½ lime and sprinkle with garlic salt. Grill steaks over medium heat for about 3 to 5 minutes per side. Do not overcook.

Mango Salsa:
2 ripe mangoes, peeled, finely chopped
1 jalapeno, seeded, finely chopped
4 green onions with tops, finely chopped
1 yellow bell pepper, seeded, finely chopped

- Mix all ingredients in bowl and squeeze remaining ½ lime over salsa. Chill while steaks cook.

Grilled, Toasty Garlic Bread

1 (16 ounce) loaf French bread, sliced
Butter
Garlic salt

- Separate slices of bread, spread butter on both sides and sprinkle with garlic salt. Lay slices across grill and cook until crispy or cook on grill wrapped in foil. If grill is overcrowded, wrap in foil and warm in oven at 325° for 10 to 15 minutes.

Grilled Veggie Kabobs

8 small white onions, peeled
1 pint grape tomatoes
2 green and 2 yellow bell peppers, seeded, quartered
Button mushrooms

- Use remaining extra-virgin olive oil to coat vegetables. Place all veggies except tomatoes on skewers or in grilling basket. Put veggies on grill before swordfish steak. When veggies begin to soften, move to cooler part of grill and place swordfish and tomatoes (in grilling basket) over medium heat. Do not overcook.

Creamy-Baked Potatoes

4 baking potatoes
Butter
Sour cream
1 (8 ounce) package shredded cheddar cheese

- Wash potatoes and stick fork in each. Wrap in paper towels and microwave on HIGH for about 5 to 6 minutes. Turn potatoes and microwave additional 5 to 6 minutes or until potatoes are tender.
- Split potatoes, scoop pulp in bowl, but leave ½-inch on skins. Mash potatoes, mix with butter, sour cream and cheese and place mixture in potato shells. Place in oven at 275° to keep warm.

Assorted French Pastries

Buy assorted French pastries from neighborhood bakery.

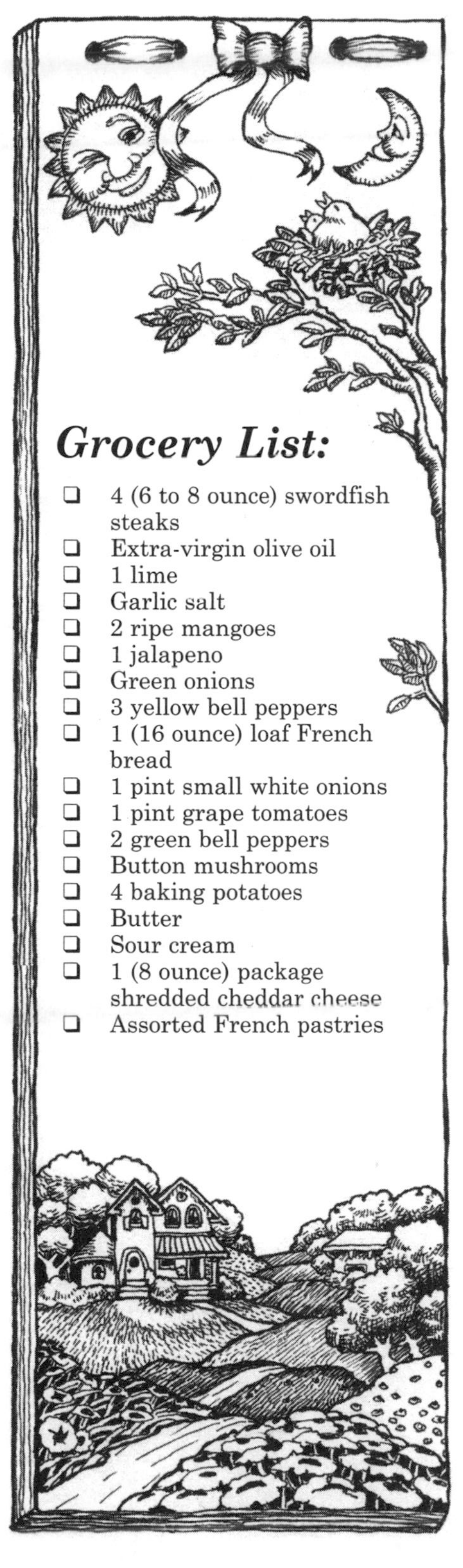

Grocery List:

- ❑ 4 (6 to 8 ounce) swordfish steaks
- ❑ Extra-virgin olive oil
- ❑ 1 lime
- ❑ Garlic salt
- ❑ 2 ripe mangoes
- ❑ 1 jalapeno
- ❑ Green onions
- ❑ 3 yellow bell peppers
- ❑ 1 (16 ounce) loaf French bread
- ❑ 1 pint small white onions
- ❑ 1 pint grape tomatoes
- ❑ 2 green bell peppers
- ❑ Button mushrooms
- ❑ 4 baking potatoes
- ❑ Butter
- ❑ Sour cream
- ❑ 1 (8 ounce) package shredded cheddar cheese
- ❑ Assorted French pastries

Neptune's Special

Grilled Tuna with Mediterranean Salsa
Potatoes Au Gratin
Cashew-Pea Salad
Jello Cups

Grilled Tuna

5 to 6 (1-inch thick) fresh tuna steaks
½ teaspoon seasoned salt
½ teaspoon minced garlic
½ teaspoon black pepper

Mediterranean Salsa:

1 (4 ounce) can chopped ripe olives, drained
1 tomato, chopped
⅓ cup olive oil, ⅓ cup crumbled feta cheese
1 teaspoon dried basil

- Sprinkle tuna steaks with seasoned salt, minced garlic and pepper.
- In small bowl, combine ripe olives, tomato, oil, feta cheese and basil. Brush salsa mixture over tuna steaks and refrigerate any leftover mixture.
- Grill tuna steaks over medium to high heat about 3 to 5 minutes. Gently turn tuna steaks and continue grilling 3 to 5 minutes. When serving, top each steak with remaining salsa.

Potatoes Au Gratin

2 to 3 (15 ounce) cans Del Monte® Savory Sides™ potatoes au gratin
1 (2.8 ounce) can french-fried onion rings

- Preheat oven to 350°. In sprayed 7 x 11-inch baking dish, place potatoes and sprinkle with onion rings. Bake about 15 minutes.

Cashew-Pea Salad

1 (16 ounce) package frozen baby peas, thawed, drained
¾ cup chopped celery, ¼ cup chopped red bell pepper, chilled
1 cup cashew pieces, chilled
½ to ¾ cup mayonnaise

- In bowl with lid, combine drained peas, celery, red bell pepper and cashews and toss.
- Add ½ cup mayonnaise and mix well. (If you want the salad creamier, add remaining ¼ cup mayonnaise.) Chill.

Jello Cups

1 package assorted gelatin dessert cups

I like a little zip in this salad and instead of ½ cup mayonnaise, I use ¼ cup regular mayonnaise and ¼ cup chipotle-chili mayonnaise. It will make you sit up and take notice of this salad.

Grocery List:

- ❑ 5 or 6 (1-inch thick) fresh tuna steaks
- ❑ Seasoned salt, minced garlic
- ❑ 1 (4 ounce) can chopped ripe olives
- ❑ 1 tomato
- ❑ Olive oil
- ❑ 1 (8 ounce) carton feta cheese
- ❑ Dried basil
- ❑ 2 or 3 (15 ounce) cans Del Monte® Savory Sides™ potatoes au gratin
- ❑ 1 (2.8 ounce) can french-fried onion rings
- ❑ 1 (16 ounce) package frozen baby peas
- ❑ Celery, sweet red bell pepper
- ❑ 1 sweet red bell pepper
- ❑ 1 cup cashews or cashew pieces
- ❑ Mayonnaise
- ❑ French's® GourMayo™ chipotle-chili mayonnaise, optional
- ❑ 1 package assorted gelatin dessert cups

Back Yard Buffet

Re-Refried Beans, Cheese and Chips
Cucumber Square
Cottage Dip With Veggies
Jalapeno Bites

Re-Refried Beans, Cheese And Chips

1 (15 ounce) can refried beans
⅓ cup chunky salsa, drained
½ teaspoon cayenne pepper
1 (8 ounce) package shredded cheddar cheese

- Preheat oven to 350°. Place refried beans in glass pie plate and stir in salsa and cayenne pepper.
- Smooth out top of beans with spoon. Heat uncovered for about 10 minutes.
- Sprinkle cheese over top of beans and return to oven for 4 to 5 minutes. Serve with chips.

Cucumber Squares

Small (3 x 3-inch) rye bread
1 (8 ounce) package cream cheese, softened
2 cucumbers, grated
1 (1 ounce) envelope dry ranch-style salad dressing mix

- Beat cream cheese in mixing bowl until creamy. Use paper towels to dry liquid completely out of cucumbers. Add cucumbers and dressing to cream cheese mixture.
- Spread on slices of small (3 x 3-inch) rye bread.

Cottage Dip With Veggies

1 (16 ounce) carton small-curd cottage cheese, drained
1 (1 ounce) envelope dry onion soup mix
Mayonnaise
Garlic powder

Veggies:
Broccoli florets
Carrot sticks
Celery sticks
Cauliflower

- Blend all ingredients well and serve with veggies.

Jalapeno Bites

1 (12 ounce) can jalapeno peppers, drained
2 cups grated cheddar cheese
4 eggs, beaten
¼ cup whole milk or cream

- Seed and chop peppers and place in greased 9-inch pie plate. Sprinkle cheese over peppers.
- Pour eggs over cheese. Bake at 375° for about 22 minutes. Cut into small slices to serve.

Grocery List:

- ❑ 1 (15 ounce) can refried beans
- ❑ Chunky salsa
- ❑ Cayenne pepper
- ❑ 1 (16 ounce) package shredded cheddar cheese
- ❑ 1 loaf party rye bread
- ❑ 1 (8 ounce) package cream cheese
- ❑ 2 cucumbers
- ❑ 1 (1 ounce) envelope dry ranch-style salad dressing mix
- ❑ 1 (16 ounce) carton small curd cottage cheese
- ❑ 1 (1 ounce) envelope dry onion dip mix
- ❑ Mayonnaise
- ❑ Garlic powder
- ❑ Broccoli
- ❑ Carrots
- ❑ Celery
- ❑ Cauliflower
- ❑ 1 (12 ounce) can jalapeno peppers
- ❑ 4 eggs
- ❑ Whole milk

Come One, Come All

Supper Salad Supreme
Cream Cheese Sandwiches
and Party Sandwiches
Cottage Dip and Chips or Veggies
Assorted Fresh Fruit

Supper Salad Supreme

2 (15 ounce) cans great northern beans, rinsed, drained
1 pound deli ham, cut into chunks
2 bunches fresh broccoli, cut into florets
1 each red bell pepper and 1 orange bell pepper, julienned
¾ pound Swiss cheese, cut into chunks

- In large bowl, combine beans, ham chunks, broccoli florets, bell peppers and chunks of Swiss cheese. Toss with garlic vinaigrette dressing.

Cream Cheese Sandwiches

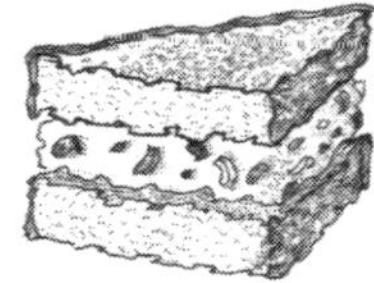

2 (8 ounce) packages cream cheese, softened
1 (4 ounce) can black olives, chopped
¾ cup finely chopped pecans
Pumpernickel rye

- Beat cream cheese until creamy and fold in olives and pecans.
- Trim crust on bread and spread cream cheese mixture on bread.
- Slice sandwiches into 3 finger strips.

Cottage Dip and Chips or Veggies

1 (16 ounce) carton small-curd cottage cheese, well drained
1 (8 ounce) package shredded Mexican 4-cheese blend
1 (1 ounce) envelope dry onion dip mix
½ cup mayonnaise

- Blend all ingredients well. Serve with chips or carrot sticks, celery sticks, jicama sticks or assorted vegetables.

Party Sandwiches

Use white bread for these sandwiches.

1 (8 ounce) package cream cheese, softened
⅔ cup mayonnaise
⅓ cup chopped stuffed olives with 2 tablespoons liquid
½ cup finely chopped pecans
6 slices pre-cooked bacon, crumbled

- ◆ In mixing bowl with mixer, beat cream cheese, mayonnaise and olive juice until smooth. Fold in olives, pecans and crumbled bacon.
- ◆ To serve, spread mixture on thin-sliced white bread (crusts removed) and cut in 4 triangles.

Assorted Fresh Fruit

Nectarines, washed, sliced
Green and red grapes, washed
Apples
Pears

- ◆ Combine sliced fruit in serving bowl and serve.

Grocery List:

- ❑ 2 (15 ounce) cans great northern beans
- ❑ 1 pound deli ham
- ❑ 2 bunches fresh broccoli
- ❑ 1 red and 1 orange bell pepper
- ❑ ¾ pound Swiss cheese
- ❑ Garlic vinaigrette dressing
- ❑ 3 (8 ounce) packages cream cheese
- ❑ 1 (4 ounce) can black olives
- ❑ ¾ cup finely chopped pecans
- ❑ Pumpernickle rye
- ❑ White bread
- ❑ Mayonnaise
- ❑ 1 (8 ounce) bottle stuffed green olives
- ❑ ½ cup chopped pecans
- ❑ 6 slices pre-cooked bacon
- ❑ 1 (16 ounce) carton small-curd cottage cheese
- ❑ 1 (8 ounce) package shredded Mexican 4-cheese blend
- ❑ 1 (1 ounce) envelope dry onion dip mix
- ❑ Red and green grapes, nectarines, apples and pears

A Twist on the Classic

A Different Sandwich
Tomato-French Onion Soup
Dill Pickle Spears
Double-Chocolate Layer Cake

A Different Sandwich

Dressing:
½ cup mayonnaise
⅓ cup dijon-style mustard
¼ cup prepared horseradish

Bread:
6 (7-inch) Italian focaccia flatbreads

Ingredients:
1 pound deli-shaved roast beef
1 (12 ounce) jar roasted red bell peppers, julienned
6 slices mozzarella cheese
Baby romaine lettuce

- In small bowl, combine dressing ingredients.
- Using serrated knife, slice bread shells in half horizontally. Spread generous amount dressing on one side of bread .
- Top with several slices roast beef, roasted peppers, cheese, romaine and remaining bread half. To serve, cut sandwiches in half.

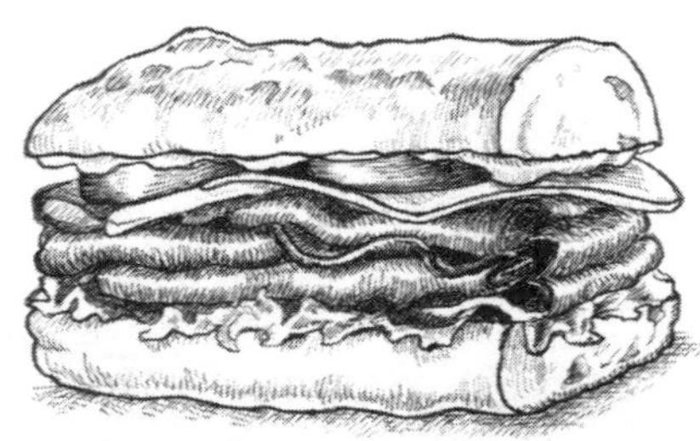

Tomato-French Onion Soup

1 (10 ounce) can fiesta nacho cheese soup
2 (10 ounce) cans french-onion soup
Grated parmesan cheese
Croutons

◆ In saucepan, combine soups and 2 soup cans of water and heat thoroughly. Serve in bowls topped with croutons and sprinkle with cheese.

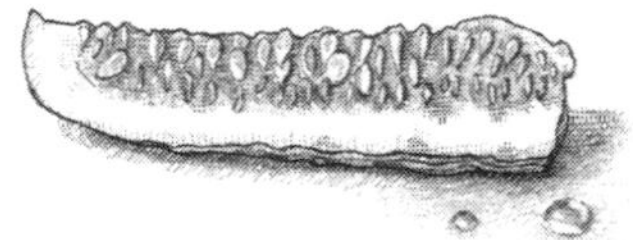

Dill Pickle Spears

1 (16 ounce) jar dill pickle spears

◆ Drain and place on serving tray.

Double Chocolate Layer Cake

1 (22 ounce) frozen double chocolate layer cake, thawed

◆ Slice and serve on dessert plates.

This sandwich with the horseradish, roast beef and mozzarella is a great blend of flavors. You've got a real "twist and shout" supper.

Grocery List:

- ❑ Mayonnaise
- ❑ Dijon mustard
- ❑ Prepared horseradish
- ❑ 6 (7-inch) Italian focaccia flatbreads
- ❑ 1 pound deli-shaved roast beef
- ❑ 1 (12 ounce) jar roasted red bell peppers
- ❑ 6 slices mozzarella cheese
- ❑ Baby romaine lettuce
- ❑ 1 (10 ounce) can fiesta nacho cheese coup
- ❑ 2 (10 ounce) cans french-onion soup
- ❑ Grated parmesan cheese
- ❑ Croutons
- ❑ 1 (16 ounce) jar dill pickle spears
- ❑ 1 (22 ounce) frozen double chocolate layer cake

Meatball Subs

1 (18 ounce) package frozen meatballs, thawed
1 (28 ounce) jar chunky spaghetti sauce
6 submarine or hoagie buns
1 (12 ounce) package shredded mozzarella cheese

- Preheat oven to 450°. In saucepan, combine meatballs and spaghetti sauce and heat until hot.
- Prepare buns by shaving thin layer off top of each roll. With fork, remove some of soft interior of bun to make "trough".
- Place rolls on large baking pan and spoon about 3 heaping tablespoons cheese in bottom of roll. Bake about 5 minutes or until buns are light brown and cheese melts.
- Spoon about ¼ cup spaghetti sauce into buns and 2 to 3 meatballs in each. Top subs with a little more sauce and generous topping of cheese. Serve hot.

Sunshine Salad

3 (11 ounce) cans mexicorn, drained, chilled
1 (15 ounce) can green peas, drained, chilled
2 (15 ounce) cans yellow wax beans, rinsed, drained, chilled
1 (8 ounce) bottle Italian dressing, chilled

- In serving bowl with lid, combine mexicorn, peas and beans and pour dressing over vegetables. Refrigerate. When serving, use slotted spoon.

Potato Chips and Pickles

Potato chips
Dill pickle spears

◆ Arrange on serving tray.

Cherry Macaroons

1 (14 ounce) can sweetened condensed milk
1 (14 ounce) package shredded coconut
¼ cup candied chopped cherries

◆ Combine and mix all ingredients. Drop by teaspoonfuls onto greased cookie sheet and bake at 350° for about 10 minutes or until light brown. Cool and remove from pan.

Tip: Place extra cherry halves in center of each macaroon before baking.

Frozen meatballs really simplify the preparation of this hearty meal.

Grocery List:

- ❑ 1 (18 ounce) package frozen meatballs
- ❑ 1 (28 ounce) jar chunky spaghetti sauce
- ❑ 6 submarine or hoagie buns
- ❑ 1 (12 ounce) package shredded mozzarella cheese
- ❑ 3 (11 ounce) cans mexicorn
- ❑ 1 (15 ounce) can green peas
- ❑ 1 (15 ounce) can yellow wax beans
- ❑ 1 (8 ounce) bottle Italian dressing
- ❑ Potato chips
- ❑ Dill pickle spears
- ❑ 1 (14 ounce) can sweetened condensed milk
- ❑ 1 (14 ounce) package shredded coconut
- ❑ Candied chopped cherries

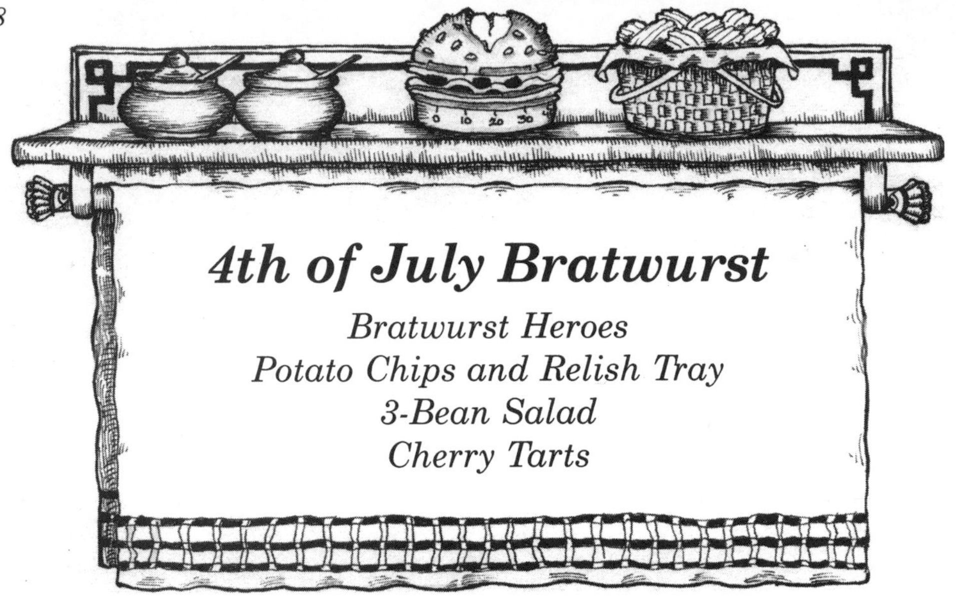

4th of July Bratwurst

Bratwurst Heroes
Potato Chips and Relish Tray
3-Bean Salad
Cherry Tarts

Bratwurst Heroes

Use hot dog buns for this recipe.

1 (6 to 8 count) package cooked bratwurst sausages
1 (8 ounce) jar roasted bell peppers
1 cup refrigerated marinara sauce
6 to 8 slices pepper-jack cheese

- Heat bratwurst on grill until hot and turn frequently. When brats are just about done, toast buns cut side down on grill.
- In saucepan, heat marinara sauce and place brats on toasted buns. Layer bell peppers, marinara sauce and cheese over bratwurst.

Potato Chips and Relish Tray

Potato chips
1 (14 ounce) jar baby dill pickles
1 (8 ounce) jar green olives
1 bunch fresh green onions

- Place potato chips in serving bowl and arrange pickles, olives and green onions on serving tray.

3-Bean Salad

2 (15 ounce) can 3-bean salad, chilled
1 (15 ounce) whole kernel corn

- Mix in serving bowl.

Cherry Tarts

1 (8 count) package graham cracker tart cups
1 (20 ounce) can cherry or blueberry pie filling
1 (8 ounce) carton whipped topping

- Place tart cups on individual dessert plates or on platter. Fill with cherry pie filling and top with large spoonful of whipped topping.

Every American is a hero on the 4th of July. Top off the day with a super-duper bratwurst hot dog, chips, pickles and holiday salad. Don't forget the cherry or blueberry tarts! Top it all off with whipped topping for a red, white and blue celebration.

Grocery List:

- ❑ 1 (6 to 8 count) package cooked bratwurst sausages
- ❑ 1 (8 ounce) jar roasted bell peppers
- ❑ 1 (8 ounce) carton refrigerated marinara sauce
- ❑ 6 to 8 slices pepper-jack cheese
- ❑ Potato chips
- ❑ Baby dill pickles
- ❑ 1 (8 ounce) jar green olives
- ❑ 1 bunch fresh green onions
- ❑ 2 (15 ounce) cans 3-bean salad
- ❑ 1 (15 ounce) can whole kernel corn
- ❑ 1 (8 count) individual graham cracker tart cups
- ❑ 1 (20 ounce) can cherry or blueberry pie filling
- ❑ 1 (8 ounce) carton whipped topping

Turkey Surprise

1 pound deli-shaved smoked turkey slices
1 (8 ounce) package provolone cheese slices
2 or 3 avocados, 2 green apples
1 (24 ounce) loaf oatnut bread or whole wheat bread

- To make 6 sandwiches, place 6 slices bread on counter and spread very slight amount of mayonnaise on each slice.
- Place several pieces of turkey on each slice of bread and layer provolone cheese and several slices avocado with dash salt.
- Now for the surprise! Peel and core apples and with your very best knife, cut very, very thin slices of apple and place over avocado.
- Spread mayonnaise on 6 more slices bread and top sandwich with remaining bread.

Bacon-Potato Soup

2 (14 ounce) cans chicken broth seasoned with garlic
2 potatoes, peeled, cubed
1 onion, finely chopped
6 slices bacon, cooked, crumbled

- In large saucepan, combine broth, potatoes and onion. Bring to a boil, reduce heat to medium high and boil about 10 minutes or until potatoes are tender. Season with pepper. Ladle into bowls and sprinkle with crumbled bacon.

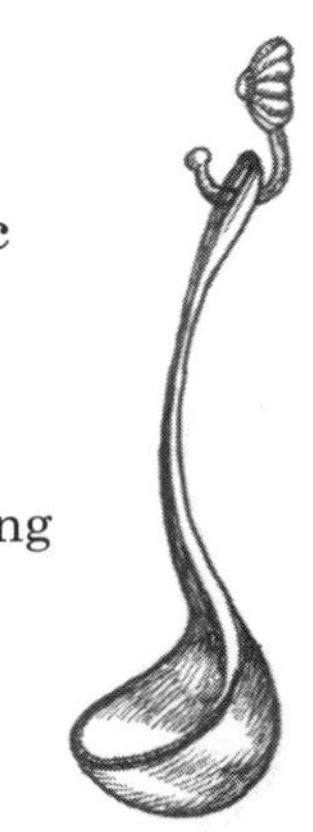

Stuffed Banana Peppers and Potato Chips

6 large banana peppers, sliced in half lengthwise, seeded
Potato chips

Stuffing:
1 (6 ounce) can tuna packed in water, drained
½ cup sweet pickle relish
2 hard-boiled eggs, mashed
Mayonnaise, seasoned salt and pepper

- ◆ With fork, mash tuna until it looks shredded. Add pickle relish, eggs, seasoned salt and pepper and enough mayonnaise to hold ingredients together.
- ◆ Stuff each banana pepper half and place on serving plate with potato chips.

Chilled Fruit Salad

1 or 2 (12 ounce) jars refrigerated mixed fruit

- ◆ Spoon fruit into serving bowl.

The thin, sweet and crunchy slices of apple in this turkey sandwich will leave everybody guessing about your "secret ingredient".

Grocery List:

- ❑ 1 pound deli-shaved smoked turkey slices
- ❑ 1 (8 ounce) package provolone cheese slices
- ❑ 2 or 3 avocados
- ❑ 2 green apples
- ❑ 1 (24 ounce) loaf oatnut bread or whole wheat bread
- ❑ 2 (14 ounce) cans chicken broth with garlic
- ❑ 2 potatoes
- ❑ 1 onion
- ❑ 6 slices bacon
- ❑ 6 large banana peppers
- ❑ Potato chips
- ❑ 1 (6 ounce) can tuna packed in water
- ❑ Sweet pickle relish
- ❑ 2 hard-boiled eggs
- ❑ Mayonnaise
- ❑ Seasoned salt, pepper
- ❑ 1 or 2 (12 ounce) jars refrigerated mixed fruit

Straight-from-the-Pantry Sandwiches

Too tired for even a 30-minute dinner? The sandwich is the answer! The easy thing about sandwiches or burgers is that you can place everything on the table and let each person build their own sandwich.

A few years ago, who would have ever thought to add the things we now add to a sandwich: cucumbers, green chilies, cream cheese, pizza sauce, olives, bean sprouts, meatballs, horseradish, coleslaw, avocados and more. Our options are endless!

Don't stop at an ordinary sandwich. Let your imagination run wild and bring a "different sandwich" to the table! This cookbook has lots of suggestions. My all-time favorite is the Turkey Surprise on page 260. Every time I make this sandwich, I get this question: "What is that delicious crunch?"

All sandwiches need bread, buns or English muffins.

Turkey-Cranberry Croissant

1 (8 ounce) package cream cheese, softened
¼ cup orange marmalade
1 pound thinly sliced deli turkey
6 large croissants, split

- In mixing bowl with mixer, beat cream cheese and orange marmalade and spread evenly on cut sides of croissants.

Hot Bunwiches

Use hamburger buns for these sandwiches.

8 slices Swiss cheese
8 slices ham
8 slices deli turkey
8 slices American cheese

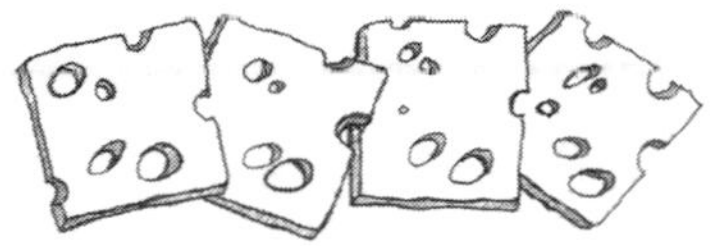

- Lay out all 8 buns. On bottom, place slices of Swiss cheese, ham, turkey and American cheese and place top bun over American cheese.
- Wrap each bunwich individually in foil. Freeze. Remove from freezer 2 to 3 hours before serving and thaw in refrigerator. Heat at 325° for about 30 minutes. Serve hot.

Pizza Sandwich

Use English muffins for these sandwiches.

1 pound bulk sausage, cooked, drained
1½ cups pizza sauce
1 (4 ounce) can sliced mushrooms, drained
1 (8 ounce) package shredded mozzarella cheese

- Split muffins and layer ingredients on each muffin half and end with cheese. Broil until cheese melts. Place top muffin over cheese and serve hot.

Turkey-Spinach Sandwiches

Use walnut bread for these sandwiches.

⅔ cup mayonnaise
2 teaspoons minced garlic
1 pound deli thin-sliced, cooked turkey breasts
8 ounces brie cheese, cut into ¼-inch thick slices
1 to 2 cups fresh spinach leaves

- In medium bowl, combine mayonnaise, garlic and cayenne pepper and spread on 12 slices bread.
- On 6 slices, layer turkey, brie and lots of spinach leaves. Cover with another slice bread.

Reuben Sandwiches

Use dark rye bread for these sandwiches.

4 slices Swiss cheese
4 generous slices deli corned beef
8 tablespoons sauerkraut
Dijon mustard

- Butter bread on 1 side and place butter side down in skillet over low heat. Layer bread for each sandwich with cheese, corned beef and 2 tablespoons sauerkraut. Spread mustard on 1 side of remaining bread and butter on other side.
- Place bread butter side up on sauerkraut and cook until bottom browns. Turn carefully and brown other side.

Turkey-Asparagus Sandwiches

Use English muffins for these sandwiches.

4 slices cheddar cheese
½ pound thinly-sliced turkey
1 (15 ounce) can asparagus spears, drained
1 package hollandaise sauce mix

- Place cheese slice on each muffin half and top evenly with turkey. Cut asparagus spears to fit muffin halves and top each sandwich with 3 to 4 spears. (Reserve remaining asparagus for more sandwiches or for another use.)
- Prepare hollandaise sauce mix according to package directions. (You only need butter for the sauce.) Pour sauce evenly over sandwiches.

Peppered-Roast Beef Sandwiches

Use crusty French rolls for these sandwiches.

⅓ cup mayonnaise, 1 tablespoon dijon mustard
2 tablespoons prepared horseradish
⅔ pound thin-sliced, cooked deli-peppered roast beef
6 Swiss cheese slices

- In medium bowl, combine mayonnaise, prepared horseradish and dijon mustard. Spread on both sides of rolls.
- Top bottom rolls with slices peppered roast beef and cheese slices. Cover with top half of rolls.

Party Sandwiches

Use 1 loaf party rye bread.

1 (8 ounce) package cream cheese, softened
½ cup mayonnaise
⅓ cup stuffed olives with liquid, chopped
6 slices bacon, cooked, crumbled or pre-cooked bacon

- In mixing bowl with mixer, beat cream cheese, mayonnaise and 2 tablespoons olive juice until smooth.
- Fold in olives and crumbled bacon and spread on party rye bread.

Serve sandwiches open-faced. Store leftovers in airtight container.

Provolone-Pepper Burgers

Use Kaiser rolls for these sandwiches.

1 pound lean ground beef
¼ cup diced roasted red bell peppers
4 slices provolone cheese
French's® Gourmayo™ chipotle-chili mayonnaise

- In bowl, mix ground beef, roasted peppers, onion and a little salt and pepper. Shape into 4 or 5 patties.
- Grill, covered, over medium to high heat for 5 minutes on each side or until meat is no longer pink.
- Place meat on heated bottom rolls and add provolone cheese. Spread a little chipotle mayonnaise on top roll and serve hot.

Meatball Hoagies

Use hoagie buns for these sandwiches.

1 onion, cut into thin slices, separated into rings
1 green bell pepper, diced
1 (15 ounce) can sloppy joe sauce
16 to 20 frozen, cooked meatballs, thawed

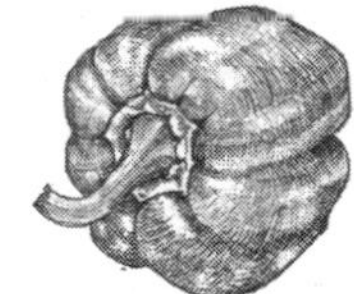

- In large skillet, saute onion and pepper in 1 tablespoon oil. Add sloppy joe sauce, black pepper and meatballs, cook about 10 minutes or until meatballs heat through and stir occasionally. Spoon mixture evenly on hoagie buns and serve hot.

Wrap-Up the Goodies

For a nice change of pace, try one of these versatile wraps. They are easy fixes and provide an excellent way to use leftover meats.

Use flour tortillas for all wraps.

Black Bean Wraps

Hot chipotle salsa
1 or 2 (12 ounce) jars black bean dip
1 (8 ounce) package shredded Mexican 4-cheese blend
¾ cup finely-chopped onion, optional

- Spread tortillas with hot chipotle salsa and wrap up all ingredients.

Chicken Taco Wraps

1 cup cilantro salsa
Sprinkle with 1 packet taco seasoning
1 (7 ounce) package non-refrigerated premium chicken breasts, shredded
1 (8 ounce) package shredded Mexican processed cheese

- Spread with 1 cup cilantro salsa, season with a little taco seasoning and wrap up all ingredients. Heat in microwave if desired.

Beefy Burger Wraps

½ cup mayonnaise, ½ cup honey mustard
¾ pound deli-shaved roast beef slices
8 slices muenster cheese
1 (12 ounce) jar roasted bell peppers

- Mix mayonnaise and honey-mustard, spread on flour tortillas and wrap up all ingredients.

Shrimp Wraps

1 quart deli shrimp salad
1 (8 ounce) package shredded American cheese
1 (7 ounce) can chopped green chilies
1 (10 ounce) package shredded lettuce

◆ Spread shrimp salad on flour tortillas and wrap up all ingredients.

Wrapped-Up Tuna

Mayonnaise
1 (7 ounce) package non-refrigerated tuna, shredded
1 (12 ounce) jar sweet pickle relish, well-drained
8 ounces American cheese, shredded
Shredded lettuce

◆ Spread mayo on flour tortillas and wrap up all ingredients.

Wrapped-Up Prime Beef Plus

Hot chipotle salsa
1 (10 ounce) package fully-cooked ground beef, shredded
1 (8 ounce) package shredded cheddar cheese
1 (15 ounce) bottle nopalito strips, well-drained
Shredded fresh spinach leaves

◆ Spread flour tortillas with chipotle spread and wrap up all ingredients.

Cheesy Wraps

1 (16 ounce) carton jalapeno-pimento cheese
1 (15 ounce) jar nopalitos strips
1½ cups shredded (deli or leftover) ham
Dry-roasted sunflower kernels
Shredded lettuce

◆ Spread with pimento cheese on flour tortillas and wrap up all ingredients.

Change-of-Pace Spreads for Sandwiches

Horseradish Mayonnaise
Remoulade Spread
Sesame-Ginger Mayonnaise
Garlic Mayonnaise
Quick Guacamole
Chutney Spread

Horseradish Mayonnaise

½ cup mayonnaise
1 tablespoon chopped fresh chives
1 tablespoon prepared horseradish
¼ teaspoon seasoned salt

- Combine all ingredients and refrigerate.

Remoulade Spread

½ cup mayonnaise
2 tablespoons chunky salsa
1 teaspoon sweet pickle relish
1 teaspoon dijon-style mustard

- Combine all ingredients and refrigerate.

Sesame-Ginger Mayonnaise

⅔ mayonnaise
1 tablespoon honey
1 tablespoon toasted sesame seeds
2 teaspoons fresh chopped gingerroot

- Combine all ingredients and refrigerate.

Garlic Mayonnaise

⅔ cup mayonnaise
1 tablespoon minced garlic
1 tablespoon finely minced onion
⅛ teaspoon salt

- Combine all ingredients and refrigerate.

Quick Guacamole

1 (1 ounce) envelope dry onion soup mix
2 (8 ounce) cartons prepared avocado dip
2 green onions, finely chopped
½ teaspoon crushed dill weed

- Combine all ingredients and refrigerate.

Chutney Spread

⅓ cup peach preserves
½ cup chopped fresh peaches
2 teaspoons finely chopped green onion
½ teaspoon balsamic vinegar

- Combine all ingredients and refrigerate. Add ½ teaspoon crushed red pepper flakes for zip.

Yummy Sandwiches with a Twist

Here are a few ideas to help you make last-minute sandwiches. Maybe some of these combinations help use whatever you have in the pantry and refrigerator. Sometimes we get in a rut with meals as simple as sandwiches.

Pastrami-Slaw Sandwiches

Use hoagie rolls for these sandwiches.

Honey mustard
Pastrami slices
Muenster cheese slices
Deli coleslaw, well drained

Ham-Sprouts Sandwiches

Use pita bread for these sandwiches.

Horseradish mayonnaise - p.268
Ham slices
Mozzarella cheese slices
Bean sprouts

Deli Special

Use French bread for these sandwiches.

Remoulade mayonnaise - p.268
Deli turkey and roast beef slices
Monterey Jack cheese slices
Romaine lettuce and tomato slices

Deluxe Egg-Salad Sandwiches

Use kaiser rolls for these sandwiches.

Softened cream cheese with chives
Deli egg salad
American cheese slices
Fresh bean sprouts

Provolone-Corned Beef Special

Use Italian sesame seed rolls for these sandwiches.

Provolone cheese slices
Deli-shaved corned beef slices
Fresh spinach leaves
Chutney spread - p.269

Crab-Salad Sandwiches

Use oatnut bread for these sandwiches.

Deli crab salad
Avocado slices with salt
Tomato slices
Fresh spinach leaves

Turkey-Havarti Sandwiches

Use multi-grain bread for these sandwiches.

Garlic mayonnaise - p.269
Deli turkey slices
Havarti cheese slices
Bibb lettuce

Pumpernickle-Beef Sandwiches

Use pumpernickel bread for these sandwiches.

Quick guacamole spread - p.269
Deli sliced roast beef
Tomato slices
Fresh spinach leaves

Island Chicken Sandwiches

Use kaiser rolls for these sandwiches.

Sesame-ginger mayonnaise - p.269
Grilled chicken breasts (leftovers)
Canned pineapple slices
Brie cheese, sliced thin
Leaf lettuce

Bacon-Turkey-Avocado Special

Use honey nut bread for these sandwiches.

Remoulade mayonnaise - p.268
Crisp cooked bacon slices
Turkey slices
Avocado slices
Leaf lettuce

Burgers with Flair

Here are some suggested additions to your basic hamburger—for a little "change of pace." Be a little adventurous and give your friends and family something to talk about.

Basic Burger

You will need 4 or 5 hamburger buns for this recipe.

1¼ pounds lean ground beef
1 egg
2 teaspoons worcestershire sauce
½ teaspoon salt

- In mixing bowl, mix ground beef with egg, worcestershire, salt and pepper. Form meat into 4 or 5 patties about ½-inch thick and about 4 inches in diameter.
- Cook on grill about 5 to 6 minutes on each side or in skillet 4 to 5 minutes on each side. (Ground beef should not be rare.)
- Toast hamburger buns and spread with mayonnaise or mustard. Add lettuce, tomatoes and onion slices.

Super Hamburger I

Add 2 slices crisp, cooked bacon, American and Swiss cheese slices for each bun.

Mexicali Burger

Instead of mayonnaise, spread deli-prepared guacamole and sliced hot peppers.

Garden Burger

Instead of lettuce, spread about 3 tablespoons deli-prepared slaw and a few sunflower seeds.

Crunch Burger

Add thin apple slices and chopped peanuts.

Cucumber Burger

Add thin cucumber slices, sliced olives and slices pepper-jack cheese.

Monterey Jack Burger

Use 2 slices of Monterey Jack cheese and prepared guacamole instead of mayonnaise or mustard.

Italian Burger

Add pastrami slices and slices of mozzarella cheese. Substitute fresh bean sprouts for lettuce.

Salami Burger

Add slices of salami and Swiss cheese. Use chipotle salsa instead of mayonnaise.

Guacamole Burger

Add slices of avocados with mayonnaise (not mustard), bacon slices and sliced hot peppers.

Roasted-Pepper Burger

Add 2 tablespoons prepared horseradish, mayonnaise and several strips roasted red bell peppers.

Monster Burger

Add several slices deli-shaved corned beef and 2 slices muenster cheese.

Pizza Burger

Instead of mustard, add pizza sauce mixed with 2 scant teaspoons minced garlic and thin slices fresh mushrooms.

Mushroom Burger

Add to each grilled burger 1 slice portobello mushroom and 2 slices provolone cheese.

Baked Brie Burger

Substitute salsa for mayonnaise and spinach leaves for lettuce. Add thin slices brie cheese and broil until cheese begins to melt.

4 Ingredient Recipes for 30 Minute Meals

Menu Index

asfsdf

Menu Index Continued

4 Ingredient Recipes for 30 Minute Meals Recipe Index

C

F

G

H

O

P

Q

R

S

COOKBOOKS PUBLISHED BY COOKBOOK RESOURCES, LLC

The Ultimate Cooking With 4 Ingredients
Easy Cooking With 5 Ingredients
The Best of Cooking With 3 Ingredients
Easy Gourmet-Style Cooking With 5 Ingredients
Gourmet Cooking With 5 Ingredients
Healthy Cooking With 4 Ingredients
Diabetic Cooking With 4 Ingredients
Easy Dessert Cooking With 5 Ingredients
4-Ingredient Recipes And 30-Minute Meals
Easy Slow-Cooker Cooking
Quick Fixes With Cake Mixes
Casseroles To The Rescue
Holiday Recipes
Kitchen Keepsakes/More Kitchen Keepsakes
Mother's Recipes
Recipe Keepsakes
Cookie Dough Secrets
Gifts For The Cookie Jar
Brownies In A Jar
Muffins In A Jar
101 Best Brownies
Cookie Jar Magic
Quilters' Cooking Companion
Classic Southern Cooking
Classic Tex-Mex and Texas Cooking
Classic Southwest Cooking
Classic Pennsylvania-Dutch Cooking
Classic New England Cooking
The Great Canadian Cookbook
The Best of Lone Star Legacy Cookbook
Lone Star Legacy
Lone Star Legacy II
Cookbook 25 Years
Pass The Plate
Authorized Texas Ranger Cookbook
Texas Longhorn Cookbook
Trophy Hunters' Guide To Cooking
Mealtimes and Memories
Homecoming
Little Taste of Texas
Little Taste of Texas II
Texas Peppers
Southwest Sizzler
Southwest Ole
Class Treats
Leaving Home

cookbook resources® LLC